From Chaos to Mission

Other books by
Gerald Arbuckle

Strategies for Growth in Religious Life
(Alba House/St Paul Publications)

Out of Chaos: Refounding Religious Congregations
(Paulist Press/Geoffrey Chapman)

Earthing the Gospel: An Inculturation Handbook for Pastoral Workers
(Geoffrey Chapman/Orbis Books)

Grieving for Change: A Spirituality for Refounding Gospel Communities
(Geoffrey Chapman/St Paul Publications)

Change, Grief, and Renewal in the Church: A Spirituality for a New Era
(Christian Classics)

Refounding the Church: Dissent for Leadership
(Geoffrey Chapman/Orbis Books/St Paul Publications)

From Chaos to Mission

Refounding Religious Life Formation

Gerald A. Arbuckle SM

GEOFFREY
CHAPMAN

Geoffrey Chapman
A Cassell imprint
Wellington House, 125 Strand, London WC2R 0BB

First published 1996

British Library Cataloguing-in-Publication Data
A catalogue record for this book is available from the British Library.

ISBN 0-225-66806-8

Typeset by Keystroke, Jacaranda Lodge
Printed and bound in Great Britain by Redwood Books,
Trowbridge, Wiltshire

Contents

For:

Mary, Joseph, Allan, Brian, Brenda, Denis, John, Michael

Then Jesus was led by the Spirit into the wilderness . . .

(Matt 4:1)

[They] confessed themselves no more than strangers or passing travellers on earth. . . . If their hearts had been in the country they had left, they could have found opportunity to return. Instead, we find them longing for a better country. . . .

(Heb 11:13, 15)

Acknowledgements

My thanks to Ruth McCurry, of Geoffrey Chapman, for her encouragement to write this book; to my colleague Michael Mullins SM for his constant support and willingness to share his experience of formation with me; to James Murphy SM and Ms Catherine Duncan for reading and commenting on the text. These people, however, are in no way responsible for the book's inadequacies. I thank the editor of *Human Development* for permission to quote from articles by Joel Giallanza, 'Postnovitiate religious formation' (vol. 10, 1989) and L. Malarkey and D. Marron, 'Evaluating community interaction' (vol. 3, 1982); the editor of *Religious Life Review* for permission to use an article of mine, 'Is the Neo-Catechumenate way compatible with religious life' (January–February 1994); the editor of *Review for Religious* to use material from articles by Jane Ferdon, 'Religious formation: a contemplative realignment' (September–October 1989) and myself, 'Planning the novitiate process' (July–August 1984), 'Prophecy or restorationism' (May–June 1993) and 'Multiculturalism, internationality, and religious life' (May–June 1995). The last two articles are also to be found in *The Church and Consecrated Life* (St Louis: Review for Religious, 1996). I also thank the editor of Alba House for permission to revise a chapter in my book *Strategies for Growth in Religious Life* (1987). Excerpts from the New Jerusalem Bible, copyright 1985 by Doubleday, a division of Bantam, Doubleday, Dell Publishing Group, Inc. and Darton, Longman and Todd Ltd, are used by permission of the publishers.

25 January 1996

Introduction

God will scorn their leaders and make them wander in chaos.
But God will lift up the poor . . .
Let the wise listen and wonder at God's great love.

(Ps 107:40–41, 43)

Make your own the mind of Christ Jesus . . . (He) emptied himself . . .
And for this God raised him high . . . .

(Phil 2:5, 7, 9)

Most religious congregations founded since the thirteenth century were formed for prophetic ministry to a world in change, yet for centuries before Vatican II, their candidates were rarely trained explicitly for this task. Through years of quasi-indoctrination and voluntary incarceration they were taught, in a monastic atmosphere of unchanging order, that the world was evil and to be avoided. Information was handed down from above to be received without question. Conformity to a theological, ecclesiastical and pastoral *status quo* was *the* most esteemed value in a candidate, and testimony to the success of the training programme.

However, training for religious life must now be *radically* reformed. Vatican II called religious congregations to return to the identity and energy of their founding roots, but this has caused active religious congregations (that is, mendicant and apostolic communities) to fall into a state of malaise or chaos. After centuries of being in the forefront of supporting order in the Church, they have no road maps or models to direct them in developing educational programmes that would stimulate their candidates to be radically creative in ministry.

This book does not claim to offer precise road maps or ready-made answers to the problems of contemporary formation. Its purpose is to create a framework for radical thinking about the critical issue of formation of religious for mission today.

Background: call to refound formation

The book shows that the problem is deeper than the lack of models to guide creation of new training initiatives. There are internal and external factors at work that make the radical rethinking of formation extremely difficult, if not impossible, for many religious communities today. Internally, many members of active congregations are uncertain about their very identity. Either they do not believe prophetic ministry is at the heart of their identity, or they lack the energy and the skills for this ministry. Therefore they cannot create suitable formation processes for their initiates.

On the external level, both the world and the Church – the objects of prophetic ministry – make it difficult for religious to develop innovative formation programmes. The world that Vatican II called Catholics to evangelize was beginning in the 1960s to show signs of a most profound revolution in thinking and acting. For several centuries it had been assumed that rational order could be imposed on all aspects of life. In *modernity*, as the period is called (see Chapter 2), people had come to believe in 'linear progress, absolute truths, and [the] rational planning of ideal social orders'.[1] The human mind was not to tolerate lack of certitude about anything. Chaos, that is, the radical breakdown of the predictable, was an aberration, the greatest of all evils. Consequently there was an unrelenting drive at all levels of human endeavour to remove the haphazard and destroy the spontaneous.

Signs of a *postmodern* world began to catch the attention of culture-watchers in the early 1970s, its way 'paved by the psychedelic, academic, racial and political upheavals of the 1960s'.[2] The sense of order and certitude that people had unquestioningly espoused for several centuries began to break apart. In the sciences and society we began to hear that chaos is normal. Now it became assumed that the 'unexpected [is] the norm . . . that most, if not all, relationships are non-linear . . . . Stability is the unwanted exception',[3] and that absolute truths were impossible to obtain. Chaos was seen as a combination of order and disorder in which patterns of behaviour continually unfold in unpredictable but yet similar, familiar yet irregular, forms.[4] Today postmodern thought is passing into a new stage intimately connected 'to the explosion of information and communication technologies, the global mass-media economy of images, the ever-increasing determination of many men and women to reconstruct traditional ideas about sex and gender'.[5]

The Church, protected for several hundred years behind its secure ghetto walls, was thoroughly unprepared to interact with the world of modernity following Vatican II, let alone with emerging postmodernity. Many Catholics have been unable to cope with the dramatic speed and the nature of changes in both the Church and the world. Yearning for the stability and certitudes of the past, some have formed a vocal and powerful restorationist movement in the Church (see Chapter 3) which is supported by significant sections of the hierarchy. It demands the return by the Church to many irrelevant values and structures of the pre-Vatican II era. Restorationists regret that the Council ever occurred. Other Catholics, increasingly impatient about this escapism and the Vatican's ongoing support for patriarchal and monolithic values and structures, are themselves becoming more vocal. Recently, for example, in Germany and Austria a growing minority of Catholics – two million of them – has been challenging the Vatican over its refusal to consider the ordination of women, but the Vatican has responded with restorationist passion by raising the claim of infallibility in an attempt to put an end to this type of questioning and debate.[6]

Religious congregations must develop training programmes that reject restorationism and equip their candidates not just to survive these tumultuous times, but to be pastorally innovative in today's chaos. Signs of the ineffectiveness of traditional training methods are everywhere. One commentator claims that if thousands of priests and religious have 'given up' over the years since the Council 'it is not least of all because they had not been prepared for the cultural, sociological, and theological changes that called everything into question. This is why', he concluded, 'they could not cope with the changes.'[7] I agree.

The two important words in the title of this book are *refounding* and *formation*. By *refounding* I mean the process of returning to the founding experience of an organization or group in order to rediscover and re-own the vision and driving energy of the pioneers. Inspired by this vision and energy, people are moved to make quantum leap creative responses that tackle the causes of contemporary problems. *Renewal*, on the other hand, is a process of improving *existing* responses to problems. It does not go to the causes of problems (see Chapter 4).

In previous publications I have applied this distinction between refounding and renewal to religious congregations. The refounding of a religious congregation is the re-entering as individuals and communities into the heart of the gospel message through the eyes of the founding person, to rediscover the power of the mission given them by the Father. Energized by this power, religious commit themselves to create quantum leap pastoral responses to the most urgent needs of today.[8] I have also written of the need to refound the Church, that is, of finding and implementing radically new forms of bringing the faith/justice good news to the world. I argued in these books that refounding is a process more akin to the phoenix – a rebirth – than the gentle, refreshing breeze that 'renewal' has come to connote since Vatican II.[9] Refounding is not synonymous with any managerial technique or planning. Ultimately refounding is a grace of God, demanding of us a prayerful pilgrimage into a world of gospel faith, ongoing conversion to Jesus Christ and at times discernment in the midst of agonizing darkness and chaos. No amount of *merely* human effort or experimentation on our part will bring about the refounding of any religious congregation or the Church.[10]

In this book I claim that we should no longer speak of renewing *formation* structures and processes, but of *refounding* them. To *refound* formation is to re-enter the sacred times of the founding of religious life itself and our particular congregation. There, having re-identified with

Christ and his prophetic mission to the world, we then struggle collaboratively to build radically new formation structures and processes in harmony with Christ's mission to the Church and world. *Renewing* formation, however, means efforts to adapt traditional formation methods to the realities of today. These methods remain substantially the same as they were before Vatican II, with but minor adjustments. Given the radicality of the theological readjustments of the Council, and the complexity of contemporary cultures and changes, the renewal of traditional methods is totally inadequate.

Focus and structure of this book

In this book I explain the nature of refounding (Chapters 1 and 4), the reasons why the refounding of congregations and their formation processes is an imperative of the gospel itself, the context in which refounding must take place (Chapters 2 and 3) and principles for refounding (Chapters 4 to 8). The principles are based on two assumptions: first, that the primary task of active religious congregations is to be prophetic in ministry to the world in change; second, that training for religious today is to be based on the principles of adult experiential learning. Didactic teaching, which was characteristic of the educational programmes for religious in the pre-Vatican II Church, resulted in learning taking place most often only at the cognitive level. Although didactic teaching has its importance, it should not be the primary method of forming contemporary religious.

Experiential training aims to involve as many different dimensions of the learner as is possible. Its purpose is to foster integrated learning at the spiritual, cognitive, affective and behavioural levels, so that there are real attitudinal and behavioural changes in people. This form of education demands far more of both teacher and learner than for didactic teaching. It is a collaborative process involving 'all participants, teachers and learners alike, in a process of mutual vulnerability and risk taking, of personal challenge and learning'.[11] Staff members must be competent in their subject at the levels of theory *and* experience; they must be prepared to be flexible and adapt their approach to the learner's current knowledge and experience.

As in my previous publications on the theme of refounding I draw on the insights of several disciplines – for example, history, theology and scripture – but the main models of analysis come from social anthropology. Anthropology is no new messiah. It is a fallible, human discipline like theology,[12] but it can help to lay bare the cultural forces that motivate people, though they are so often unconscious of these forces' existence and their power to influence behaviour. Culture, says anthropologist Clifford Geertz, is made up of 'webs of significance'[13] or meaning. The anthropologist's expertise is to help us unravel these complex webs of significance, for example through the use of cultural *models* and *case studies*.[14] A *model* is the highlighting of particular social acts or relationships taken from a number of concrete examples of societies. It never describes the total reality, but merely helps us to obtain insights into a complex cultural situation. The model is then used to deepen the understanding of other specific communities.

Religious life formation is a *rite of passage*, that is, a process of initiation for candidates into a particular vocation in life. However, in the Western world we have lost the *group* art of experiencing life-transitions through rites of passage. In modern society, writes Eric Neumann, 'collective rites no longer exist, and the problems related to [life's] transitions devolve upon the individual' so that he/she becomes 'so overburdened that psychic disorders are frequent'.[15] For example, traditional initiatory rites of young people into adult society have been allowed 'to atrophy with disuse', comments Anthony Stevens, 'because our "elders" have lost confidence in the values of which they are the custodians and no longer possess any certain knowledge as to what it may be that they are initiating young people for'.[16] Therefore, because the collective art of initiation has disappeared in our society and to a lesser extent in the Church itself, I draw heavily on a model of initiation that anthropologists have devised after researching many traditional cultures in which such rituals remain essential for the survival and growth of the collectivity as well as the individual (see Chapter 5). This model of symbolic death and rebirth, which is made up of three stages – separation, transition/liminality and re-aggregation – also has a powerful scriptural foundation as will be explained in the text. Ritual elders fulfil crucial functions in this model. They are the confident custodians of sacred knowledge that gives identity and a sense of purpose to group life and they are charged by society to share this wisdom with initiates in ways that maximize learning. A deeper understanding of this model provides contemporary formators, as congregational ritual elders, with structural guidelines to assist them in the refounding of their formation processes.

Case studies are also used in most chapters. A case study is a detailed description of a particular human experience of individuals and/or groups that illustrates theoretical principles of a chapter. Generalizations cannot be made from a case study. All it does is to give a first-hand feel for the realities of social life. Accidental details in the case studies in this book have been changed in order to preserve the anonymity of people and places.

This book is written primarily for the use of active congregations, that is, communities generally referred to as mendicant and apostolic, though many insights are relevant to the refounding of formation in monastic life. However, although the book is about religious life formation, its basic theme, namely the dynamics of initiation rituals, is relevant to any individual or group concerned about their future. In general there is now a widespread 'initiation hunger' in contemporary Western societies, specially around the mid-life, employment changes and other major cross-roads for men and women, but they are at a loss to know what to do.[17] I believe this book can help them. In particular, people committed to liturgical reform, the Christian Initiation of Adults, the training of clergy and lay ministers, will find Chapters 4 to 8 a response to their need for theoretical and practical information about initiation rituals.

Personal reflections of a formator

I was on the staff of a religious seminary of my congregation from 1965 to 1970 and then its rector from 1976 to 1981. Later as an assistant-general of my congregation in the early 1980s, I discovered that the difficulties I had encountered as a formator and rector had been common to many formators both within and outside my congregation. In 1992 I was invited to conduct a workshop on formation for the National Association of Formation Directors in Canada, and the helpful reactions of the participants further confirmed the relevance of my insights.

During my period as rector I headed an institution that had been founded 80 years before in a remote part of my country to educate priests of an apostolic congregation. The institutional culture, eleven years after Vatican II, was still basically monastic. The rector, by tradition and legislation, held enormous power, but it was fundamentally the power to maintain the *status quo*. Like some medieval Benedictine abbot, he was responsible for the educational side of the seminary but most of his time was taken up overseeing sheep and cattle farms, deciding when grapes should be picked for commercial winemaking, defending property rights. Few had questioned the spending of time on issues which had very little to do with the primary purpose of a seminary for apostolic life.

It was my hope that the monastic system could be deconstructed within a few years and that a new culture based on the educational needs of an apostolic congregation in the contemporary world would emerge in its place. This did not happen, mainly because I made several mistakes that are relevant to the theme of this book. In retrospect I recognize that far more time should have been given to clarifying with the provincial administration and staff the primary purpose of an apostolic congregation and therefore to developing together a shared vision for the seminary. Consequently, for example, initial screening procedures of candidates lacked a sharpness of focus and insufficient time was given to reimagining alternative forms of training religious for ministry.

At the time, I thought renewal could lead automatically to refounding. That is, I incorrectly assumed that provided there were enough small changes made to the culture, then eventually there would be a radical cultural swing towards a training system focused on the demands of an apostolic congregation. Renewal often alleviates the symptoms of a problem, but the process of refounding goes to its very roots. Only over a period of time did I discover that no amount of symptomatic change will penetrate to the roots of a problem. The only solution was to refound the educational system in a collaborative way, that is to begin again, but on the foundations of a clearly stated and owned vision of what it means to be in mission as an apostolic congregation. To do this it would have been necessary to move the seminary to a totally different site – in the heart of a significant centre of population – where a new start could be made to build an appropriate culture. It is a historical and anthropological reality, that since cultures are so durable and resistant to major change, people must first experience chaos, that is the personal and cultural dislocation or breakdown of the predictable, before they are open to significant change (see Chapter 4). The transfer to a new site would provide the much-needed cultural dislocation.

Chaos, leadership and refounding

Refounding demands radical rethinking of the way we understand the Church, religious life and the world. All three have one thing in common – *chaos*! In a short space of time the cultures of the pre-Vatican II Church and religious congregations have collapsed. And society seems less and less interested in our evangelization. It is as though we are back in the time of the prophet Jeremiah when the three pivotal symbols of Jewish culture – the monarchy, the temple and Jerusalem – were threatened with destruction. Jeremiah described the scene as the return of primeval waste, but no one else wanted to acknowledge it:

> I looked to the earth – it was a formless waste;
> to the heavens, their light had gone . . .
> I looked – the fruitful land was a desert, all its
> towns in ruins before Yahweh . . .
>
> (Jer 4:23, 26)

Jeremiah was calling his listeners to reflect on the lesson of primeval chaos in the opening verses of the book of Genesis. There and throughout the bible chaos is not once and for all 'dead matter' or 'sterile nothingness'. It is described in terms of confusion, darkness, emptiness, nothingness, but it carries with it the notion of indeterminacy and potentiality. The primary motif, or symbol, in the mythological use of chaos is that through God's creative power, his mercy and human co-operation, radically new and vigorous life can spring up.[18] Jeremiah is saying, however, that chaos around him is *merely* a potentiality. And the cause: Yahweh's anger because the people fail to listen to the call to radical individual and group conversion (Jer 4:26). Jeremiah begs the Israelites to admit to the chaos and their dependence on God. If they do so, then the seemingly impossible will happen: there will be creativity beyond all human imagination: 'Look, today I have set you over the nations and kingdoms . . . to build and to plant' (Jer 1:10).[19]

Similarly, refounding the Church, religious congregations and formation begins for individuals and groups when they admit their powerlessness and their total dependence on God, letting go at the same time their attachment to the irrelevancies of the past. Vatican II destroyed for ever the assumption that a hierarchical model of the Church must be *the* only operative one, and that monasticism is *the* model of religious life. People with converting hearts must take the risk and free themselves fully from these assumptions. Only then are they free to re-imagine and create the surprisingly new out of chaos.

This is never an easy task. At times I meet considerable despondency among formators in religious congregations. Everything that was secure is collapsing around them. In the Western world they may have few, if any, candidates. Others in the Third World may be overwhelmed with candidates, but lack adequate screening methods, formation processes, staff and the understanding support of their congregational leadership. Many wonder if there is any use in attempting to refound their formation structures and processes when they look at the inertia and resistance to refounding within and outside their own congregations. These formators are right – there are few reasons to be optimistic. But optimism is not the same as hope. The virtue of hope gave meaning to believers in chaos down through the centuries although they were tempted to despair when faced with seemingly impossible situations. The face of God was hidden from them (Pss 10:11; 13:1), but they lived believing that out of the chaos there would come life, even though they never knew what forms it would take. Their trust was never misplaced.

History shows that the founding and refounding of religious communities began when small groups of religious committed themselves in hope to a clear and practical vision, though everything was against them. Despite the darkness, they had kept passionately in faith to the task of building the kingdom within the world of their time and had attracted like-minded people to join them. 'I know of few more helpful guide-lines', writes historian John Tracy Ellis about how to respond to today's chaos in the Church, 'than the lives of the Church's most original and creative minds, men and women who were [also] endowed with marked sanctity. I think, for example, of a Saint Teresa of Avila, threatened by the Inquisition because of her innovations regarding the contemplative life, yet pushing on with her reform of the Carmelites.'[20] He could also have referred to St Ignatius Loyola,[21] and to countless founding persons who remained undaunted by suffering and the threats of persecution in their struggles to build communities of faith and action. Religious communities and formation processes will today be founded and refounded in the same way, provided there are people of like calibre prepared to act on their beliefs.

8

St Paul, a formator of faith communities, had every reason to be pessimistic about the future of a fragile Church, but he had hope that Jesus Christ would bless his efforts in ways he could not imagine. That prevented him from despairing. So also for contemporary formators:

> But we hold this treasure in pots of earthenware, so that the immensity of the power is God's and not our own. We are subjected to every kind of hardship, but never distressed; we see no way out but we never despair; we are pursued but never cut off; knocked down, but still have some life in us; always we carry with us in our body the death of Jesus so that the life of Jesus, too, may be visible in our body.
>
> (2 Cor 4:7–10)

Notes

1. D. Harvey, *The Condition of Postmodernity: An Enquiry into the Origins of Cultural Change* (Oxford: Basil Blackwell, 1989), p. 27.
2. W. T. Anderson in W. T. Anderson (ed.), *The Truth About the Truth: De-Confusing and Re-Constructing the Postmodern World* (New York: Putnam Books, 1995), p. 7.
3. T. H. Nilson, *Chaos Marketing: How to Win in a Turbulent World* (London: McGraw-Hill, 1995), p. 177.
4. See R. Stacey, *Managing the Chaos* (London: Kogan Page, 1992), p. 63.
5. Anderson, op. cit., p. 7.
6. See *The Economist* (2 December 1995), p. 63.
7. Cited by W. Buhlmann in his book *The Chosen Peoples* (Slough: St Paul Publications, 1982), p. 273.
8. See G. A. Arbuckle, *Strategies for Growth in Religious Life* (Slough: St Paul Publications, 1987); *Out of Chaos: Refounding Religious Congregations* (London: Geoffrey Chapman, 1988); G. A. Arbuckle and D. L. Fleming (eds), *Religious Life: Rebirth Through Conversion* (New York: Alba House, 1990).
9. See G. A. Arbuckle, *Earthing the Gospel: An Inculturation Handbook for Pastoral Workers* (London: Geoffrey Chapman, 1990); *Refounding the Church: Dissent for Leadership* (London: Geoffrey Chapman, 1993).
10. *Grieving for Change: A Spirituality for Refounding Gospel Communities* (London: Geoffrey Chapman, 1991).
11. T. Hobbs in T. Hobbs (ed.), *Experiential Learning: Practical Guidelines* (London: Routledge, 1992), p. xiv. For the definition and explanation of experiential learning see Hobbs, pp. xiii–xv.
12. See C. H. Kraft, 'Cultural anthropology: its meaning for Christian theology', *Theology Today*, vol. 41, no. 4 (1984–85), p. 399.
13. C. Geertz, *The Interpretation of Cultures: Selected Essays* (New York: Basic Books, 1973), p. 5.
14. See J. L. Peacock, *The Anthropological Lens: Harsh Light, Soft Focus* (Cambridge: Cambridge University Press, 1986), p. 7.
15. E. Neumann, *The Child: Structure and Dynamics of the Nascent Personality* (New York: Putnam, 1973), p. 186. Also M. Douglas, *Natural Symbols: Explorations in Cosmology* (New York: Pantheon Books, 1970), pp. 1–18.
16. A. Stevens, *Archetypes: A Natural History of the Self* (New York: William

Morrow, 1982), p. 159. Also C. Coon, *The Hunting Peoples* (Boston: Atlantic, Little, Brown, 1971), pp. 392–3.

17. See L. C. Mahdi in L. C. Mahdi *et al.* (eds), *Betwixt and Between: Patterns of Masculine and Feminine Initiation* (La Salle, IL: Open Court, 1987), pp. x–xiv.
18. See Arbuckle, *Out of Chaos*, op. cit., pp. 47–62.
19. See W. Brueggemann, *Texts Under Negotiation: The Bible and Postmodern Imagination* (Minneapolis: Fortress Press, 1993), pp. 83–5, 89–91.
20. Cited by E. A. Malloy, *Culture and Commitment* (Notre Dame, IN: University of Notre Dame, 1992), p. 31.
21. See J. W. O'Malley, *The First Jesuits* (Cambridge, MA: Harvard University Press, 1993), p. 27.

1 Mission, ministry and formation: a historical sketch

> [Religious orders/congregations] are a kind of shock therapy . . . for the Church as a whole. Against the dangerous accommodations and questionable compromises that the Church . . . can always incline to, they press for the uncompromising nature of the Gospel and the imitation of Christ. In this sense they are the institutionalized form of a dangerous memory within the Church.
>
> (J. Metz)[1]

This chapter explains through historical reflection:

- the prophetic nature of religious congregations;
- that formation programmes depend on the particular prophetic emphasis of each religious congregation;
- that the refounding of religious life demands special attention to the selection and training of candidates;
- that the institutional Church still discourages the development of formation programmes based on the ministry character of active congregations.

There have always been, and I believe will continue to be, people in the Church who are so moved by love of Jesus Christ and his kingdom values that they come together, forgoing marriage, to be of service as groups to their neighbours within the Church and to society at large. They publicly commit themselves to live the Beatitudes of Jesus in a particular contemporary way. They share his concern for the outcasts and marginalized in society, his acceptance of the equality of women and his repudiation of the belief that economically and/or politically men are the special friends of God, his earnest desire to listen to children, his subversive manifesto of a new order in which compassion and communion will be substituted for domination and oppression in all cultures. It is a vision of liberating all peoples from oppressive values and systems. To achieve this prophetic mission they plan and organize themselves, as history repeatedly shows, into new or reformed, structured ways of life, calling others to join them.[2]

The founding persons of these religious movements have the ability to perceive the enormity of the gap between the gospel and the world in which they live. It deeply shocks them. Through a deep conversion to Christ, they see a particular way of bridging this chasm. They move with creative, imaginative stubbornness, with suffering and extraordinary patience to implement their vision.[3] And they explicitly or implicitly struggle to establish formation processes to mould their followers according to this vision. They are prophetic people, insisting the movements they establish be in vivid contrast to non-kingdom values wherever they exist.

Historically, once these movements cease to be prophetic, though in Church law they may remain religious congregations, they are no longer authentically religious. By sinking to the level of purely human institutions they have lost their reason for being. When this happens, new prophetic movements emerge within the Church and/or refounding people arise within existing congregations to challenge them to return to the radical demands of the Beatitudes.

In the following pages I briefly sketch the key stages in the history of religious congregations as prophetic movements and the evolution of their formation programmes. Notice throughout this complicated history the following points:

— radical religious movements, such as religious congregations, emerge or are refounded especially when the Church and/or society are in periods of deep chaos; we are in such a stage today;

— founders and refounders possess a profound knowledge of the critical needs of the Church and society, a proven intimacy with the Lord, imaginative and practical responses to the problems they so sharply see around them;

— founders and refounders, from the very depths of their beings, seek to imitate 'Jesus' obedience to God and his continuous confrontation with Mammon';[4]

— the primary emphasis in founding and refounding is on the call for personal and community conversion, or on the mission of Christ to the Church and society; formation programmes and structures for ministry are established in light of this mission;

— community life is an essential requirement in all congregations, though its form differs according to the particular mission of each congregation;

— failure to screen candidates adequately and to provide appropriate formation seriously contributes to the decline of the prophetic function of religious communities; congregations become the people they recruit;

12

– from the thirteenth century, the institutional Church has attempted, often with considerable success, to domesticate the prophetic function of religious congregations; this is most notably the case with women's groups.

Monasticism: some reflections on formation[5]

Significant movements to establish organized religious life emerged about the second half of the third century, especially in reaction to abuses of eremitical life. People like Antony (*c.* 251–356), Pachomius (*c.* 290–346) and Augustine of Hippo (354–430) recognized that people living alone and committed to gospel values can easily delude themselves. Stable communities are needed so that people are helped by one another to keep to the authentic path of holiness. Though these groups emphasized the priority of personal holiness, there was a strong prophetic dimension to them as well. For example, the rule of Augustine was formed at the time the Peace of Constantine (AD 313) was profoundly influencing the life of the Church following a long period of persecution. While this peace allowed the Church to function freely, the Church often uncritically absorbed negative aspects of the imperial culture. For example, bishops adopted the power or authority symbols of royalty; priests emphasized their authority *over* people and downplayed their role as servants *within* the community. Worship left the home and entered grand and impersonal basilicas. Not only did the Church and its officials become increasingly wealthy, with women being more and more excluded from leadership positions, but undesirable aspects of Roman legalism also began to have a deep impact on Christian living. Sin, which had earlier been thought of as a fracturing of the relationship of love and trust between members of the community, and as a violation of the covenant relationships between the community and God, was now presented in legal terms as breaking an impersonal divine or ecclesiastical *law*.[6] In contrast to these movements and the accompanying abuse of ecclesiastical and civil power, Augustine's rule emphasized union with others in a common love of God and poverty. The superior, in order to counter the abuse of authority in the Church and society, was to model his behaviour on Christ the humble servant by fostering unity in charity.

The Benedictine revolution

St Benedict of Nursia (*c.* 480–547) also reacted prophetically to the growing chaos within civil and ecclesiastical societies. As the Roman Empire crumbled and Europe became subject to destructive invasions from outside, Benedict, influenced by people such as Basil, the father of

Eastern monasticism, fostered a fraternal and socially-conscious monasticism centred on the local Church. Benedict's rule, again in opposition to the individualism, materialism and authoritarianism of feudalism, offered an alternative vision of society founded on the kingdom values of interdependence, love and justice. Benedict dreamt of communities in which class discrimination would have no place. To prevent the clericalism already existing in the Church from entering monastic life, Benedict insisted that priestly ordination be rare. The number of priests in each monastery would be determined by the community's eucharistic needs; the priest's sole role was to celebrate the eucharist. The abbot's task as the major formator in the community was to be persuasive, not coercive.[7] Not only was he to be elected by all the monks, but he was to make important decisions only after listening to the whole community. Special consideration was to be given to younger members because, says the rule, 'the Lord often reveals what is better to the younger . . . . If less important business in the monastery is to be transacted, (the Abbot) shall take counsel with the seniors only.'[8]

Benedict, in one of the longest chapters of the rule, shrewdly insists that would-be followers must be thoroughly tested during their formation, according to definite criteria: 'When anyone newly comes to be a monk, let him not be granted an easy admittance; but, as the apostle says: Test the spirits, to see whether they come from God . . . . And let a senior be assigned to them who is skilled in winning souls, that he may watch over them with the utmost care. Let him examine whether the novice truly seeks God, and whether he is zealous for the Work of God, for obedience, and for humiliations. Let him be told all the hardships and trials through which we travel to God.'[9]

In brief, although monastic life stressed the primacy of individual and community union with Christ, at the same time the Benedictine rule demanded of its followers a way of life that was strongly prophetic. Unfortunately, over time Benedict's brilliantly humane, lay-inspired and egalitarian movement itself fell victim to clericalism, individualism and materialism. These abuses provoked efforts over the centuries to refound the Benedictine vision. The first refounding movement came in the late eighth century under Benedict of Aniane who attempted a new interpretation of the rule. Then came the establishment of Benedictine life at Cluny in the tenth century. More than a thousand monasteries became dependent on Cluny and this refounding movement was the first to become directly accountable to the pope, in an effort to remove its monasteries from the destructive interference of local bishops. But even the Cluny reform eventually lost its fervour; it succumbed to the materialism and authoritarianism of the day. St Bernard of Clairvaux (1090–1153), a refounder himself, openly charged Cluny monasteries with corruption: 'I have seen an abbot with sixty horses after him, and even more. Would you not think, as you see them pass, that they were not fathers of monasteries, but lords of castles – not shepherds of souls, but princes of provinces?'[10]

Among other causes of the decline of monastic radicality, there are two particularly relevant to the theme of this book, and they are described by historian David Knowles:

> Success brought recruits in flocks. Under Hugh (abbot 1048–1109) numbers grew from 100 to 300, and under Peter (abbot 1122–56) they reached nearly 400. This caused serious physical and psychological strain. Similarly, in the order outside the walls of Cluny, the vast numbers were unmanageable . . . . There was at Cluny in Hugh's last years a failure to test vocations and train recruits . . . . Yet another cause of decline was the overemphasis laid on the liturgical element in the monastic life . . . . Not only was time short for private prayer and reading, but physical work had all but disappeared as part of the monastic life.[11]

Benedict's insistence on adequate screening and formation was ignored with disastrous consequences for the monastic movement.

At Cîteaux in 1098 there was founded what became known as the Cistercian order. It was an effort to return to the original tenets of the Benedictine rule, but by the end of the thirteenth century most of these new communities had themselves become guilty of monastically relaxed behaviour.[12] The order founded as a protest against monastic riches and power 'had acquired for itself an unenviable reputation for avarice and group acquisitiveness'.[13] The Carthusian way of life initiated by St Bruno (1032–1101) was far more successful in the long term as a refounding of the Benedictine vision. Bruno's rigorous vision placed, in his own words, 'God, and God alone, in solitude!' Although still insisting on community, Bruno nonetheless greatly emphasized the solitary experience of the individual member. From the beginning, the order demanded of candidates the qualities necessary for its way of life, and this fact has been one of the main reasons why the order has never needed a reform.[14]

The overall decline of Benedictine monasticism became increasingly obvious by the thirteenth century. Monastic groups had lost sight of their primary task; they had become settled communities in which the customs of ages suffocated spiritual creativity and dynamism. No one expected the monks to be generators of new ideas or new expressions of spiritual life.[15] At the same time, however, Europe was changing economically and socially; an urban way of life was beginning to develop and the Benedictines, long accustomed to rural life, were unable to adapt. The mendicant form of religious life would emerge in response to the new pastoral needs; it would have its own criteria for the admission and formation of candidates.

Women's congregations

No reference has been made thus far explicitly to the establishment of religious communities of women. There is evidence of communities of consecrated virgins even before the time of Benedict. St Jerome wrote enthusiastically in the late fourth century of female-inspired Roman religious communities under the direction of Marcella:

> I had the joy of seeing Rome transformed into another Jerusalem. Monastic establishments for virgins became numerous, and of hermits there were countless numbers. In fact so many were the servants of God that monasticism, which has been a term of reproach, became subsequently one of honour.[16]

Similar establishments were made in Egypt by Melania, a wealthy widow of Roman patrician status. Some argue that they were formed as a protest against the exclusion of women from the male-oriented Roman Church.[17] Certainly, they offered a creatively different alternative to the then prevailing secular and ecclesiastical power structures and wealth.

Benedict of Nursia did not plan for religious life for women. However, his rule was adopted by women in England and from the middle of the eighth century until the twelfth century it was commonly their only directive. Women's congregations emerged as counterparts to the men's orders and were often dependent on them in various ways, for example liturgically. The prejudice of the male-oriented culture of these centuries effectively stifled efforts by women to act alone in devising new forms of religious life and appropriate formation programmes. Female orders were usually far more enclosed than their male counterparts, a practice reinforced by society's belief that unmarried and unenclosed women would be in danger of exploitation.[18]

Friars: emphasis on ministry and appropriate formation

> In the vast majority of orders and congregations founded since the 13th century, ministry has been at the center of their self-understanding. Definitions and descriptions of religious life that fail to take full account of this indisputable fact are . . . misleading and harmful.
>
> (J. W. O'Malley)[19]

The radical economic, social and political turmoil of the twelfth and, especially, the thirteenth centuries had a dramatic impact on the development of religious life. As Europe became richer and more commercially oriented, so also the need for places of learning intensified; Oxford University was founded in 1167 and Cambridge in 1200. As lay people became more literate they were more prepared to question clericalism and its oppressive power over their lives. People began to yearn for a simple gospel piety, simplicity and poverty of life-style – things that the contemporary ecclesiastical and monastic structures were rarely able to provide. There arose in response to people's spiritual needs and in protest against the wealth and clericalism of Church life a wide variety of radical enthusiastic religious movements, especially in the developing urban centres. These lay-inspired movements were commonly led by itinerant preachers and ascetics. For them, ministry was not to be confined to clerics; they believed that all are called to preach evangelical simplicity in word and action.

The mendicant friars emerged within this stimulating milieu. Because of the radicality of the changes they introduced in their congregations by way of mission, ministry, life-styles and government, they virtually refounded religious life itself. They renounced some pivotal principles that had characterized monastic religious life for centuries; for example, instead of giving priority to personal holiness, they emphasized ministry to the world. This did not downgrade the importance of holiness, but it was to be seen now as a requirement for effective ministry to others. The friars abandoned the geographical isolation of monasteries and enclosure in order to minister especially to the new urban populations. They developed a passion for the ministry of preaching and the simplicity of the gospel: there were to be no spiritual elites in the Church, but all were called to holiness in whatever state they were living. And as a protest against the wealth of monasteries and their involvement in commerce, the friars opted for a rule of corporate poverty. For centuries it had been assumed that orders must own property to maintain themselves, but the friars refused to accept this and chose instead to support themselves through begging. These radical changes naturally meant that new forms of formation were required. Monasteries trained candidates for a life of rigorous predictability; friars needed candidates who could adapt to rapid change.

In the early thirteenth century St Dominic Guzman (1170–1221) founded the Dominican clerical order (and later an order of women) to combat heresy through preaching. It was to be preaching founded exclusively on the power of the Word of God and the Holy Spirit. He demanded that his followers adopt a life-style of gospel simplicity and poverty in order to be effective evangelizers. Dominic himself developed administrative structures to suit the preaching apostolate; in fact, every-thing – organizational structures, studies, rules about poverty and liturgy – had to be subordinated to this task.[20] Though many monastic customs were kept for the internal running of communities, Dominic significantly and readily allowed dispensations to be given if pastoral and study require-ments demanded them. The revolutionary contribution of Dominic, however, is to be found in the government structures of the order; for example, every superior was not only elected, but had to be accountable to his community for his stewardship. Dominic also provided for the establishment of administrative units, that is, provinces, but the central administration was to retain overall authority to a greater degree than had been customary in monastic orders.

St Francis of Assisi (1182–1226), unlike Dominic, founded a lay movement, though it later – contrary to his vision – became clericalized. While Dominic's aim was to battle heresy, the concern of Francis was to form a group of followers committed in brotherhood to radical corporate poverty and simplicity of life. The stress on poverty was peculiarly Franciscan and its radicality would eventually cause considerable tension and division among the followers of Francis. Like Dominic he was shocked by the wealth and misuse of power within existing orders and the Church in general, but unlike Dominic, Francis emphasized in his preaching, life-style and the formation of his followers the radical imitation of Christ the Poor One.

The poverty of Francis was not primarily personally ascetical; rather, it was to be evangelical or prophetic and christological. According to Francis, his followers 'must rejoice when they live among people (who are considered to be) of little worth and who are looked down upon, among the poor and powerless, the sick and the lepers, and the beggars by the wayside'.[21] Christ had freely chosen poverty, thus revealing the humility of God himself. Above all, Francis loved Jesus in the crib, on the cross and in the eucharist because in these realities God's powerlessness, his vulnerability and his littleness were so dramatically revealed. For the Benedictine, obedience to God was stressed, not poverty; poverty for a Benedictine was the denial of self-will – the actual poor were to be fed *outside* the enclosure of the monastery. Little wonder, therefore, that the formation of Benedictines and Franciscans would differ radically. To be true to the vision of Francis, recruits must experience what it means to be powerless by being educated in the midst of the poor. If their ministry is to be among the poor, then that is where they must be formed. Francis, unlike Benedict and Dominic, had few organizational skills and to his annoyance his followers adapted large sections of the Dominican governmental organization as well as their apostolate to the universities.[22]

Ministry and community for mendicants

In traditional monastic life the predictable structures and stable daily rhythm of community life, for example the hierarchical role and authority of the superior, the cultivation of humility, obedience and mutual love, the periods of community and private prayer, exist primarily to facilitate the individual's and the community's contemplative and ascetical search for God. Benedict believed that the necessary predictability and stability could not be achieved unless monks resided in the same place throughout their lives: a fixed locality was integral to monastic life. Not so for Dominic and Francis. They refused to accept locality and the internal detailed predictability of monastic structures as essential conditions for their forms of religious life. Communities must be mobile, that is, they must be prepared to move wherever the most urgent apostolic needs are to be found. The direct ministry of individual members is to foster a community that witnesses to kingdom values; in so doing, of course, members themselves feel encouraged to develop their talents in the service of the community. The role of the superior, who, unlike an abbot, was not to be appointed for life, was to facilitate the interaction or dialogue of members in the community for the sake of this prophetic mission to the world.[23]

Ministry to the world was to be essential to their identity for mendicants, not something conditional upon ordination. The prophetic radicality of this emphasis on ministry cannot be overstated. Over the centuries the right to ministry had become synonymous with the clerical state; bishops bestowed the ministry of preaching and of distributing the sacraments on certain people ordained for this task. And bishops supervised this ministry. Now Dominic and Francis went back to apostolic times and insisted that the right to preach the Word of God belonged to *every* Christian by virtue of their baptism. It did not originate in or depend on the power of bishops. The reformers recognized that local bishops would obstruct the work of their followers because of its radicality, so they obtained permission to be answerable directly and only to Rome for their ministry. This exemption allowed the friars to emphasize the model of the Church as Herald of the Good News rather than the Church as Sacrament.[24]

In order to be prepared for ministry, mendicants clustered around the newly established universities, building houses of studies. This was a significant move away from the apprenticeship model of formation then common in the training of diocesan priests, in which a candidate was expected to learn what was required for any ministry from a master on a one-to-one basis. The ministry of the Word demanded the more rigorous method of the classroom.[25] The spiritual formation of mendicants was still shaped, however, in various ways by monastic experience. As historian John O'Malley notes: 'Their novitiates and convents, modeled on the monasteries, were where that commitment could be further evoked and sustained . . . . In the convents a regimen of discipline and liturgy prevailed that provided for what we might call the ongoing spiritual formation of the friar, providing for him in this regard what the university did not.'[26]

During this period women religious were not given the same creative space as men, though there were attempts to do so. The most remarkable effort to achieve apostolic freedom of movement was that undertaken by the Beguines. They were groups of laywomen who developed within the same world that gave rise to the friars and they came together to practise a new form of religious life. They desired to live in voluntary poverty in imitation of Christ, but *within* the new urban setting. In order to enter these communities, individuals were expected to renounce their personal wealth, have a simple life-style, be prepared to assist the poor and sick and to support themselves in various ways, including begging. In marked contrast to tradition, although they promised to observe chastity while members of their communities, they could freely choose to leave and marry. As in the case of friars, the formation of the Beguines was to be done close to the poor whom they sought to serve. However, by the middle of the thirteenth century the Beguines became the targets of increasing criticism; they were particularly attacked for their lack of enclosure and clerical supervision. This effectively crushed their capacity for prophetic mission. In fact, the insistence that women religious be subject to strict rules of cloister became universal, and these restrictions would oppress women in religious congregations right through to Vatican II. Men's congregations would also suffer through the indiscriminate imposition of monastic structures but to a lesser degree than their female counterparts. This point will be explained further below.

The breakdown of recruitment and formation standards

By the fifteenth century the general picture of religious orders, including their methods of recruitment and formation, was far from good. Benedictine monasticism was marked by general decay and mediocrity. Recruitment to monasteries had commonly become aristocratically exclusive in order to bolster their institutional grandeur and income. The quality of community life – and therefore the formation of candidates – had disintegrated, and few looked to monasteries to provide ascetical challenges.[27] Even among the friars there had been a decline in spiritual and missionary fervour. Originally, as we have seen, these reforming orders, especially the Franciscans, had protested against the rise of clericalism in the Church, but they themselves also fell victim to this disease. Within these groups and in the Church in general, 'the laity were squeezed out or relegated to an inferior status because there was no important role for them'.[28]

In addition to clericalism there developed a commonly held belief that monks and nuns formed the spiritual elite in the Church, so there was no need for them to be interested in matters that concerned lay people. In the year 1092, Pope Urban II had issued a Bull in which he asserted that 'from the beginning the Church has always offered two types of life to her children: one to aid the insufficiency of the weak, the other to bring to perfection the goodness of the strong'.[29] 'The strong' referred to religious. The early mendicants would not accept this view, but in time many of their followers adopted it without question. Elitism would plague religious congregations down the centuries until Vatican II, and it fostered formation processes that removed candidates from any meaningful contact with lay people or the 'evil world'. As the laity were at a lower level of gospel life, religious order candidates had to be kept away from them lest they were tempted to slip back to this inferior spiritual status. The laity, it was assumed, had nothing of importance to teach the elite class in the Church.

There were some efforts at reform; for example, the Brethren of the

Common Life was a movement initiated originally as a lay action by Geert Groote in the fourteenth century. He inspired a trend towards mystical piety, commonly referred to as *devotio moderna* to emphasize that it was different from the piety encouraged by Benedictines and mendicants. The Brethren of the Common Life, though visibly like existing orders, embracing poverty, celibacy and obedience, differed radically in that they did not take vows. Groote was the last reformer of this age to attempt to unite clergy and laity in a single community. His mystical piety, open to all Christians, stressed an affective devotion to the humanity of Christ rather than a piety based primarily on clergy-centred liturgies. Eventually efforts to keep clericalism out of this movement failed.

Apostolic congregations and formation

The early years of the sixteenth century brought about a widespread chaos in the Church's life, with dramatic consequences for the evolution of religious life. The major cause of the chaos was the drive against corruption within the Church by people like Martin Luther in Germany and Ulrich Zwingli in Zurich. They initiated the Protestant Reformation which ultimately led to the Counter-Reformation in the Roman Church. It is important to identify some reactions to these tumultuous times by the Church and society in general in order to appreciate the quality and kinds of refounding in religious life and their impact on the formation of candidates.

The Council of Trent (1545–63), convoked in response to the Reformation, attempted to reconcile the conflicting forces in Christendom and to foster reform within the Church itself. The first aim failed, but the Council's efforts to initiate internal reforms certainly had far-reaching impact on the Church's life. People realized that the Church's survival was at stake; there was a move to redefine its boundaries to distinguish it clearly from Protestant denominations. In an act of self-defence the Church withdrew within itself, becoming the 'ghetto' or 'fortress' Church, discouraging structural and pastoral experimentation, fostering papal institutional and bureaucratic centralization. It now assumed that the changing world had to adapt to the Church and not vice versa.[30] Any change was seen as a capitulation to Protestant reformers.

The Council adopted some much-needed reforms for religious orders, for example steps to reorganize novitiate training, but there was much that would henceforth negatively affect religious, especially women. For example, the overall emphasis by the Council on the maintenance of order throughout Church life stifled many efforts by congregations to be true to the creative founding charism of religious life itself, namely the call to be ever-prophetic and innovative in challenging the Church and society to kingdom values. As far as women were concerned, the Council reaffirmed the practice that all nuns without exception had to be cloistered, even asking secular authorities to force dissidents to conform. Pope Pius V in 1566 repeated the pro-cloister stand of Trent, closing any loopholes that had been missed by the Council's decree.[31] The downgrading of the world-oriented prophetic emphasis in religious life radically affected the way vows were viewed. Religious life had evolved because people wanted to serve Jesus Christ in a particular way; the vows logically followed this commitment. Now, however, the vows became *the* major focus for religious, divorced often from personal commitment to Jesus the Prophet to the world. The vows became impersonal rules to be obeyed.[32]

The sixteenth century was also one of European colonial expansion accompanied by energetic missionary activity. The Church, however, in the eyes of many evangelizers and ecclesiastical authorities, had become so interwined with European culture that no distinction could be made between them. Conversion meant accepting European cultural expressions of faith, the very evil that the Council of Jerusalem in the early Church had condemned. And, again in reaction to the Reformation, the primary theological stress moved away from the evangelization of the community to the salvation of the individual soul. The overall goal of missionary action became the implantation of the Church as an unchanging European institution – a monarchical, clerical and hierarchical entity, and the sole instrument of individual salvation and welfare. The institutional Church had the total truth; it was the perfect society equipped with truths and pre-structured answers for any pastoral situation that might emerge. According to this model of ecclesiology and evangelization, there was little need for missionaries to understand culture(s). Only the soul mattered. Christians were to show compassion, for example through medical and educational services, but such efforts were incidental to the main evangelizing thrust, namely the conversion of the individual soul to God. Culture had little or nothing to do with this salvation. Religious life among missionaries to lands outside Europe and the formation of locally-born candidates there inevitably reflected these theological and Eurocentric assumptions. Religious congregations were planted even in tropical countries with little adaptation to the diversity of cultures and climate.[33] It is not surprising, therefore, that the models of religious life in non-European lands even now remain fundamentally Western.

This negative view of non-European cultures, namely that the Spirit was saying nothing through them about God's creative and revealing power, extended to the emerging physics. This physics used mechanistic concepts to explain the world, based on the mathematical model of Isaac Newton (1642–1727), the philosophy of René Descartes (1596–1650) and the scientific methodology devised by Francis Bacon (1561–1626). As this soon-to-be influential physics developed, the Church refused all dialogue with it. Yet, paradoxically, it did absorb aspects of the new scientific thinking; for example, Catholic thinkers also began to *over-stress* the rational part of human thinking. Without realizing it, they accepted

22

Descartes' statement 'I think, therefore I am', and came to equate personal identity with the rational mind rather than with the whole organism. The integration of body, mind and spirit nearly disappeared as a concept. This encouraged people to forget to use their bodies as agents of knowing and to separate themselves from their natural and *affective* environment.[34] This downplaying of our affective life was to damage the formation of religious for centuries.

The anti-kingdom values of the Church after the Council of Trent were challenged by founders of several new congregations. Within a Church which actively discouraged any radical change of structures or established order, these reformers started with the missionary imperative to evangelize a world in change. They held that personal holiness and structures of religious life, for example community, must be shaped by this mission and not by a pre-set monastic model.

Ignatius Loyola: ministry, refounding and formation emphases

St Ignatius Loyola (1491–1556), the greatest of these founders, decided that ministry to the world was to be *the* priority for his followers. As O'Malley explains: 'The most obvious and fundamental decision (of the early Jesuits) was the commitment to ministry, more exigent and clear-cut than the stated goals of any previous religious order. What the early companions did made them what they were, and they did ministry.'[35] Jesuits were to be ever-creative and adaptive to changing pastoral situations. Their efforts must always be measured by the axiom: let all things be for 'the greater glory of God'; this norm would call Jesuits to be always searching for *better* ways to preach the mission of Christ. Community life was at the service of the mission to the world, and here Ignatius made a profound jump in thinking and refounding religious life itself. For Benedict, Dominic and Francis, community life was the primary focus for religious, but for Ignatius it was the ministry to the world by individual Jesuits that was primary, not the community. This does not lessen the importance of community. On the contrary, community was to be an essential support for the ministry of Jesuits to the world. Ignatius' model freed individual Jesuits to enter any ministry that furthers the mission of Christ to the world, even if on occasion that ministry required the Jesuit to live alone. Community life had to be so flexible that it fostered this diversity of ministries. Jeronimo Nadal, the vicar-general of Ignatius, summarized the priority of mission over predetermined structures of community: 'The principal and most characteristic dwelling for Jesuits is not in the professed houses, but in journeyings. . . . I declare that the characteristic and most perfect house of the society is the journeys of the professed, by which they diligently seek to gain for Christ the sheep that are perishing.'[36]

Since Jesuits were not to depend on a set of uniform and detailed rules to hold them together in community, Ignatius especially emphasized the importance of their inner conversion to the Lord. He devised his *Spiritual Exercises* as the instrument through which Jesuits would seek to discover God's will for themselves so that they could be better able to serve the mission of Christ co-operatively with one another. He called his followers to seek God in all things, that is, to be contemplatives in action. This meant that they did not have to withdraw into cloisters to find God, but had to develop the art of being open to God's presence wherever they found themselves. This went against the wisdom of his day, because the belief had grown up that authentic prayer was possible only through withdrawing from one's activities.

Like the founders of the mendicants, Ignatius emphasized not priesthood as such but ministry determined by the needs of the people. Priesthood for Jesuits, writes Thomas Rausch, is to be 'prophetic, a priesthood focused on preaching and evangelization'.[37] And preaching is not to be confined to Mass, but is to be exercised in every way possible if the mission demands this. Ignatius' decision to have a special vow committing Jesuits to be totally available to the pope was itself an imaginative and prophetic act; by so doing, Ignatius bypassed hierarchical structures, for example parish priests, bishops, prince-bishops and secular authorities, whom he knew from experience would obstruct prophetic pastoral action.[38] The Council of Trent had reinforced the power of bishops, as well as that of priests at the parochial level, so that ministry had become even more synonymous than before with the sacramental power of ordination. Hence, Ignatius' move to make Jesuits the pope's agents was an effort to guarantee freedom for his congregation to develop any kind of creative ministry demanded by the mission. Many of his followers, even in Ignatius' lifetime, showed in their pastoral work the creativity and adaptability he stresses so much in his writings, for example St Francis Xavier, Alessandro Valignano, Matteo Ricci, Roberto de Nobili.[39] These last two men in particular fostered dialogue with non-Western cultures, contrary to the prevailing Eurocentric model of evangelization, though they were later condemned by Roman authorities for it. Without doubt Ignatius was the major contributor in this period to the refounding of religious life. Most active congregations founded after his time would model themselves on Ignatius' primary insistence on ministry to the world.

Since Ignatius expected Jesuits to be in the forefront of the Church's missionary activities, exploring new pastoral methods, living in difficult situations without the usual monastic and mendicant community supports, he recognized that candidates for his apostolic model of religious life should have particular qualities before they could be accepted. Their formation had to be shaped primarily by the radical nature of the congregation's purpose. The mission had priority, not the personal needs of the candidate.

Ignatius writes with forcefulness about the need to maintain 'the well-being of this whole body . . . avoiding the admission of a crowd, or of persons unsuitable for our Institute, even to probation'. With similar urgency he writes of the need for 'dismissals during the time of probation when it is found that some persons do not turn out to be suitable. Much less ought those to be retained who are . . . incorrigible.' Still on the theme of admission, he writes: 'But even greater strictness should be shown in admitting persons among the approved scholastics and formed coadjutors, and strictness far greater still in regard to admission to profession.' He counsels Jesuits to avoid 'leniency in regarding as fit those who are not'.[40] O'Malley notes that 'by the time Ignatius died, he had admitted to final vows only forty-eight out of a thousand Jesuits as fully professed and a mere five as spiritual coadjutors'.[41] This figure well illustrates the importance Ignatius placed on the testing of candidates in ministry and over a long period of time. If Jesuits had to be so committed to ministry, then it was but logical that they had to be assessed according to their actual performance *in* ministry. Classroom and community life assessments alone were not enough. After the death of Ignatius, Nadal became concerned about the number of Jesuits who were ineffective in ministry, so he forcefully repeated the requirement to provide better screening of candidates, quicker expulsion of those found unsuitable for ministry, and 'a moratorium on opening new schools, whose needs for ever more Jesuits had led to laxer standards for admittance and less vigorous action on dismissal'.[42]

The implications, for the training of Jesuits, of Ignatius' primary stress on ministry were already clear before he died. For example, the period for novitiate was to be two years during which novices were to participate in the full *Spiritual Exercises*. The distinguishing feature of novitiates, however, was 'not a rigorous discipline, much less long hours of prayer, but the preparation for ministry'.[43] During novitiate the novices are expected to become involved in various ministries, for example serving in hospitals, and, if priests, preaching and the administration of the sacraments. There was also a practice of sending novices on a pilgrimage during which they had to beg to sustain themselves. The purpose of this, as O'Malley points out, was not primarily to foster medieval devotional practices, but to provide the novices with the personal unpleasantness inherent in itinerant ministries. Not only were these practices to test the authenticity of the vocation of the novices, they 'were meant to help them capture for themselves the experience of the original band' of Jesuits.[44] After the novitiate the emphasis on training for ministry to the world determined the nature of the educational structures, and the type and quality of skills expected of Jesuits. If Jesuits were to serve the pastoral needs of lay people, then they had to be trained *with* them. When Ignatius died in 1556, every training institution for Jesuits was open to lay students.[45] Nadal, shortly after Ignatius' death, sharply reminded Jesuits that talents had be developed to their fullest potential – not for the sake of the individual, but in order to be as effective as possible in ministry: 'The Society wants men who are as accomplished as possible in every discipline that helps it in its purpose . . . and do not be satisfied with doing it half-way!'[46]

Other apostolic congregations

The influence of Ignatius Loyola on the development of other apostolic congregations for the next three hundred years was profound: his style of prayer, a centralized system of government to guarantee the ready placement of personnel in ministry, formation structures, the priority he gave not to monastic spirituality but to 'modern, professional, ascetic individualism – all at the service of the Church'.[47]

However, efforts to refound religious life for women in ways similar to what Ignatius did for men met with intense resistance from the Church hierarchy. St Angela Merici (1474–1540), the founder of the Ursulines, had the idea of forming apostolic religious congregations before Ignatius. She appreciated the need to develop a form of community life and a method of training candidates in accordance with her vision of serving people at their point of need. Confronted with the breakdown of family life in northern Italy, Angela felt that an appropriate pastoral response was to form women *within* the family circle, not in any institution or within a cloister. For this she needed uncloistered women prepared to live right where the problems were to be found, that is, with families them-selves if necessary. They would wear no religious habit, earn whatever money was necessary to maintain their apostolate, and take no public vows, but a private vow of chastity. Members were to be united by bonds of mutual love, not by pre-set and inflexible community structures. She had in mind something akin to a secular institute, not a religious congregation as such, though this was to come later. Though the relev-ance of her creative vision was initially accepted by papal authorities, her followers were soon forced to accept the monastic cloister, solemn vows and habits. This was a tragedy because for centuries it denied the peoples of the Church the opportunity to receive the apostolic inventiveness of women shaped by the vision of Angela Merici.

Later Mary Ward (1586–1646) and her followers faced the same appalling fate. Mary planned to evangelize in England during the days of persecution. She recognized that the cloister, habit and choir would be incompatible with this aim, so she wished to adapt the Jesuit Constitutions and formation programmes to the needs of women, but to be in no way dependent on the Society of Jesus. As she wrote:

> There is no such difference between men and women that women may not do great things. . . . And I hope to God it will be seen that women in time will do much. . . . As if we were in all things inferior to . . . the man! . . . I would to God all men understand this verity, that women if

they will be perfect, and if they would not make us believe we can do nothing, and that we are but women, we might do great things.[48]

Her imaginative designs were too much for ecclesiastics unwilling to grasp the idea that women not having a cloister could work in an apostolate, bound together only by their ties of charity and commitment to the active apostolate. Mary's desire to have her congregation governed solely by women directly responsible to the pope and independent of local bishops and men's orders was altogether too much for the authorities to accept. Mary persisted, suffering considerable personal hardship for her prophetic stand, but she failed to have her insightful vision for the congregation approved.[49] Religious women without solemn vows, habit and cloister could not be imagined.

Two other notable efforts were made to allow women to enter the active apostolate. St Francis de Sales (1567–1622) tried unsuccessfully to develop a congregation without the restrictions of the cloister. St Vincent de Paul was more successful because he shrewdly avoided calling his Daughters of Charity a religious order. The Daughters, he claimed, had to go to where the poor lived and the needs of the latter would dictate their timetable and community structures: 'Leave the grandeur of religious women to themselves. . . . Daughters of Charity are bound to go everywhere.'[50] In order to get his vision accepted by ecclesiastical authorities, Vincent established the Daughters as a pious society, with annual simple vows and without habit or cloister: 'you will easily see that it is not necessary to be closed up in a cloister in order to acquire the sanctity which God asks of you. The religious state is truly holy but it does not follow that only those who embrace it will be sanctified.'[51] They would be sanctified without the cloister through a life of dedicated charity to the poor. As he said to his sisters: 'When you leave your prayers for the bedside of a patient, you are leaving God for God. Looking after the sick is praying.'[52]

Domesticating apostolic congregations: nineteenth–twentieth centuries

The nineteenth century was a period of intense growth in the number of religious congregations since about six hundred new communities were formed worldwide in that period. Many founders opted for the apostolic model developed by Ignatius Loyola. This was possible even for women's communities, since Rome finally acknowledged at the *theoretical* level in the early part of the century that this model had validity for both men *and* women. In *practice*, however, Rome insisted that many inappropriate monastic and conventual customs had to be integrated into the constitutions of these congregations, as if it still assumed that the ideal form of religious life was monastic and anything else was not quite authentic.

The dynamic founding energy of these communities was thus quickly suffocated by rules, for example the requirement to wear habits, and to maintain at least a semi-cloister, which Rome decreed should be integral to all approved forms of religious life. The fossilization of apostolic religious life intensified following publication of the 1918 Code of Canon Law. The practice of imposing structures inimical to the values of apostolic religious life was now fully supported by a universal Church law. For example, one apostolic congregation in its 1922 edition of its constitution no longer envisioned sisters caring for people in private houses, but *only* in institutions ('hospitals and asylums'). The primary emphasis in its founding story that sisters should serve the poor *where* they are living was now formally rejected.[53]

For this reason it is correct to say that many apostolic communities in this era were never founded; they were forced at birth into becoming precisely what their founders did not want, namely highly structured, rule-oriented communities ill-equipped for apostolic mobility and creativity. So, fundamentally it is not a question today of *re*founding but of *founding* them for the first time. The same can be said for their formation structures and programmes.

There were other factors that made it difficult for the newly formed apostolic communities to be true to their founding vision. Commonly these congregations confined their energy to the development of institutional apostolates, especially schools and to a lesser degree hospitals. These apostolates, while certainly needed, were considered especially for religious women culturally acceptable, and ecclesiastical hierarchies could more readily control them. Schools became the place for educating the masses in the faith and for providing them with secular skills to gain entrance into societies that were often opposed to Catholicism, for example Britain, the United States, Australia and New Zealand.[54] These institutions became immensely successful in achieving their aims, but at the same time they severely restricted at times the apostolic creativity of religious who loyally staffed them. Often teachers were poorly trained or had to acquire academic skills while still teaching long hours. There was little energy left to imagine other ways of responding to the apostolic needs of people in a changing world. Teaching sisters were dependent financially, particularly on parish priests; criticism of this situation was seen as an attack on the priests and hierarchy itself. The money religious sisters received for their teaching in parish schools was rarely enough to support them, hence they committed themselves to music instruction outside school hours in order to cover the costs of living.[55]

There were dangers in priests from religious orders accepting parish duties. Priesthood, as we have seen, was not intended to be *the* identifying characteristic of their vocation, but rather commitment to prophetic ministry was to be their distinguishing quality. For this ministry they had to be able to move quickly and creatively to respond to the most urgent pastoral needs. In practice, parish ministry had become over time the arena for sacral/ritualistic, not prophetic, action by the priest, within very set geographical boundaries. Ignatius[56] and founders who followed his apostolic model were most reluctant to permit their followers to assume an apostolate demanding long-term commitment, such as a parish, simply because this would hinder or prevent them from living out their prophetic congregational charisms. Once a congregational priest entered the parish structure most commonly he became absorbed in maintaining the cultic *status quo* and an agent of the bishop supporting an institutionalized ghetto-Church. In fact many mendicant and apostolic congregations did accept parishes and in practice often became indistinguishable in their ministry from diocesan clergy.

In summary, the formation of mendicant and apostolic religious in this period reflected the prevailing attitudes of the institutional Church: ghettoism, anti-world, anti-change or fear of prophetic questioning of the *status quo*, and nostalgia for monasticism as the ideal form of religious life. Candidates for ministry to the world were trained as though the world did not exist. The educational process could be summed up in the phrase: *quasi-indoctrination and voluntary incarceration to foster in candidates for religious life submission to the ecclesiastical and pastoral status quo*. The words are somewhat dramatic perhaps, but they do describe the overall aim of the formation processes. The pattern for the training of religious men, for example, was the same the world over: rules forbidding contact with lay people, even parents, for long periods of time; rote learning of lecture material; access to libraries discouraged; refusal to accept the social sciences in the curriculum; long and regular monastic liturgies; monastic customs, for example no speaking at most meals; opportunities for affective and creative development severely discouraged; cultivation of spiritual elitism. The formation culture aimed to produce candidates who would loyally maintain the *status quo* with attitudes inimical to apostolic creativity. The formation of religious women was even more controlling. For those who did not experience formation in those times the stories are almost unbelievable, for example, the refusal of permission by superiors for sisters to attend the funerals of their parents; or the insistence that sisters who had accidentally broken crockery attach the remains to their cinctures for a period of time. In the light of these and other examples the words 'indoctrination' and 'incarceration' do not exaggerate the reality. Although the gospel was calling religious to take up an autonomy as men and women in a faith communion, the Church by its formation directives was demanding that they comply to a culture of rigid, detailed rules and dependency on authority figures.

Vatican II: the challenge to refound formation

Something dramatic had to happen for the creative pastoral forces of mendicant and apostolic religious life to be released. In fact, at least in the United States, the move came prior to Vatican II from a surprising source, Rome itself! In the United States in the early 1950s the National Catholic Education Association became disturbed by the low level of professional training for sisters. The Sister Formation Conference was formed as a committee of this organization in order to challenge congregational leaders to allow sisters to enter teacher training programmes. This they did, even though it meant reducing for periods of time the number of religious in schools. Bishops and parish priests objected in vain to this policy. This initiative led to all kinds of educational programmes to train sisters in theology, secular sciences and formation. Within the United States, prior to Vatican II, as in no other country, there developed an ever-increasing number of highly educated religious women who were less and less prepared to tolerate attitudes and structures in formation and apostolates that had nothing to do with the essentials of active religious life.[57] When the time was right, many would seek to mould their congregations and formation programmes according to the values of their founding vision.

Rome supported these initiatives to improve the professional skills of members of religious congregations, especially sisters. In 1952 Pope Pius XII called an international gathering for the superiors general of women's congregations at which he insisted on the need for professional qualifications for sisters. At the same convention a high Vatican official, Archbishop A. Larraona, criticized archaic religious habits, the existence of class distinctions within communities, and the use of Latin in the office.[58] These initiatives helped to create an ethos in which religious, women in particular, could begin to question a culture of religious life that had held them back from discovering the true nature of active religious life and the formation needed to live it. Eventually Vatican II would provide officially-approved space for religious to rediscover the prophetic nature of religious life and what must be done to form candidates for it.

Vatican II challenged religious to return to their founding vision and to apply it to the contemporary world. However, the document on religious life (*Perfectae Caritatis*), having opened with this imperative, proceeds to describe in 23 sections what is assumed to be the ideal model of religious life – monasticism: the search for personal holiness through self-discipline and the three vows.[59] Only *two* sections are concerned with ministry, 'despite the fact that since the thirteenth century most orders of men were founded for ministry and since the seventeenth century most orders of women'.[60]

The restorationist movement in the Church[61] (to be explained more fully in Chapter 3), which has gathered considerable momentum since the 1980s, continues to deny that many congregations are defined primarily in terms of ministry. For restorationists the pursuit of personal holiness is *the* priority. In 1983 Rome published a document called *The Essential Elements of Religious Life*, which aimed to summarize what it considered to be the relevant points of the Church's teaching on religious life. It aroused considerable controversy since, *inter alia*, it sought to reintroduce into apostolic congregations and their formation programmes various monastic or conventual attitudes/structures which had rightly been removed after Vatican II. John Lozano, a historian of the development of religious life, commented that the document 'descends from a generic concept of religious life . . . and then adds the apostolic aspect, instead of reflectively following the genesis itself of our institutes in the Church, in which we have become religious in order to better develop a ministry required by the People of God'.[62]

The *Lineamenta* prepared for the 1994 Synod on Religious Life evoked widespread negative reactions[63] because it ignored the fact that the primary task of religious life is to be prophetic, that is, to challenge the Church and society to be true to kingdom values. Secondly, it failed to acknowledge that most congregations are defined by their ministry and that formation programmes must be in accordance with this vision. The working document (*Instrumentum Laboris*) that was finally produced for the Synod in response to widespread criticism from religious world-wide was more realistic, but one senses still some hesitancy to accept these two points.[64] In the section on inculturation, however, the document is particularly positive and forceful, for example: 'It is not merely a question of adapting certain customs, but rather of a profound transformation of mentalities and ways of living . . . . (The) structures of the consecrated life drawn up in rural societies in the Middle Ages or those coming from the period of the industrial revolution . . . do not always seem appropriate for expressing the needs and desires of today's women and men.'[65]

Practical reflections for formators

In the light of this chapter we can already suggest some *initial* practical conclusions and guidelines for formators. Their relevance will be more fully explained in subsequent chapters.

1. The mission of a congregation ultimately defines how formation programmes are to be established.

2. For centuries, even in the post-Vatican II world, *active* congregations have been prevented or at least hindered from developing appropriate *ministry-oriented* formation programmes. Consequently there is considerable malaise about matters relating to formation among major superiors and formators within these congregations. Therefore, there must be a refounding of formation programmes for these congregations. For this to happen, we require people of refounding qualities who are in touch with the original vision of the founding persons and contemporary pastoral needs to devise and evaluate such programmes.

The refounding of formation programmes may evoke tension with the institutional Church, but congregational leaders and formators must prophetically persist in their efforts. If they wish to be true to the founding vision of their communities they have no alternative.

3. Until this refounding is well established, formation programmes will continue without a sharp and authentic focus. As a consequence unsuitable candidates, with personal agendas contrary to the founding vision of the congregations, will be accepted because the criteria for their assessment are inadequate, and suitable recruits will not apply because the founding vision of ministry is neither articulated nor concretized in appropriate formation processes and communities.

4. Only those candidates should be accepted and professed who have the potential to contribute to the ongoing refounding and prophetic work of the congregation.

Formation processes need to be structured in such a way that the prophetic gifts of candidates are discerned, tested and fostered. If the congregations are ministry oriented, then testing must be done while candidates are actually involved in ministry over a significant period.

Summary

A religious congregation is authentic only when it is prophetically challenging anti-gospel values of society and the Church itself. When existing congregations are failing to fulfil this function there commonly emerge successful or unsuccessful efforts to refound them or form entirely new communities. That is the lesson of history.

The formation programmes of each congregation depend on the purpose for which they were established. Since the thirteenth century most men's orders were founded for ministry, attempting in consequence to establish appropriate formation programmes; likewise, since the seventeenth century most orders of women. For various reasons, the institutional Church over the centuries imposed on active congregations structures and formation processes that were contrary to their ministry. They became crippled by irrelevant monastic values and customs. Although Vatican II encouraged these congregations (i.e. the mendicant and apostolic communities) to return to their ministry-oriented identity, the Council and many subsequent ecclesial documents ignored or downplayed it.

Notes

1. J. Metz, *Followers of Christ: The Religious Life and the Church* (London: Burns and Oates, 1978), p. 12.

2. See K. Rahner, *The Religious Life Today* (London: Burns and Oates, 1976), pp. 11–12. For an excellent analysis of the prophetic values and actions of Jesus see W. Wink, *Engaging the Powers: Discernment and Resistance in a World of Domination* (Minneapolis: Fortress Press, 1992), pp. 45–9.

3. See G. A. Arbuckle, *Out of Chaos: Refounding Religious Congregations* (London: Geoffrey Chapman, 1988), pp. 88–111.

4. A. Pieris, 'The religious vows and the Reign of God', *The Way Supplement*, no. 65 (1989), p. 10.

5. I am specially grateful to J. Padberg for his overview of the history of religious life. See his analysis 'Understanding a tradition of religious life' in G. A. Arbuckle and D. L Fleming (eds), *Religious Life: Rebirth Through Conversion* (New York: Alba House, 1990), pp. 3–19. Also A. Arthur, 'Lessons of experience and imagination' in *Refounding Religious Life From Within: Strategies for Leadership* (Sydney: Australian Conference of Major Superiors, 1989), pp. 81–130 and L. Cada *et al.*, *Shaping the Coming Age of Religious Life* (New York: Seabury Press, 1979), pp. 11–46.

6. See G. Arbuckle, *Earthing the Gospel: An Inculturation Handbook for Pastoral Workers* (London: Geoffrey Chapman, 1990), pp. 11–12.

7. See T. Kardong, 'The Abbot as leader', *The American Benedictine Review*, vol. 42, no. 1 (1991), p. 69 and passim.

8. T. Fry (ed.), *R.B.: The Rule of St Benedict* (Collegeville, MN: Liturgical Press, 1981), pp. 179–80.

9. Ibid., ch. 58. For a commentary on the rule's directives about formation see ibid., pp. 437–66.

10. Cited by I. C. Hannah, *Christian Monasticism* (New York: Macmillan, 1925), p. 53.

11. D. Knowles, 'The rise and decline of Cluny' in P. Huizing and W. Basset (eds), *The Future of the Religious Life* (New York: Seabury Press, 1974), pp. 21–2.

12. See R. W. Southern, *Western Society and the Church in the Middle Ages* (Harmondsworth: Pelican, 1970), p. 269.

13. C. H. Lawrence, *Medieval Monasticism* (London: Longman, 1984), p. 198. See also C. B. Bouchard, *Holy Entrepreneurs: Cistercians, Knights, and Economic Exchange in Twelfth-Century Burgundy* (Ithaca, NY: Cornell University Press, 1991), passim.

14. See T. Merton, *The Silent Life* (New York: Farrar, Straus and Giroux, 1975), p. 140.

15. See Southern, op. cit., pp. 230–40.

16. Cited by J. Simpson, 'Women and asceticism in the fourth century: a question of interpretation', *The Journal of Religious History* (Sydney), vol. 15, no. 1 (1988), p. 53.

17. See Simpson, op. cit., pp. 52–3.

18. See E. A. Wynne, *Traditional Catholic Religious Orders: Living in Community* (New Brunswick: Transaction Books, 1988), pp. 136–7; Lawrence, op. cit., pp. 216–30; Padberg, op. cit., p. 6.

19. J. W. O'Malley, 'Priesthood, ministry, and religious life: some historical and historiographical considerations', *Theological Studies*, vol. 49, no. 2 (1988), p. 255.

20. See Southern, op. cit., p. 283.

21. R. Armstrong and I. Brady, *Francis and Clare: The Complete Works* (New York: Paulist, 1982), p. 108.

22. See Southern, op. cit., p. 248.

23. See G. A. Arbuckle, *Refounding the Church: Dissent for Leadership* (London: Geoffrey Chapman, 1993), pp. 159–61.
24. See O'Malley, op. cit., pp. 231–7. Exemption is an example of a refounding axiom 'the new belongs elsewhere' that will be explained in Chapter 4.
25. See J. W. O'Malley, 'Diocesan and religious models of priestly formation: historical perspectives' in R. Wister (ed.), *Priests: Identity and Ministry* (Wilmington, DE: Michael Glazier, 1990), p. 55.
26. Ibid.
27. See Lawrence, op. cit., pp. 274–90.
28. Southern, op. cit., p. 352.
29. Cited by J. Lozano, *Discipleship: Towards an Understanding of Religious Life* (Chicago: Claret, 1980), p. 53.
30. See P. Bernier, *Ministry in the Church: A Historical and Pastoral Approach* (Mystic, CT: Twenty-Third Publications, 1992), pp. 176–201.
31. See J. R. Cain, 'Cloister and the apostolate of religious women', *Review for Religious*, vol. 27, no. 2 (1968), pp. 270–3.
32. See Arbuckle, *Out of Chaos*, op. cit., pp. 70–1. For comments on the role of the vows in religious life see J. Lozano, *A Gospel Path: The Religious Life* (Brussels: Lumen Vitae, 1975), p. 101.
33. See Arbuckle, *Out of Chaos*, op. cit., pp. 70–1 and *Earthing the Gospel*, op. cit., pp. 12–13.
34. See F. Capra, *The Turning Point: Science, Society and the Rising Culture* (London: HarperCollins, 1983), pp. 32–3.
35. J. W. O'Malley, *The First Jesuits* (Cambridge, MA: Harvard University Press, 1993), p. 363.
36. Quoted by J. W. O'Malley, 'Travel to any part of the world: Jeronimo Nadal and the Jesuit vocation', *Studies in the Spirituality of Jesuits*, vol. 1, no. 3 (1968), p. 136.
37. T. Rausch, *Priesthood Today: An Appraisal* (New York: Paulist, 1992), p. 91.
38. See W. Dirks, 'The monks' response' in Huizing and Basset, op. cit., p. 16.
39. See A. Dulles, 'St Ignatius and the Jesuit theological tradition', *Studies in the Spirituality of Jesuits*, vol. 14, no. 2 (1981), pp. 5–9.
40. Quotations from Ignatius by M. J. Buckley, 'Mission in companionship of Jesuit community and communion', *Studies in the Spirituality of Jesuits*, vol. 12, no. 4 (1979), pp. 45–6, 36.
41. O'Malley, *The First Jesuits*, op. cit., p. 346.
42. Ibid., p. 61.
43. Ibid., p. 316.
44. Ibid., p. 317.
45. See O'Malley, 'Diocesan and religious models of priestly formation: historical perspectives', op. cit., p. 61.
46. Cited by O'Malley, *The First Jesuits*, op. cit., p. 61.
47. T. F. O'Meara, *Theology of Ministry* (New York: Paulist, 1983), p. 121.
48. Cited by Cain, op. cit., vol. 27, no. 4 (1968), p. 663.
49. For a historical reflection on Mary Ward see Cain, ibid., pp. 659–71.
50. Cited by Cain, ibid., p. 665.
51. Ibid.
52. Cited by C. J. Kauffman, *Ministry and Meaning: A Religious History of Catholic Health Care in the United States* (New York: Crossroad, 1995), p. 2.
53. See J. P. Dolan et al., *Transforming Parish Ministry: The Changing Roles of Catholic Clergy, Laity, and Women Religious* (New York: Crossroad, 1990), p. 117.

54. See Cada *et al.*, op. cit., pp. 39–43.

55. See Dolan, op. cit., pp. 123–8.

56. See O'Malley, *The First Jesuits*, op. cit., p. 364.

57. See L. A. Quinoz and M. D. Turner, *The Transformation of American Catholic Sisters* (Philadelphia: Temple University Press, 1922), pp. 6–11.

58. Ibid., pp. 12–17.

59. See O'Malley's insightful article 'Priesthood, ministry, and religious life: some historical and historiographical considerations', op. cit., pp. 223–57.

60. O'Malley, 'Diocesan and religious models of priestly formation: historical perspectives', op. cit., p. 67.

61. For an explanation of restorationism see Arbuckle, *Refounding the Church*, op. cit., pp. 1–157. See comments by P. Wittberg, *The Rise and Decline of Catholic Religious Orders: A Social Movement Perspective* (Albany, NY: SUNY, 1994), pp. 213–23.

62. J. Lozano, 'The theology of the "essential elements" in the teaching of the Church' in R. J. Daly *et al.* (eds), *Religious Life in the US Church: The New Dialogue* (New York: Paulist Press, 1984), p. 130.

63. See G. A. Arbuckle, 'The *Lineamenta*: the survival of religious life?', *Religious Life Review*, vol. 32, no. 160 (1994), pp. 130–7.

64. See Document *Instrumentum Laboris* for the Synod of Bishops, *Consecrated Life and Its Role in the Church and the World* (Vatican: Vatican Press, 1994), paras 71–72.

65. Ibid., para. 93.

2 The purpose of formation: to foster the art of inculturation

> Inculturation is not achieved through hasty and superficial adaptation. The discernment of what is essential involves the following: a lengthy contemplation on the mystery of God; a freedom of heart; . . . familiarity with the Word of God; . . . great love for people . . . deep knowledge of the (culture) and history of each people.
>
> (*Instrumentum Laboris*)[1]

This chapter explains:

- inculturation as a gospel imperative and why it must be the focus in forming candidates for religious life ministry;

- the complexity of culture;

- four models of culture that formators and candidates for religious life need to know in order to be effective agents of inculturation.

Religious are committed to be prophetic leaders in evangelization. But evangelization *is* the process of inculturation, that is, interaction between the gospel message and cultures. Hence, formation must foster as a priority in candidates the art of inculturation, a process demanding 'discernment, seriousness, respect and competence'.[2] The main purpose of this chapter, after briefly defining inculturation, is to clarify the nature of culture and describe several significant culture models that have particular implications for evangelization and formation today. Candidates for formation are 'many-cultured people'. They carry with them the cultural influences of their nation, family, school, university, peer group. And they enter into an educational process that has its own culture, a reflection of the wider culture of the congregation which they hope eventually to join more fully. In order to become competent in the art of inculturation candidates will need first to become aware of the power of these cultural influences on their own lives.

Clarifying terms

Inculturation

Inculturation emerged as a theological term in the 1970s in an effort to spell out two primary aspects of evangelization: the object, and the actual method or process of evangelization. Evangelization is to be directed at cultures: 'what matters is to evangelize human culture and cultures (not in a purely decorative way, as it were by applying a thin veneer, but in a vital way, in depth and right to their very roots)'.[3] Secondly, inculturation is a process whereby the Christian life and message become incarnated within 'a particular culture, in such a way that this experience not only finds expression through elements proper to the culture in question, but becomes a principle that animates, directs and unifies the culture, transforming and remaking it so as to bring about a "new creation"'.[4]

The definition highlights the reality of the faith-founded nature of inculturation. It is a movement of conversion at the invitation of God. Evangelizers, with Christ, struggle to call people and cultures to this radical turning to God. Michael Amaladoss notes that three mysteries of our faith are especially involved in the process: the re-living of the incarnation, the dying of cultures to what is not of God, the elevation through union with Christ in his paschal mystery, of attitudes, values and customs that are in conformity with Christ's message, and the creative, Pentecostal energizing of people and cultures to share their love of Jesus with others.[5]

The process of inculturation therefore involves liberation, a freeing of a people and cultures from all forms of domination or injustice. But the unmasking of cultural domination, for example prejudices and discrimination, is an extremely difficult process. People on their own, even the most oppressed, are often unable to identify the insidious nature of domination in their lives, assuming it is something natural and that nothing can be done about it.[6] Hence, in addition to the other requirements for effective inculturation, such as a deepening union with Christ and appropriate theological knowledge, candidates need to develop the skills of cultural discernment in order to perceive objectively the ways in which people, including themselves, are oppressed by cultural influences or contribute to the cultural oppression of others. As it is very difficult, if not impossible, to do this discernment alone, candidates must become aware of the need for community reflection and its appropriate skills.

The process of inculturation, therefore, demands that candidates (and of course, formators) become skilled in cultural analysis, that is, the ability to assess the inner dynamics of this or that culture and the forces inhibiting or fostering gospel liberation. The first critical stage in this analysis is the process of reflecting on one's own culture and its impact on one's life. The inability to feel the power of culture in one's own life, and to identify and articulate its complex forces, will inhibit candidates from developing compassion and empathy with people of other cultures. In the following paragraphs I define and explain the nature of culture. Several cultures are then described because they are relevant particularly to formators as they plan formation programmes and search for ways to know better the cultures of their candidates.

Culture and cultural analysis

A traditional definition, popular last century in anthropology and widely held by non-specialists today, views culture as a visible, comprehensible entity, the conscious creation of rational minds.[7] The definition stresses the need to detail *observable* phenomena, for example, foods, literature, dances, and to ignore how people *feel* about what they do. Cultures are then able to be graded aesthetically, for example one culture may be considered to have more artistic dances than another. The definition has grave deficiencies, for example, it overstresses historical life-styles or customs of ethnic groups and downplays their struggles to adapt to the world in which they live. It freezes a culture in a time period and encourages romantic or fossilized views of a people's way of living in the past. In brief, this definition of culture likens a culture to a machine – something with visible, rationally constructed and interconnecting parts; each part, such as a custom or institution, can be readily replaced by another component without people experiencing any sense of hurt or difficulty.

A second definition of culture gives priority to a group's ideas *and* feelings: culture is a 'system of shared ideas, a system of concepts and rules and meanings that underlie and are expressed in the way that humans live, not what they do and make'.[8] Anthropologist Clifford Geertz in a similar way refers to culture as 'the fabric of meaning in terms of which human beings interpret their experience and guide their actions'.[9] For him 'human behaviour is seen as symbolic action', that is, actions which are generated and interpreted according to 'the fabric of meanings'.[10] Culture is not primarily an entity but a process that is actively or persuasively at work, particularly in the unconscious of the group and individuals. It is a pattern of shared assumptions or values, expressed in its constituent parts, namely symbols, myths and rituals, that have been invented, discovered or developed by a group as it struggles to cope with problems of external adaptation and internal cohesion. Its primary function is to provide *felt meaning* or a sense of order in the process of living because what we most fear as humans is the world of chaos or disorder.

This instrumental view of culture, while it assumes the importance of factual history and visible phenomena, emphasizes *first* the developmental, or ever-evolving, survival role of culture for a people in a world of change, prejudice and discrimination and *second*, that culture is not one facet of life along with, for example, religious, political or economic activity, which is a view particularly popular among contemporary management writers.[11] On the contrary, culture is the complete set of feelings affecting all behaviour of individuals and groups to some degree.[12] Formators and evangelizers ignore this understanding of culture at their peril. People may change with relative ease their *visible* actions, especially under external pressure, not so their feelings![13]

Finally, because a culture is essentially a living construct of meanings encased primarily in symbols and myths, the feeling of belonging to it is basically inaccessible to outsiders. The experience of being culturally different or of confronting a history of prejudice and discrimination produces in a people a set of memories or feelings that are not easily shared with outsiders. The non-member of a culture may gain some understanding from participation in the visible activities of the group, for example dances, food rituals, but the inner experiences and feelings of a cultural group are still difficult, if not impossible, to comprehend fully. In fact these feelings are so deep within a culture that people find it difficult to identify and name them in their *own* culture. Often all they can say is: 'we just feel we belong together'. Or 'we feel different from the people of another culture'. Anthropologist Edward Hall aptly comments:

> Deep cultural undercurrents structure life in subtle but highly consistent ways that are not consciously formulated. Like the invisible jet streams in the skies that determine the course of a storm, these hidden currents shape our lives; yet their influence is only beginning to be identified.[14]

Feeling the power of symbols and myths

Anthropologically rituals are visible behaviour or 'what people are seen to do'. They are the concrete expressions of symbols and myths – the less visible but the more powerful forces in any culture.[15] Symbols are *experienced* or *felt* meanings; symbols are multivocal, that is one symbol will have many meanings at the same time and this in itself makes it difficult to find out what precise meaning is operative for an individual or group at a particular time and place. Symbolic meanings are *felt*, that is they cannot be fully articulated in words or rational statements, so people struggle at times to express meanings of symbols through such mediums as art, music and dance. A myth, a set of narrative symbols, is a story or a tradition that claims to reveal to people, in an *imaginative way*, a fundamental truth about the world and themselves. This truth is considered *authoritative* by those who accept it, for example the exodus myth for the Israelites. In short, myths inspiringly or feelingly tell people who they are, what is good and bad, and how they are to organize themselves and maintain their feeling of unique identity in the world. Rollo May writes that 'myths are like the beams in a house: not exposed to outside view, they are the structure which holds the house together so people can live in it'.[16]

The most powerful and essential myth in every culture is its creation myth, since it provides people with their *primary* source of identity as a distinct group.[17] When the creation myth's existence is threatened, even when intellectual assent is given to what is happening, people commonly experience degrees of anxiety, anger, numbness, sadness; the Israelites poignantly articulate these feelings of lostness in their lamentation psalms of exile (e.g. Ps 137:1). At least three kinds of creation myths can be identified: the public, the operative and the residual. The *public* myth is a set of stated ideals that people openly claim bind them together, for example the ideals or stories contained in a congregation's constitutions or mission statements. In practice, these ideals may have little if any effective cohesive force. The *operative* myth, however, is what *actually* at a point in time gives people their felt cohesive identity. The operative myth can and often does differ dramatically from the public myth, though people are rarely conscious of this discrepancy.

A *residual* myth normally has little or no daily impact on a group's life, but at times it can surface and become a powerful operative myth. For example, a candidate can claim that the congregation's charism, the public myth, is deeply affecting his/her behaviour, even though in fact a residual myth characteristic of an adolescent subculture is presently operative. Or a candidate may have come from a restorationist sub-culture[18] in the Church. He/she may believe conversion to the values of Vatican II has occurred and restorationist mythology no longer influences them, but in practice on occasions this mythology becomes operative and affects their lives. If candidates do not learn to recognize these different kinds of creation myths and how they affect their lives, they will not see them in the lives of those they seek to evangelize.

To begin to appreciate another's culture we need the gifts of empathy and an openness to dialogue. Empathetic listening means trying to become aware not only of another's feelings, but also of *how* he or she experiences them and to feel similarly insofar as that is possible.[19] Dialogue, a consequence of empathy, is the interaction between people in which each person aims to give himself/herself as they are and seeks also to know the other as the other is. Dialogue, an integral requirement of inculturation, presumes that one is prepared to learn from others and their cultures; this means that one lets go of attachments to those areas of one's culture that interfere with the growth of mutuality. Yet here is the problem: unless people are sensitive to the forces at work in their own lives, for example their creation myth and cultural prejudices, they will be unaware of what they need to let go of before authentic dialogue can begin and develop.

Case study: Cultural dislocation succeeds

George, two years after novitiate in his home country, England, was assigned to a mission zone of his congregation in a poorer part of Africa for two years. On arrival he was at first enthusiastic about seeing different places and people. He felt that the way of life of the people was so relaxed and joyful that 'no better culture in the world exists'. He was heard to say: 'I want to so identify with these people that I forget the corruption and materialism of our Western culture. In fact I don't think I have a culture of any worth at all!' Within a month, however, his feelings changed dramatically. Now he found the food difficult to take and he had constantly to seek help, even in little things, from people whose language he could not speak. He became at times depressed, condemnatory of local customs, angry that he had to depend on uneducated people for day-to-day information. He yearned for home.

After several months, with a professional supervisor, he became critically aware for the first time of the many positive and negative cultural influences on his behaviour in an experiential way. By having to depend on local people, he started to discover values in their lives that he had been insensitive to in the early months of first contact. At the same time he became more reflective and objective about his own culture of origin, seeing there both negative and positive values.

People are generally so enmeshed in their culture that it requires the shock[20] of contact with a significantly different culture for them to realize, sometimes dramatically, that they have a culture and that it intimately influences them. The case study above illustrates this. George experiences a wide range of reactions. At first he is caught in *cultural romanticism*, the belief that a particular culture is perfect and no other culture, even his culture of origin, has anything to offer people by way of comparison. His view of culture is the traditional one, that is, he thinks culture is synonymous with what he sees. This assumption begins to change when George finds that all is not perfect before him; he is humbled also by his dependence on people with little or no education. It is a positive experience, because the formation staff have judged he has enough personal integration in order to learn from the pastoral exposure programme. George has a skilled supervisor who knows what to do, that is, not to rush in to save him from the pain of the culture exposure process. Through the supervision George is able to get in touch with his feelings which leads to a more mature sensitivity to the power of culture in himself and in the lives of the people. Disorientation was an essential condition of George's learning.

At some stage in the formation process, therefore, candidates should be assigned to a ministry where there are few or no familiar cultural supports. The exposure to a significantly different culture must be for a lengthy period (e.g. one to two years), otherwise learning cannot take place.

Cultures: some insights

Given the daunting number and array of cultures and subcultures in the world, formators ask whether there is some way to place them into manageable and describable categories in order to understand them better. If this information is obtainable, then formators will better understand the cultural influences on their candidates and the cultures that must be the focus of their formation for evangelization.

To answer questions of this kind, anthropologists construct culture models or types. An anthropological model is not a perfect representation of the real world at all, but a highlighting of major emphases to be found in cultures. Nuanced explanations or details are omitted to allow us to grasp a little more clearly what is in reality a highly complex situation. Any particular culture is then compared with the model to see to what extent it resembles it or not. Four culture models are briefly described below, though particular attention is given to postmodernism since it commands considerable global influence today. In practice a culture may well have elements of all four models at the same time, though one model will tend to predominate at a particular time (see Table 2.1).

Table 2.1 Culture models

	Premodern	Modern	Postmodern	Paramodern
Significant people	Aquinas	Descartes Newton Bacon Locke Hume	Nietzsche Darwin/Marx Freud/Jung Sartre Heidegger Derrida	Teilhard de Chardin Bergson Eliade Panikkar Derrida Turner
Significant events		Renaissance Reformation Enlightenment	New sciences World War II Revolution of Expressive Disorder Vatican II	
Primary identity source	Predetermined group	Autonomous self	Self: fiction	Relationships freely chosen
Pivotal symbols	Group/ tradition/ fate	Self/progress/ orderly world/ rationality	Chaos/ narcissism	Chaos and order
Founding myth	Tradition	Perfectibility and progress: materialism	Progress questioned: chaos	Order/ chaos

Table 2.1 Culture models cont.

	Premodern	Modern	Postmodern	Paramodern
			Meaning: episodic/ fragmented	
Cosmology	Sacred and profane one: theistic Life subject to fate/magic	Sacred and profane separate	Real world unknowable	Life: process/ interconnected
		Universe orderly/ knowable/ controllable	Questioning order	Patterns observable in chaos
	Humans and environment interdependent	Environment separate from and subject to humankind	Environment to be used at will	Humans and environment interdependent
	Sin: social	Sin: individual guilt	Sin: failure to achieve	Sin: social and ecological
Education	Experience based	Institutional/ abstract	Institutional questioned	Experience based
Theology	God-centred: secrets of universe belong to God Salvation: obey commandments	Universe: coherent, intelligible, law-abiding system God's existence knowable through reason	Reason not able to know God; faith alone Scripture centred Reason downplayed	Breakdown of patriarchal theology
		God the transcendent	Incarnational theology	Creation theology
	Institutional Church Patriarchal	Ghetto Church Patriarchal	Restorationist Church irrelevant Kingdom values: justice and peace	Models: Pilgrim People of God Protest Churches Interdependence theology: feminine/ masculine/ ecological
Religious life	Counter-culture Monastic	Counter-culture: e.g. Francis, Ignatius, Merici	Chaos: restorationist/ prophetic	New forms: e.g. mixed gender

cont.

Table 2.1 Culture models cont.

	Premodern	Modern	Postmodern	Paramodern
Image of cultures	Organic whole: humans and environment	Mechanistic/ impersonal	Cultures inter-relate through violence	Organic whole: humans and environment
Language emphasis	Concrete/ imagination/ story-telling	Rational/ abstract/ concise	Feelings Intellect distrusted	Intuition and reason
Social organization	Priority: group order Kinship based	Priority: individual Society contract-based		Priority: interdependence/ collaboration
	Government: autocratic/ hierarchical	Government: strong/ self-confident democracy based on consensus Common good stressed: welfare state or individual rights	No consensus Welfare state breakdown: individual rights over group	Communitarian
Economic structures	Subsistence/ personalized small trading	Capitalism: extreme or modified Bureaucratic/ specialization/ impersonal	Extreme capitalism	
Minorities	Tribal societies oppressive/ federate	Oppressed: survival of fittest	Struggle for rights	Multiculturalism
Social control	Order before justice: informal sanctions, e.g. shame/honour	Justice over order: formal sanctions	Fear of violence	
Gender emphasis	Male dominant	Male domination reinforced	Male domination questioned	Equality Feminism overcoming inferiority/ superiority based on gender

Model 1: Premodern culture

This culture type, found commonly in Asia, Africa, parts of Middle and South America, and the South Pacific today, and throughout Europe up to the Reformation period, is one in which behaviour is highly traditional. The individual's identity is inseparable from the group he/she is born into, such as the extended family, clan or tribe.

Founding myths exalt the stability and sacredness of tradition, not change; the culture is a gift of the gods/ancestors so it must not be questioned. The fear of ostracism, of being mocked, laughed at or punished by spirits if one goes against tradition, enforces conformity to the group's norms. Because tradition is pivotal, harmony and unity must be maintained within the group at all costs, even if the objective norms of justice are broken in the process. To be expelled from the group, as Cain found after murdering Abel (Gen 4:10, 12–13), is the severest form of punishment possible, because then the individual loses all sense of identity and rights. Respect for patriarchal values is also a strong force in maintaining the *status quo*. If women misbehave, then men, who are the guardians of tradition and stability, experience shame; to avoid this shame and maintain a sense of male honour, women must be kept in their inferior status and fully under men's control.

Case study: Excessive group control

A missionary from Europe after several months as a formator in a large formation house for clerical religious of his congregation in the Philippines remarked to a visitor: 'The quality of community life here is just so perfect, so Christian. There is a gentleness and a humility in the way the candidates relate to one another. No one steps out of line. No one feels lonely. There is so much harmony here. Just so different from the individualism of the Western world.' Two years later the same formator commented: 'I was wrong. There is considerable unresolved tension between the students. Many feel oppressed by the group and fear to challenge it for this.'

This case study illustrates some key points of the premodern culture model. In the Philippines faithfulness to the group, called *bayanihan*, is emphasized. A key expression in that culture is *pakikisama*, and this underlies virtually the entire structure of social relationships. Priority is to be given to smooth interpersonal relationships at all times and *pakikisama* is a primary way of achieving such smoothness. It means 'giving in', 'following the lead or suggestion of another', in a word, 'concession', even when one knows that concession is objectively the wrong thing to do. *Pakikisama* favours avoidance of direct confrontation that could lead to open and violent aggressive behaviour. The desire for frictionless relationships can result in extensive use of euphemism in conversation, and speech is loaded with metaphors that convey a message with minimum risk of offence. *Pakikisama* certainly has its positive side, for example the need to be concerned about how others feel, but it also has negative effects and the case study shows some of them. It can so overstress group loyalty and the maintenance of smooth relationships that members find it extremely difficult to develop and own individual autonomy and self-assertiveness. Moreover, the group can become so consumed with maintaining the external facade of peace that issues of importance to the group's identity and purpose cannot surface. The missionary in the above case study is insensitive at first to all these dynamics. Formators working in cultures of this type, therefore, need to provide ample opportunity and guidance for individuals to become their autonomous selves.

Case study: Syncretism

An African religious, finally professed 20 years ago and educated at training centres of the congregation in Europe, was diagnosed recently as having cancer. He recounts his reactions: 'I was personally shattered. Why me? What have I done to deserve this? My relatives said I should consult a particular witch-doctor (i.e. a diviner or one who seeks the secret causes of things). I eventually sought his advice and he said I was being secretly attacked by a witch, a close relative I do not relate to easily. My immediate family demanded and received compensation for this bewitching. I had radiation treatment, but also I do what he said I should, that is, I carry special charms to ward off further witch attacks – just in case. Now I think about all this and wonder if it is a good thing according to the gospel. We had not talked about witch attacks in our formation years. We were told just to believe in Jesus and forget these things. I think we should have talked about them.'

Evil in traditional cultures is commonly seen as that which destroys life, health, good status and prosperity. These premodern cultures recognize the immediate and rational causes of evil, for example, that cancer causes death, that for every misfortune there is always an answer to the question 'how?' (physical or natural causes), but the further question, namely 'the why?' (the ultimate, determining cause(s)), must be answered in other ways. As in the above case study people readily acknowledge the visible causes ('the how?') of the misfortunes, but the answer to the question 'why?' is far more difficult. Often they believe that the ultimate cause of evil is ancestors who punish the living for not showing respect to them or for breaking tribal taboos. The living can also harm others through the intentional or unconscious use of magical forces. Tribal cultures have a variety of specialists (e.g. shamans, diviners) and methods to discern precisely which spirit or person is causing the evil and what are the necessary remedies.[21]

Syncretism in social anthropology is any synthesis of two or more culturally diverse beliefs or practices. No judgement is made about whether or not the believers are morally good or bad. Syncretism from a Christian perspective, however, is 'any theologically untenable amalgam'.[22] St Paul writes against this latter kind of syncretism: 'It is for freedom that Christ has set us free' and he adds the corollary 'Stand fast therefore and do not fall back into slavery again' (Gal 5:1). Formation programmes fostering in religious only an intellectual assent to this call to freedom and not challenging them to conversion deep within their hearts and cultures are themselves forms of slavery. The religious in the above case study of syncretism rightly criticizes his formation programme. He and others were told not to think about witchcraft dynamics in their culture. However, unless candidates are encouraged to reflect on such issues in the light of the gospel, conversion deep within themselves cannot take place. Unchallenged feelings about witchcraft dynamics formed a residual myth for this religious, waiting to surface and become an operative myth when the circumstances were right. One African formator summarized for me the challenge in this way, and I believe pastorally correctly:

> Our candidates come from cultures where magic, witchcraft, sorcery and divination are as real to them as the air we breathe. My experience is that our candidates and professed religious commonly develop a split-level way of thinking. On the one hand, they intellectually assert that these behaviour patterns make no rational sense and conflict with the gospel. On the other hand, at the feeling level they are influenced, especially at times of illness, by those cultural forces. I believe this dual way of reacting, plus our failure to raise these issues honestly with them, is significantly obstructing our formation work. Inculturation demands our candidates reflect together on their cultural experiences, otherwise we give them knowledge that stops at the head. I call this a process of 'self-inculturation'.

Model 2: Modern culture

[The Enlightenment was the belief in] 'linear progress, absolute truths, and rational planning of ideal social orders'.
(D. Harvey)[23]

Since about the sixteenth century, reinforced by the writings of the Enlightenment period in the eighteenth and nineteenth centuries, the pivotal principle of modern culture has been the *self*, not the group as in premodern culture. As Daniel Bell writes: 'The fundamental assumption of modernity, the thread that has run through Western civilization since the sixteenth century, is that the social unit of society is not the group, the guild, the tribe or the city, but the person. The Western ideal was the autonomous man [*sic*] who, in becoming self-determining, would have freedom.'[24] Such autonomous persons through reason and the sciences attain objective knowledge of a reality and discover lasting truths about an orderly world. The founding myth of modernity asserts that the human person is perfectible through his or her own efforts; progress is open to all who try hard enough.

The pre-eminent position of the person and the assumption that progress is inevitable for humankind found support in the emergence of classical physics, as mentioned in Chapter 1. Matter was thought to be the foundation of all life and the material world was assumed to be a huge orderly machine consisting of elementary parts. These assumptions of classical physics were adopted by scientists and Western society in general and they deeply affected the thinking of politicians, social commentators, economists and philosophers.

Descartes' influence on the evolution of this culture model has been profound in at least two ways. First, with his famous axiom 'I think, therefore I am' it was concluded that individuals must equate their identity with their rational mind. The idea of an integrated body, mind and spirit was not considered. This encouraged people to overlook the need to use their bodies as avenues of knowing and, unlike the premodern culture model, to separate themselves from the natural environment. Living organisms were thought to be machines built from separate parts; so also cultures. The latter could be divided up and sections destroyed without any sense of guilt because machines do not feel. Such a view supported a ruthless colonialism and extreme capitalism.[25] Second, given Descartes' emphasis on rationality, forms of knowledge that do not fit the norms of precise logical thinking are considered of no value whatsoever. Hence, knowledge through symbols and myths is not considered valid. As poetry, metaphysics and theology could not measure up to the need for clear and distinct ideas they were considered unworthy of the authentic thinking person. Patriarchy was a powerful force in the evolution and maintenance of this type of culture model, since it was believed that only men could undertake logical, rational thinking.

The emphasis on rationality impacted on people's views of God. To some, Isaac Newton's view of the cosmos as an ordered entity pointed to God's omnipotence and wisdom. As the cosmos was so neatly ordered, so also would society be if we left things to God; the deity would reconcile conflicting interests of individuals just as the creator keeps the planets at peace with one another. This viewpoint, however, eventually gave way to the assumption that the law-like behaviour of the natural world showed it did not need God. God was dispensed with. Materialism and secularism thus became acceptable in the modern culture. With the 'death of God', sin lost its previous meaning: the breaking of one's relationship with God. The focus moved to self and the imperative of self-fulfilment; when this happened sin could become synonymous with the failure to get ahead in life through using one's own initiative and resources. If minority groups became obstacles to one's self-fulfilment, then they had to be destroyed and their resources used in ways that foster an 'orderly' world. For example, the Nazis followed this thinking when for their own advantage they murdered millions of Jews.

National, even world order was seen to be possible if enough people come to a consensus that it is good to work together; self-fulfilment is impossible if order is lacking in society. This kind of rational thinking about the conditions necessary for achieving self-fulfilment paradoxically contributed to the emergence of the welfare state, for example in Britain, the British Commonwealth countries, France and to a much more limited extent, the United States.

The Roman Church, because of its withdrawal into a fortress culture following the Reformation in the sixteenth century, appeared to escape the impact of what this culture model represents, unlike its Protestant counterparts. As I mentioned briefly in Chapter 1, this is not entirely true. The rational arguments of Protestants against the Church were to be countered by more powerful rational responses. The Roman Church's theology became highly rational, removed from the world of experience and feeling, with scripture used only to support logical argumentation. Formation houses, especially those for the training of clerics and clerical religious, became models of educational order; it became an age of manuals in which philosophy and theology were reduced to neat and orderly pages so that students could learn, by heart if necessary, logically presented material that they were not to challenge. Theology became a cold and uninspiring discipline. Students were not expected to think for themselves; such freedom would disrupt the orderly structure of the formation system and the life of the Church itself. Thus the Church and its institutions had in their own way become seduced by Descartes' over-stress on the rational and the logical.[26] While seeking to remain aloof from the rising modern sciences, which it frequently considered dangerous to faith, the Church in fact became deeply affected by their emphasis on rationality and order. It was an unacceptable syncretism that few theologians or ecclesiastics challenged.

In this culture model there is a striking gap between rational thinking, scientific knowledge and technological skills on the one hand and wisdom, spirituality and ethics on the other. With the tragedies of two world wars, concentration camps and atomic explosions in Japan, the myth of orderly human technological and social progress at the foundation of modern culture, without ethical restraints, has been destroyed. This has contributed to the emergence of a new culture described in model 3.

Model 3: Postmodern culture

> The human mind [to the postmodernist] now appears to be anything but a neat thinking machine that – when properly operated – poses right questions and prints out right answers.
>
> (W. T. Anderson)[27]

In this culture model, which began to emerge visibly in the 1950s and 1960s, the assumptions that reality is ordered in a way which can be laid bare by the human mind and that it is possible to build a universal human culture upon a foundation of rational thought are rejected. Nor is it assumed any longer that progress is inevitable. Postmodernism connotes an extensive cultural malaise noted for its cynicism, pragmatism, deconstructionism, narcissism, scepticism, relativism and nihilism.[28] Critical realist assertions like truth and ethics are considered without foundation and in their place there is a *relativistic* construction of the world through language and narrative.[29] That is, the major theme of postmodern culture is the decline of '*meta*narratives', such as foundational theories legitimating a universal morality and social progress. There is a massive breakdown of certainty, writes Jean-François Lyotard, 'a loss of a central, organizing principle governing society and a unitary standard of cultural excellence or morality, and a decline in the belief of a unitary, coherent self'.[30]

Several factors have influenced this rejection of modernity, and this consequent cultural chaos. For example, as physicists reflected on the random behaviour of atomic and subatomic phenomena it became clear to them that the emphasis of classical physics on an orderly world could no longer be accepted. There was also a growing disillusionment among many people, especially in the 1960s, with the belief that more and more technological achievements must mean progress. There broke out in the Western world what can be called the Revolution of Expressive Disorder. It was a middle-class revolt against all certainties and boundaries – political, moral, sexual, educational, artistic and social. It was an intense effort to enshrine the rights of the individual as a feeling, free person rejecting all forms of impersonal bureaucracy, political manipulation and hypocrisy. The revolution began as a form of cultural revolution among a small group of radical activists, and climaxed by changing some of the most profound habits and assumptions of Western society. Within the United States, for example, it eventually killed the imperialist presidency of Richard Nixon, provoked a legal and political slide and weakened centuries of discrimination against blacks.[31] Sociologist Bernice Martin[32] notes that the most common quality of this revolution was the symbolism of 'anti-structure', 'anti-order': gaudy dress, long hairstyles and new beat music of pop stars like the Beatles, or the art forms of painters like Andy Warhol.

Inevitably this revolution caused a massive erosion of the legitimacy of traditional institutions: business, government, education, the Churches, the family. These institutions were seen to have compromised values such as freedom, creativity or self-expression, the dignity of the person. The continuous and competitive pursuit of money, the involvement in foreign wars, for example in Vietnam, and the maintenance of colonies was also in conflict with these values. Little wonder, therefore, that the post-modern culture model assumed that it is impossible to achieve consensus on any values. Any consensus smacks of order, a taboo word in post-modernism.[33] Within the Expressive Revolution, however, there is a major paradox. On the one hand, there is the earnest effort to develop structureless individualism with its burning zeal for immediate self-fulfilment and liberation from all restraints on freedom, but on the other hand, there is also the push towards collectivity, for example through commune-style living, uniformity in anti-structure clothing or hairstyles.

As regards the first part of the paradox, the self is no longer the modern coherent being, but instead the creative story-teller and maker; there are as many potential selves as there are innovative story-tellers. This idea of self as 'continuously revised biographical narratives'[34] is an attempt to achieve some meaning in a world where it is assumed that reality cannot be depthed to any degree. There is a constant search for personal identity, but one is always aware that even when it is achieved to some degree, it ultimately remains a fiction because there is no way to prove its objective truth. Mary Jo Leddy says that in postmodernism meaning is something which happens from time to time,[35] that is, a particular incident or episode in life offers a fleeting insight into one's identity. An individual may keep retelling what happened in an effort to reassure himself/herself that life does have meaning. Along comes another incident unrelated to the previous one, and life becomes a series of often disparate, unsatisfying meaning-giving episodes which lack an underlying, uniting and objectively knowable foundation giving meaning to whatever happens. So there is a constant, even manic, search for new experiences in the hope that ultimately some persuasive meaning will emerge, but there is the feeling at the same time that this is not possible or merely a figment of the imagination.

Inevitably this ongoing search by individuals for sustained meaning in life in the midst of a rapidly changing world produces many very fragile, insecure, highly narcissistic and depressed people. We cannot assume that candidates for religious life are exceptions. They may present themselves to the world as highly sophisticated and professional, but they may lack an integrated sense of self maturely relating to the world around them. Narcissism exists in modern culture, but it is more markedly in post-modernism. A narcissist is not a self-sufficient egomaniac, but one whose ego is in fact too weak to support an independent self. He/she is a deft manipulator of appearances and feelings, outwardly cool, yet fleeing from all lasting commitments and deeply dependent upon others' praise to make up for the emptiness that is felt. Because the narcissist's image of self is so weak, and envy such a powerful force, there is constructed a frail structure of grandiosity through devaluing others. The narcissist is focused only on the self and others have meaning only as they relate to it. Relationship and commitments of all kinds are highly fragile for the narcissist; every relationship, even marriage, is dispensable if it fails to serve the self-fulfilment aspirations of the narcissist.[36]

Richard Stivers argues that cynicism is a consequence of postmodern thinking: we cannot know reality as it is and there is nothing one can do about it. Cynicism makes things worse than they are in that it renders the current situation permanent, providing no hope of transcending it. And such cynicism, with its fatalistic foundation, breaks out into scorn and derision. Stivers points to contemporary humour, for example television programmes such as *Monty Python* and *Saturday Night Live* and individual comedians like Roseanne. Their humour has become extremely aggressive: 'It's not enough to point out the foibles and incongruities of human existence and to laugh with the other; instead one must show contempt for the stupidity and absurdity of the other. The other is a failure; I, the scorner, am the success.'[37] Readers may like to compare the old television family sitcoms, such as *The Brady Bunch* and the Cunninghams in *Happy Days*, with today's popular *The Simpsons*. The first two programmes represent the modern culture where in the ideal family all problems can be resolved and people are open to change. *The Simpsons*, however, reflects postmodern culture: the family is dysfunctional, members do not change, there is an atmosphere of hopelessness and aggression, authority figures are presented in ridiculous and cynical ways. People have become bored with the impossible task of finding their self-identities by themselves; boredom breeds both cynicism and envy.

Envy, a problem in any age and culture, is especially powerful in postmodern culture. Envy is the sadness I feel because someone else has what I want and if I cannot get it I seek to destroy the object and cut the person down to my size.[38] If a person is genuinely happy and integrated, he/she becomes the object of destructive envy to those whose self-image is poor – a common phenomenon of depression-ridden postmodernism.

Zygmunt Bauman believes that vagabonds or vagrants offer an apposite metaphor of the postmodernist. What keeps vagabonds moving is their disillusionment with the last place of rest and the hope that eventually the right locale will be found to give them a long-awaited sense of meaning. But meaning is never achieved, though the wandering continues; the postmodernist is a vagabond, like a pilgrim without roots or destination, 'a nomad without an itinerary'.[39] The tourist is another metaphor. The tourist lives without any commitment to, or any in-depth social or spiritual encounters with, the people he or she sees while travelling. Ultimately it is a dehumanizing experience: 'One thing that the vagabond's and the tourist's lives are not designed to contain, and most often are excused from containing, is the cumbersome, incapacitating, joy-killing, insomniogenic moral responsibility.'[40]

Now to reflect on the push towards *collectivity*, the polar opposite of individualism in postmodernism. Youth subculture emerged as an entirely new phenomenon in the mid-1950s at the time that postmodernism was beginning to develop. Factors such as the increased spending power of young people, the lengthening educational requirements for work, the growth and power of the mass media helped to foster this distinctive subculture that is markedly anti-adult, anti-order.[41] It fuelled the Revolution of Expressive Disorder. Rejecting institutional life, including traditional churches, younger people yearned for intimacy in community life, clarity of meaning and direction in their lives and the chance to assert independence before an adult world that looked so orderly and spiritless. New or renewed sects and cults were appealing movements through which they could achieve these goals. Lost in the cultural turmoil of the late 1960s, many were prepared to forgo their freedom for the sake of belonging. These collectivity-oriented movements, demanding *total* commitment in all areas of life, provided their adherents with security, a culture of dependency and the chance to make a protest against the adult world that viewed sects and cults with growing anxiety.[42]

Case study: A formator reflects

An informant reflects on his two experiences as a formator, one immediately before Vatican II and the other from 1968 to 1974:

'From 1953 to 1963 I was on the staff of a large seminary for clerical religious students in a First World country. The qualities that most marked these students when they entered the seminary were: clarity about the ministry they were to be part of, self-assurance, the desire to serve others, unquestioning commitment to the institutional Church which they deeply admired, submissiveness to authority, refusal, even inability, to question the structures of formation.

'I returned to the same seminary in 1968 and the contrast was vivid. These are some qualities I found in students: a questioning of *everything* – from seminary structures to ministry; an earnest desire for intimate, experienced sharing in community – if they did not *feel* community then they concluded there was no community life; beneath a facade of self-assurance, even maturity, a feeling of deep personal inadequacy or fragility; the desire to feel that they were praying, otherwise they thought they were not praying to God; a growing interest in scriptural studies; a self-centredness verging at times on the narcissistic; verbal concern for social justice but an unwillingness to become involved; a general weariness . . . . They were so serious. Everything needed analysing. Sure, there were many good values and attitudes in their lives, for example their questioning of the *status quo*, their intolerance of depersonalizing community structures, their search for new forms of prayer. I had the feeling of group and individual depression, a sense of sadness and a restless urge to experience "highs" through periods of sudden intense activities. I recognize that Vatican II had caused the breakdown of the centuries-old Catholic culture and this would have affected the students, but there were deeper influences operating and I believe they came from the cultural turmoil in the Western world.'

The formator is correct; the candidates after 1963 were coming from a Western culture in the midst of its postmodern revolution and this was reflected in their behaviour.

By the early 1970s, governments began to recover from the post-modernist attack on their legitimacy. The political new right emerged with its distinctive set of values and clear-cut answers to contemporary socio-economic challenges. Although condemning the narcissism of post-modernism by claiming to stand for traditional values, they nonetheless adopted with vigour its individualism. Devotees viewed the breakdown in morality and the growing government support for welfare services as ways of undermining a nation's local and international power. For them it became patriotic to support a *laissez-faire* capitalism, economic rationalism and decreasing aid to the poor and minorities. They claimed that people had the power to make something of their own lives, but would not do so as long as governments continued to organize their own welfare and affirmative action programmes; the poor are poor through their own fault. Politicians like Ronald Reagan and Margaret Thatcher – with much middle-class support – sought to destroy the welfare state and replace it with structures to encourage the revitalized Victorian virtues of *individual* self-help, and enterprise, and the survival of the fittest.[43] The breakup of the welfare state was seen as essentially a process of 'putting moral responsibility where it traditionally was thought to belong' – that is, among the *private* concerns of individuals.[44] So while outwardly rejecting postmodernism this political fundamentalism in fact became energized by several of its values, for example distrust of selectively chosen institutions, importance of individualism, the selfishness of narcissism.

Though all mainline Churches have been deeply influenced by post-modernism, the Roman Catholic Church has been especially affected. Vatican II challenged Catholics to leave the securities of their ghetto culture and go out into the world to listen and to evangelize, but few were prepared for this task, and certainly not for the turmoil of the Expressive Revolution. Catholics were expected to adjust to the demands of the modern era – something they had in many ways been protected from for centuries – and to the turmoil of the emerging postmodernist age at the *same time*. The effects of the combined impact of the Council, the Expressive Revolution, modern and postmodern cultures were traumatic for many Catholics: their meaning system, if it had been the coherent and well-integrated world-view of the ghetto-Church, collapsed with remarkable suddenness. Significant numbers of young people felt that the Church, like other mainline denominations, had so compromised with secular values, or had become so out-of-touch with contemporary issues, that it could no longer provide the desired haven of understanding and meaning. One section of the Church took Vatican II very seriously and fostered theology based on experience of people's needs, for example liberation and feminist theologies. One vociferous section opted, not for the Council's theology, but for the return of pre-Vatican II theology with its highly privatized individualistic piety and selfish non-involvement in the world – paradoxically supported by postmodernist emphases on individualism and lack of concern for social justice.[45]

Another group in the Church accepted the postmodern rejection of the rational emphases in modern culture; their assumption is that reason cannot grapple with questions of ultimate concern. With the post-modernist emphasis on subjectivity and the distrust of objective reality there is no possibility of finding any firm ground from which to articulate a world-view or universal truths.[46] As Huston Smith comments: 'Instead of "These are the compelling reasons, grounded in the nature of things, why you should believe in God," the approach of the Church to the world today tends to be "This community of faith invites you to share in its venture of trust and commitment".'[47] Faith, not reason, has moved now to centre-stage in theology. To this extent postmodernism has invaded even theology.

The positive consequences of this invasion are already emerging; people are rarely convinced now by rational arguments in favour of Christianity, but rather by example. They expect the Church to prove its legititimacy from the gospel quality of the lives of its members, not from history. Scripture scholar Walter Brueggemann sees that postmodernity can help us to use scripture in liberating ways. Under the influence of modernity, he argues, we made the text fit our orderly modes of know-ledge and control, but postmodernism has destroyed the legitimacy of such order and control. In a spirit of hope, he writes: 'As we stand before the text, no longer its master, but as its advocate, we will have to find new methods of reading.'[48] If we allow ourselves to reflect imaginatively on biblical texts, putting aside the unnecessary baggage of modern culture, we will become prophetically subversive within society and the Church through ministry and liturgical prayer.

Model 4: Paramodern culture

> The time is, for all its . . . complexity and dissonance, a moment of great beauty and opportunity. We glimpse new ways of thinking about ourselves, new possibilities for coexisting with others – even profoundly different others.
>
> (W. T. Anderson)[49]

This model reflects trends still emerging in a wide range of scientific, philosophical and social thinking to critique, on the one hand, the excessive optimism about human progress within modern culture and, on the other, the in-built pessimism of postmodernism. Among the factors that have influenced the as yet tentative development of this culture type are theologians such as Teilhard de Chardin, philosophers like Jacques Derrida, cross-cultural scholars like Mircea Eliade and Raimon Panikkar, cultural anthropologists like Victor Turner, the new physics, feminism, concern for the environment and the growing demand by minority peoples for multiculturalism.

In the area of philosophy, Derrida with his deconstructionist method-ology fits primarily within this paramodern culture model (though this may well be a controversial claim). Derrida deconstructs a text, explains Glenn Larner,[50] not to oppose or subvert it, but (like psychoanalysis) to uncover what it seeks to exclude and suppress, and to examine its conceptual and ideological schema. Deconstruction is not a matter of opposing modern discourse, 'but of unceasingly analysing the whole conceptual machinery, and its disinterestedness',[51] that is, showing how it is used or manipulated for political power and ideological purposes. The postmodernist view of self as a story-teller, based on the assumption that the self cannot get in touch with any deeper reality within, is challenged by the deconstructionists. They aim to peel aside the layers of stories and expose reality; out of this process people will then freely be able to construct a reality-based sense of self. Deconstruction is for the sake of *construction*.[52] Deconstructionism in management studies, for example, uncovers how patriarchal values dominate organizational life making it very difficult, if not impossible, for women to assume leadership. Once these values are identified, then action can be taken to allow feminine qualities to enter organizations to counter masculine dominance. The more 'feminine virtues' of mutual responsibility, compassion, gentleness and love are given space, the more a partnership or systemic society will emerge[53] – a distinctive quality of paramodern culture yet to be signi-ficantly realized. The greatest cultural deconstruction/construction process ever will be one that leads to removal of patriarchalism and emergence of authentic gender partnership.

Scientists during this century have become increasingly aware that classical physics no longer has the categories to cope with what they are finding. Instead of the machine-like universe of modern culture, they are discovering a world that is 'a harmonious indivisible whole; a network of dynamic relationships that include the human observer in an essential way'.[54] The world is seen systematically in terms of relationships between living organisms that are essentially co-operative and characterized by co-existence, relational interdependence and symbiosis. All organisms, from the smallest bacteria to humans, are integrated wholes and living systems, interdependent and interrelated. The greater whole is the biosphere itself – the planetary ecosystem – which is a dynamic and highly integrated web of living and nonliving forms.

In an effort to describe this reality that was no longer seen to be neatly ordered, scientists have evolved what is popularly called the *chaos theory*, simply explained as 'the science of process rather than state, of becoming rather than being . . . (resulting in) a science of the global nature of systems',[55] or what has also become known as the study of complexity.[56] Traditionally all our ways of thinking have been founded on linear relationships. If we add two to six we expect to have eight. But the insight of the new physics is that very few relationships are in fact linear, rather they are 'chaotic'. By 'chaotic' behaviour scientists now mean

56

patterns and events that are apparently random, but which are in fact causally determined. They are therefore predictable, at least in theory. In practice, chaotic events are unpredictable because they are 'non-linear' effects of many causes, that is, minute changes in causes can lead to surprisingly large changes in the effect. One commonly used example is the weather: the beating of a butterfly's wings could affect the future weather of places thousands of miles distant but it is not possible to check each butterfly (or all the other influencing factors), so the distant weather remains a surprise.

In brief, the study of wholeness and change is the science of chaos, a discipline responsive to the global nature of systems. Applications of this theory and methodology are to be seen increasingly in social sciences, for example economics,[57] literary criticism and decision-making negotiations.[58] The impact of the theory on management studies is of considerable importance. Leaders must have the skills to be comfortable with chaos, that is with uncertainty and rapid change; if they cannot manage or lead in change, then their organizations will certainly fail.[59] This is a radical break with pre-existing notions of leadership, as articulated within the modern culture model: leaders in the modern culture model had to be above all managers aiming to achieve harmony and predictability. In the paramodern model leaders must have the skills to cope positively with ongoing unpredictability; proactive, not managerial, qualities are demanded of leaders. As Ralph Stacey, an authority on leadership and chaos, comments: 'Chaos (theory) focuses attention on the importance, for strategic direction (in the midst of chaos), of intuitive thinking, insight, judgement.'[60]

The problem the multicultural movement faces has been inherent in thinking from premodern times: few, if any, cultures teach how to be multicultural. Cartesian duality – the us/them dichotomy – helps to make it difficult to reach out and embrace differences rather than fearing them or feeling threatened by them. The more the language of interdependence and systems displaces Cartesian thought, the more likely it is for authentic multiculturalism to occur.

Practical reflections for formators

Today's candidates for religious life are confronted not by the characteristics of one of the preceding culture models, but by *all* models at the same time, even in the Third World, as a consequence of the globalization of the information media. One model may at a particular time and place have more impact than the others, but in today's chaotic world this can change with considerable rapidity.

The consequences are obvious: candidates must understand all the models theoretically and experientially, if they are to be effective agents of inculturation. They must be people who are not afraid of change, but have the ability to use it for the sake of the kingdom. Moreover, candidates for religious life are most likely to evangelize in postmodern and paramodern milieus. If they do not themselves have proactive leadership qualities so as to be agents of inculturation within cultures that approximate to these culture models, they must be able to co-operate with those who do, otherwise they should not be accepted into religious life. Formators for their part should realize the personal consequences of the cultures of origin on candidates and adapt their formation processes accordingly. For example, candidates that are deeply influenced by postmodernism may present themselves with a high level of social and intellectual sophistication but lack personal integration. The following are some practical reflections for formators in light of this chapter:

1. The ability to foster inculturation is an essential requirement for religious in active congregations. Candidates for religious life, therefore, require:
   - a deepening union with Jesus Christ;
   - an appropriate level of philosophy and theology;
   - an ability to empathize with people and develop faith communities in which the process of inculturation actually takes place;
   - the skill of cultural self-analysis and an understanding of the dynamics of culture change;
   - skills to lead proactively in the midst of change.

2. By *cultural self-analysis* candidates identify the impact of culture and culture change in their lives, which is a prerequisite to helping other people to do the same. This skill is to be achieved through:

   2.1 the study of history and the social sciences, *particularly* social anthropology, which is the study of cultures and change;

   2.2 the development of their imaginative and creative qualities, for example appreciation of art and literature in all their forms;

   2.3 cultural exposure programmes, that is, being placed for a sufficient period of time (e.g. one to two years) in culture(s) *significantly different* from their own. Formators must discern when this learning experience will be especially positive for each candidate and guarantee on-site professional supervision;

   2.4 developing community-building talents.

3. No culture is unchanging, but all cultures have in-built resistance to change. The more radical the change, the more people feel a sense of cultural and personal lostness and insecurity. In this situation powerful movements of resistance emerge, for example sects and cults. Candidates must understand the dynamics of cultural change and its impact on their

own lives and on people around them. There is need to develop a vigorous faith life as a defence against excessive dependence on culture as a source of identity.

4. If there is no well-founded hope that candidates can develop the skills to be pastoral catalysts for inculturation, then they must not be accepted into religious life nor allowed to continue their training. And if a congregation is unable to provide educational facilities, including skilled formators, to train people in the art of inculturation, it should cease to recruit candidates.

Summary

Religious commit themselves to be specialists in the art of inculturation, and this demands that candidates be selected and trained with this task primarily in mind. If a religious congregation cannot provide the facilities to form people in this competence, it should cease to recruit candidates. This pastoral skill presupposes not only an ever-deepening personal relationship with Jesus Christ, community development skills, an adequate knowledge of philosophy, theology and the social sciences, but also the ability to understand and react positively to the tensions of culture conflict and change.

The world candidates are being formed to evangelize is caught up in the clash of several cultures: postmodernism is revolting against the certitudes of modernity, paramodernism against the pessimism of postmodernism. Candidates do not enter religious life to escape culture change and its tensions, but to discover how they can use them creatively for evangelization. If they lack potential for this task they have no vocation for religious ministry in the world.

Notes

1. Document *Instrumentum Laboris* for the Synod of Bishops, *The Consecrated Life and Its Role in the Church and World* (Vatican: Vatican Press, 1994), para. 94.
2. Paul VI, Apostolic Letter: *On Evangelization* (Vatican: Sacred Congregation for Evangelization, 1975), para. 20.
3. Ibid.
4. P. Arrupe, cited by M. Amaladoss, 'Inculturation and internationality', *East Asian Pastoral Institute*, vol. 29, no. 3 (1992), p. 239.
5. Ibid.
6. See W. Wink, *Engaging the Powers: Discernment and Resistance in a World of Domination* (Minneapolis: Fortress, 1992), pp. 87–104.
7. See fuller explanation in G. A. Arbuckle, *Earthing the Gospel: An Inculturation Handbook for Pastoral Workers* (London: Geoffrey Chapman, 1990), pp. 26–78.

8. R. H. Keesing, *Cultural Anthropology* (New York: Holt, 1981), pp. 68–9.
9. C. Geertz, 'Ritual and social change: a Javanese example', *American Anthropologist*, vol. 59, no. 1 (1959), p. 33.
10. C. Geertz, *The Interpretation of Cultures* (London: Hutchinson, 1973), p. 10.
11. E.g. see G. Egan, *Change Agent Skills in Helping and Human Service Setting* (Monterey, CA: Brooks/Cole, 1985), pp. 277–87. P. Senge does not refer to culture at all: see his *The Fifth Discipline: The Art and Practice of the Learning Organization* (New York: Doubleday, 1990).
12. On this point I differ from Amaladoss's excellent article, 'Inculturation and internationality', op. cit., pp. 241–3.
13. See S. A. Sackman, *Cultural Knowledge in Organizations: Exploring the Collective Mind* (London: Sage, 1991), pp. 16–23.
14. E. Hall, quoted by P. R. Harris and R. T. Moran, *Managing Cultural Differences* (Houston: Gulf Publisher, 1993), p. 264.
15. For a fuller explanation of symbols and myths see Arbuckle, op. cit., pp. 26–43.
16. R. May, *The Cry for Myth* (New York: Delta, 1991), p. 15.
17. See G. A. Arbuckle, 'Mythology, revitalization and the refounding of religious life', *Review for Religious*, vol. 46, no. 1 (1987), pp. 14–43.
18. For explanation of restorationism see G. A. Arbuckle, *Refounding the Church: Dissent for Leadership* (London: Geoffrey Chapman, 1993), pp. 1–97.
19. See F. Lopez, *Pastoral Care in an Emerging World* (Sydney: Marist Centre for Pastoral Care, 1994), p. 302.
20. See Arbuckle, *Earthing the Gospel*, op. cit., pp. 203–5.
21. See M. Marwick (ed.), *Witchcraft and Sorcery* (London: Penguin, 1990), *passim*. For an excellent analysis of the witch-hunting ethos and the pastoral response see A. Shorter, *Jesus and the Witchdoctor: An Approach to Healing and Wholeness* (London: Geoffrey Chapman, 1985), passim.
22. L. J. Luzbetak, *The Church and Cultures: New Perspectives in Missiological Anthropology* (Maryknoll, NY: Orbis Books, 1988), p. 360.
23. D. Harvey, *The Condition of Postmodernity: An Enquiry into the Origins of Cultural Change* (Oxford: Basil Blackwell, 1989), p. 27.
24. D. Bell, *The Cultural Contradictions of Capitalism* (New York: Basic Books, 1976), p. 16.
25. See F. Capra, *The Turning Point: Science, Society and the Rising Culture* (London: Flamingo, 1983), pp. 1–284; L. Osborn, *Restoring the Vision: The Gospel and Modern Culture* (London: Mowbray, 1995), pp. 17–77.
26. For an analysis of the Cartesian impact on Western society see R. Tarnas, *The Passion of the Western Mind: Understanding the Ideas That Have Shaped Our World View* (New York: Ballantine, 1991), pp. 275–81.
27. W. T. Anderson (ed.), *The Truth About the Truth: De-Confusing and Re-Constructing the Postmodern World* (New York: Putnam, 1995), p. 240.
28. See C. Norris, *Uncritical Theory: Postmodernism, Intellectuals and the Gulf War* (London: Lawrence and Wishart, 1992), passim; R. Tarnas, op. cit., pp. 395–413.
29. The insights into postmodernism and paramodernism by G. Larner have been particularly helpful. See 'Para-modern family therapy: deconstructing post-modernism', *Australian and New Zealand Journal of Family Therapy*, vol. 15, no. 1 (1994), pp. 136–7.
30. J.-F. Lyotard, 'The postmodern condition' in S. Seidman (ed.), *The Postmodern Turn: New Perspectives on Social Theory* (Cambridge: Cambridge University Press, 1994), pp. 27–38.

31. See Arbuckle, *Earthing the Gospel*, op. cit., pp. 68, 119–23, 136–7; T. H. Anderson, *The Movement and the Sixties: Protest in America from Greensboro to Wounded Knee* (New York: Oxford University Press, 1995), passim.
32. B. Martin, *A Sociology of Contemporary Cultural Change* (Oxford: Basil Blackwell, 1981), passim.
33. See S. Connor, *Postmodernist Culture: An Introduction to Theories of the Contemporary* (Oxford: Basil Blackwell, 1989), p. 8 and passim.
34. A. Giddens, *Modernity and Self-Identity* (New York: Polity Press, 1991), p. 5.
35. M. J. Leddy, 'Formation in a post-modern context', *The Way Supplement*, no. 65 (1989), pp. 10–12.
36. See Arbuckle, *Refounding the Church*, op. cit., p. 170; C. Lasch, *The Culture of Narcissism: American Life in an Age of Diminishing Expectations* (New York: Warner, 1979), passim; May, op. cit., pp. 112–14.
37. R. Stivers, *The Culture of Cynicism: American Morality in Decline* (Oxford: Basil Blackwell, 1994), p. 90.
38. See G. A. Arbuckle, 'Obstacles to pastoral creativity', *Human Development*, vol. 16, no. 1 (1995), pp. 15–20.
39. Z. Bauman, *Postmodern Ethics* (Oxford: Basil Blackwell, 1994), p. 240.
40. Ibid., p. 242.
41. See Arbuckle, *Earthing the Gospel*, op. cit., pp. 130–46.
42. Ibid.
43. Ibid., p. 125. See also C. Lasch, *The True and Only Heaven: Progress and Its Critics* (New York: W. W. Norton, 1991), passim; S. Bruce, *The Rise and Fall of the New Christian Right* (Oxford: Clarendon Press, 1990), passim.
44. See Bauman, op. cit., pp. 242–3.
45. See Arbuckle, *Refounding the Church*, op. cit., pp. 15–35.
46. See Tarnas, op. cit., p. 398; E. Gellner, *Postmodernism, Reason and Religion* (London: Routledge, 1992), p. 23; P. Berry and A. Wernick (eds), *Shadow of the Spirit: Postmodernism and Religion* (London: Routledge, 1992), passim.
47. H. Smith, *Beyond the Post-Modern Mind* (New York: Crossroad, 1982), p. 12.
48. W. Brueggemann, *Texts Under Negotiation: The Bible and Postmodern Imagination* (Minneapolis: Fortress Press, 1993), p. 11. See also relevant comments by G. Davie, *Religion in Britain Since 1945: Believing Without Belonging* (Oxford: Blackwell, 1994), pp. 189–204.
49. Anderson, op. cit., p. 11.
50. See Larner, op. cit., pp. 11–16.
51. J. Derrida, 'This strange institution called literature: an interview with Jacques' in D. Attridge (ed.), *Acts of Literature* (New York: Routledge, 1992), p. 109.
52. See M. Blanchot, 'The absence of the other' in M. C. Taylor (ed.), *Deconstruction in Context: Literature and Philosophy* (Chicago: University of Chicago Press, 1986), p. 390.
53. See R. Eisler, *The Chalice and the Blade* (San Francisco: Harper and Row, 1987), p. 121.
54. Capra, *The Turning Point*, op. cit., p. 32. Capra provides an excellent introduction to paramodernism; I draw on his insights, particularly pp. 1–89. See also D. Zohar and I. Marshall, *The Quantum Society: Mind, Physics and a New Social Vision* (London: Bloomsbury, 1993), passim.
55. J. Gleick, *Chaos: Making a New Science* (New York: Penguin, 1987), p. 5.
56. See M. M. Waldrop, *Complexity: The Emerging Science at the Edge of Order and Chaos* (New York: Simon and Schuster, 1992).

57. See *The Economist* (15 August 1992), pp. 70–1; (25 June 1994), pp. 85–6. For a critique of the application of chaos theory to economic planning see ibid. (13 January 1996), pp. 73–4.
58. See N. K. Hayles, *Chaos Bound: Orderly Disorder in Contemporary Literature and Science* (New York: Cornell University Press, 1990).
59. See M. J. Wheatley, *Leadership and the New Science: Learning About Organization from an Orderly Universe* (San Francisco: Berrett-Koehler, 1992); T. H. Nilson, *Chaos Marketing: How to Win in a Turbulent World* (London: McGraw-Hill, 1995).
60. R. D. Stacey, *The Chaos Frontier: Creative Strategic Control for Business* (Oxford: Butterworth-Heinemann, 1991), p. xi.

3 In the service of the Church: some formation implications

> The inevitable gap between the Kingdom promised and the Kingdom realized to date provides the space within which the Church members can lovingly challenge the Church in order that it might be more faithful to its call and to its mission. But the key word here is *lovingly*.
>
> (R. P. McBrien)[1]

This chapter explains:

- the reasons for the contemporary turmoil in the Church and various ways of being Church today;

- the impact of this turmoil on religious congregations and its implications for formation programmes;

- some dysfunctional aspects of new religious movements and their implications for the recruitment of candidates to, and their formation in, religious congregations.

Religious life exists to be of prophetic service to the world in and through the Church. If the institutional Church is not being true to gospel values, as many now believe, then religious by profession must challenge the Church to return to these values.

This chapter explains the contemporary tensions within the Church resulting from different reactions to Vatican II. Religious life formation must be based on the values of the Council, but there are significant pressures within and outside religious congregations to prevent this happening. Formators must be aware they are to train candidates to identify these negative forces and be prepared to call not just the Church in general but the congregations they are joining to be true to the Council's principles.

Over the last few years I have conducted workshops in many parts of the world and I often ask participants (lay, religious and clerical) to describe their experience of the contemporary institutional Church. The following are representative comments of people who though critical of the institutional Church still deeply love it:

'The Church is withdrawing into itself; it has become frightened of evangelization.'

'People are moving away from the Church in their thousands, simply because the institutional Church has lost touch with the real world and its Christ-given commitment to evangelization. This makes me sad and angry. I feel utterly powerless.'

'There is no forum to air one's views. Bishops are judge and jury.'

'Bishops are being appointed without adequate consultation.'

'There is no accountability in the Church in pastoral and financial matters.'

'We women are being ignored more and more.'

'Celibacy is seen as more important than the Eucharist. No discussion is possible – there are attempts to control even our inner thoughts.'

'Any pastoral experiment is reported to the bishop by right-wing movements.'

'We cannot even debate the possibility of women being priests in the Church. Surely this is a denial of free speech! I wonder what Jesus would say about this!'

'I sense fear all around me. We feel any move to be pastorally creative will be reported upwards.'

'Right-wing movements are in. Social justice evangelization is out!'

'I feel so sad. Vatican II gave me so much hope that a new era of evangelization for kingdom values would begin. Now we are being told to run away from the Council's vision. What is more important: Christ or the Church? I feel the Church sees itself as above Christ!'

'Fundamentalism is powerfully present in the Church. Fundamentalists confuse the accidentals of history with the substance of the Gospel and there can be no dialogue with them. As far as they are concerned, we are wrong and they are right. And Rome favours them.'

These comments are actually criticisms of a significant movement in the Church today, one sanctioned and encouraged by powerful forces within the institutional leadership. As briefly explained in Chapter 1 I call this movement *restorationism*, that is a crusade to take the Church *uncritically* back to the values and structures of the pre-Vatican II era. The restorationists say the Church must return to the hierarchical structures and non-involvement with the problems of the world that existed before Vatican II. At root, the campaign is anti-Vatican II; restorationists believe, some with far more vigour than others, that the Council was an enormous mistake.[2]

Restorationism and tensions in the Church

As the preceding comments illustrate, restorationism causes deep pain to many within the Church. They see many leaders seemingly paralysed when they are challenged to take the risks that are imperative if the reforms of the Council are to be implemented. They experience a pastoral inertia, apathy and the loss of opportunities to evangelize cultures from within. They see their friends walk away from the Church as it fails to speak compassionately to them and to their contemporary needs. They are distressed because, while the hierarchy of the Church often speaks of the need for a new, creative evangelization and for justice in the world, it refuses to allow an open scrutiny of its pastoral attitudes and structures, and secretive methods of governing and financing. Ecclesiastical structures that should be encouraging communication up and down and sideways are reverting to the pre-Vatican II style of selective listening. Bishops are being appointed very often without consultation of the people within dioceses they are to serve. Collegiality is being downplayed and it is increasingly difficult for local Churches to live that diversity so clearly called for by the Council.

Back in 1950, Pius XII appreciated the need for the Church to be a body open to *responsible dissent*. There 'would be something missing from her life', he declared, 'if there were no public opinion within her', a weakness or sickness, if responsible dissent was not encouraged.[3] John Paul II agrees: 'Truth is the power of peace . . . . What should one say of the practice of combating or silencing those who do not share the same views?'[4]

These powerful words make good sense because when leaders in the Church, or in any organization, are concerned for the future they foster a reasonable degree of diversity and dissent. By dissent I mean simply the proposing of alternatives. Open organizations encourage people who propose alternative ways of doing things, because they know that cultures age and produce dead wood, that is become over-institutionalized or committed to the maintenance of the *status quo*. Only new ideas and innovative ways of doing things can guarantee that life and vitality will continue. Ageing is a process that does not have to occur in any group, provided there is a continuous openness to rejuvenation through new and creative ideas. The Church, in the post-Council era, desperately needs dissent. The world, caught up in complex and revolutionary change, urgently needs people with creative ideas and courage to bring the gospel into contact with the realities of this change.

Reactions to Vatican II

When people are confronted with the possibility of change and its inevitable disruption, they commonly act, out of anxiety and fear of the unknown, to reaffirm without any critical reassessment their culture's traditional values, structures and boundaries. Groups develop their own sanctions to keep members in line. And this is precisely what is happening today within the Church, contrary to the theoretical openness to principled dissent so well encouraged by the comments of Pius XII and John Paul II.

From a cultural anthropological perspective there are several reasons for this restorationist shift within the Church. Consider the fact that not only did the Council introduce radically new theological orientations into the living culture of the Church, it also catalysed a cultural revolution the full ramifications of which we are still trying to grasp and will continue to for generations to come. By *revolution* I mean sudden, radical change which occurs in key areas of a culture, for example in the political, religious and social fields, so that one traditional way of living or value structure is dramatically challenged and even replaced at times by another in theory and/or in practice.

Culture, as we saw in Chapter 2, is a 'silent language', in the sense that symbols and myths are often held on to without our being conscious of their pervasive influence in our lives. People claiming to act rationally, to be motivated only by reasons of efficiency, are still influenced by hidden cultural symbols and myths.[5] The most powerful myth, as we have seen, is a group's creation story; it shapes their most important images and self-conceptions, their sense of having roots.[6] And every founding myth contains within itself polarities, for example the founding story of democracy embraces two opposites – the need to respect both the rights of the individual *and* the common good *at the same time*. As the myth cannot tell people *how* these polar opposites are to be reconciled in practice, the tendency is for the group to gravitate towards one pole and to downplay commitment to its opposite. Reform movements historically arise to restore the balance. When the authenticity of a founding story is in any way questioned, even for the very best reasons, such as getting a balance within a democracy between the rights of individuals and those of the group, people will experience symptoms of cultural chaos such as anger, disillusionment, a sense of lostness and simplistic blaming or scapegoating of others for the chaos. Their felt sense of order or belonging has been disrupted and they express this in dysfunctional ways.

Vatican II: call to reform frustrated

Vatican II was an effort to reform the Church at its most basic level of identity; the Council sought to bring the Church back to its authentic founding story. For the very best theological reasons it exposed the inadequacies of the Church's founding myth as it had interpreted and lived it for at least the past three hundred years. For example, the model of the Church as hierarchical had now to be balanced by the requirements of the Church as the people of God. Likewise the priesthood as a sacrament and ministry had to be balanced with the fact that all by baptism are priests.[7] The Council did not tell us precisely how the equilibrium between the many polarities in its documents is to be achieved. Nor could it have done so. For generations many had been like little children, conforming to the detailed instructions of our clerical elders, and then overnight they were expected – laity included – to behave like adults and act on their own initiative as creative evangelizers, finding and maintaining the balance between the mythological or theological polarities in the documents of Vatican II. Little wonder that chaos occurred and continues! Historian John O'Malley concludes that the Council was another 'great reformation', resembling the Gregorian and Lutheran reformations 'in that it constructed a new paradigm that departed in significant ways from the one . . . before the Council began'.[8] He is correct. But my opinion is that the cultural chaos resulting from the Council's reformation will be seen by later generations as far more intense and disruptive than the other two reformations. Not only did the Church have to adjust to the realities of the culture of modernity, but it had to interact with a world in the cultural turmoil of postmodernism. It was ill-equipped, and remains so today, to interact constructively with the realities of both cultures.

There are three significant options for a group that has moved into the chaos stage of culture change. *First*, there is the formation of a new *status quo*, a new and revised founding mythology with appropriate structures and power systems. This is a long and often tortuous process, demanding patience, experimentation, and the ability to live in the ambiguity of the here-and-now as an updated mythology is slowly and hesitantly articulated and owned, and appropriate structures developed. The *second* possibility is a counter-revolution, the restoration of the former values and power structures. Often a short period of concessions to change by those in power, then growing rigidity and insistence on widespread conformity/ uniformity build frustration to breaking point. The *third* is the breakdown of the revolution into general disorder in which sundry conflicting groups flourish. Some actively support the values of revolution, but are denied access to appropriate power structures; others form sects characterized by elitism, quick-fix authoritarian solutions to the malaise, doom-and-gloom predictions of the future if the former structures are not restored, and intolerance of unbelievers accompanied by witch-hunting campaigns to identify 'heretics with revolutionary values'. Others, weary of the infighting, withdraw and go underground to wait for a better day, or else escape entirely from any kind of involvement whatsoever.

All three cultural reactions to the Council's mythological or theological reformation, especially the second and third, are evident today. In consequence, there are several culturally different ways of being Catholic or Church today, with important implications for the selection and training of candidates for religious life. For example, formation programmes based on the pre-Vatican II or restorationist models of Church do not accept the prophetic nature of religious life; they should be closed down or radically reoriented to the values of Vatican II. *A fortiori*, candidates should not be accepted into religious life as long as they remain attached to these models as the foundations for their apostolic life. I now describe four models of the contemporary Church and then indicate the implications of these types for the recruitment and training of candidates for religious congregations.

Group styles/structures in the Church today

Anthropologist Mary Douglas has developed a typology of cultures, using two variables – *group* and *grid* – that helps us to understand different ways of being Church today. The *group* variable connotes the degree to which people are controlled in their social interactions by their commitment to a social unit bigger than the individual. The *grid* variable, on the other hand, indicates the restraints on individuals interacting with one another *within* the group.[9] On the basis of her analysis we can identify four significant ways of being Church. They represent four distinct culture types.

Model 1: Strong group/strong grid: pre-Vatican II Church

Description
In the strong group/strong grid culture model, group boundaries are rigidly delineated. Internal structures or grid set out in minute detail how people are to relate to one another within a male-dominated hierarchical system. Conformity to unchanging tradition is the most esteemed value. Hence, this is not a culture model in which innovation is encouraged. In the religious cosmology of the culture there is a hierarchy of transcendent gods/spirits intimately concerned with the well-being of the culture and its stability; the gods at the top of the hierarchy are remote and stern, so people feel more comfortable with a range of intermediary and approachable spirits who can intercede with the higher gods. Within the culture itself there is a male hierarchy of priests mirroring the status ranking in the spirit world beyond, whose task it is to maintain the social and religious *status quo* established by the gods. Sin is primarily the infringing of the detailed rules which hold the group together.

Application to the Church
The pre-Vatican II Church approximated to this model. Recall the detailed laws controlling behaviour, for example the long list of intricate rubrics governing the celebration of Mass by the priest, the regulations concerning the amount of food permitted on fast days under pain of

mortal sin. The Pope, bishops and priests were considered to be the Church, the sacred guardians of the mysteries of faith, removed from the dangers of an evil world, ruling the Church through edicts handed down from on high. The laity were passive receivers of the expert, male, ritual/religious leadership of priests and hierarchy; they could not be trusted to save their souls alone in a dangerous world, so they were given an intricate set of rules to obey as their way to heaven. Sin was often seen as the breaking of these formally stated regulations, not the fracturing of a personal relationship with Christ.

God in pre-Vatican II times was pictured as a remote, almost Old Testament figure, the patriarchal Judaic Creator-God, one who keeps a very strict account of sin; even Christ was portrayed as someone remote from people, his transcendence being specially stressed so that he was presented more as King and Judge of a recalcitrant people who broke the rules. There was a wide range of compassionate intermediaries such as Mary and the saints. People could identify with them and relate to them personally, but it was difficult to foster a personal relationship with Christ the Transcendent, Mysterious One. His humanity was downplayed. Mary understandably became venerated as the pre-eminent saint, the warmly approachable mediator between humankind and Christ.[10] In this model of the Church change was considered unacceptable.

Model 2: Strong group/weak grid: the restorationist Church

Description

In this type of culture people have a sense of belonging to *this* group rather than to another, but there is a marked lack of agreement about the ways in which individuals relate to one another within the group. In other words, internal social cohesion is weak and social conflict is considerable. Cliques, alliances and sects form in response to people's needs for security and control in a world of uncertainty. People are suspicious of one another, feeling that others are manipulating the system against them, which destroys all sense of order and security. It is a climate in which witch-hunting or scapegoating flourishes.

Application to the Church

I feel this model represents the contemporary restorationist Church rather well. All kinds of sect-like movements flourish, some, for example Opus Dei, Neo-Catechumenate, Communion and Liberation, Blue Army,[11] yearning to restore the certainties, hierarchical structures, theological values and liturgical customs of the pre-Council Church. Claims of divine intervention, especially through God's messenger Mary, are many and at times verge on the bizarre. Often the supposed revelations emphasize the importance of returning to traditional orthodox practices such as the Rosary and the Tridentine Mass in order to avoid punishment by God.

Other groups, however, seek to live according to the values of Vatican II, but experience difficulty because the hierarchy of the Church for the most part supports the restorationist movement. They become the objects by restorationists of witch-hunting campaigns which denounce them for their so-called dangerous ideas. Especially targeted are people with little or no power within the traditional structures of the Church: feminists, creative theologians and evangelizers, and the poor.

Model 3: Strong grid/weak group culture: the accommodationist Church

Description
In this type of culture people are sturdily egalitarian, individualistic, utilitarian and competitive, but they have a very weak sense of belonging or of having obligations to the group. Alliances or relationships are very fragile because people come together only for as long as it is necessary for them to achieve their individual goals. If people feel other relationships can further their interests, they readily break the ties they have to their present group. It is a culture of lonely individuals. The gender emphasis is masculine, because the qualities thought to be required for success socially and in business are aggressiveness, impersonality, rationality and individualism. Sin is negligence in failing to use morally good or bad available means to succeed personally; if a person uses deviant means to succeed then *the* sin is to be found out. This is the culture of Watergate.

Application to the Church
In a highly secularized, capitalistic culture, God, Jesus Christ and the Church are viewed from a purely utilitarian perspective: 'How can they be an advantage to me in my struggle to succeed, to achieve status, material success and power over others?' If the Church is unable to respond to personal needs, then people will turn elsewhere, for example to New Age spirituality. Robert Wuthnow, in his analysis of support groups in the United States, significantly concludes: 'We want community, but nothing binding. We want spirituality, but we prefer the sacred to serve us instead of requiring our service.'[12] Because the individual and his/her material success are the major focus of this culture, compliant evangelizers do not emphasize the social justice obligations of Catholics especially those to the poor. The Church loses its prophetic thrust and marginalizes those who dare to be prophetic.

As a consequence of the dramatic breakdown of the pre-Vatican II culture many Catholics have opted for this accommodationist model of Church. They uncritically accept non-gospel values of the secular world around them and believe the Church's teaching must adjust to their unacceptable syncretism.

Model 4: Weak grid/weak group culture: protest communities

Description

The culture is strongly egalitarian in relationships and gender, with minimal pressures from internal and external structures to conform to group behaviour patterns or tradition. As in Model 2, groups approximating to this model are in the transition or breakdown stage, but unlike restorationists struggle to move creatively forward. To achieve this people return to their founding myth to rediscover what is essential and to be retained and what is accidental and to be let go. They recognize the need for social bonding based on mutuality and interdependence in response to a common vision. Friendships, therefore, are based on the need to work together to realize this vision of the group, not on the narcissistic wishes of individuals. A feminine aspect is evident in a 'heightened awareness of creativity, sensitivity, personal relationships and feelings, personal worth and individual differences'.[13]

Application to the Church

God in this model is transcendent *and* incarnational, revealed not only in the scriptures and tradition but also in the events of life. Jesus is the Emmaus Jesus, the compassionate challenging accompanier on the journey, the liberator from personal and structural sin. The Church of the Acts of the Apostles exemplifies significant aspects of this model: people freely and enthusiastically bound themselves together for a common mission through their personal conversion to Christ, they formed a pilgrim people with their brother and saviour Jesus Christ, recognizing their common sinfulness and their need of salvation; some women presided over house-Churches, worked as missionaries and in some instances shared a ministry with their husbands.[14]

Today within the Church there are emerging communities which struggle to live out the values of Vatican II in protest against the restorationism. Among the most notable are: Basic Christian Communities[15] particularly in the Third World, house-Churches, feminist movements and intentional or refounding communities within religious congregations. The person of Jesus Christ, the compassionate saviour and prophetic critic of wealth and power of New Testament times, is their focus. Their links with the institutional Church vary in intensity.

Post-Vatican II turmoil: implications for religious congregations

'Turmoil is going to break out among your tribes.'

(Hosea 10:14)

Anthropologically a *tribe* is a group 'of bands . . . having a feeling of unity deriving from numerous similarities in culture, frequently friendly contacts, and a certain community of interest'.[16] Of course people within a tribe commit themselves in varying degrees to its values and structures, but at least they and others know they belong to this tribe rather than to another. By this definition, before Vatican II the many bands or clans (congregations) constituted *one* tribe bound together, despite differences in founding and individual charisms, by common beliefs about the nature and purpose of religious life, for example the assumptions that the world is evil and to be avoided, and religious form the spiritual elite within the Church. Formation programmes were the same everywhere in the world and these further reinforced a sense of tribal unity.

Since Vatican II this tribal unity no longer exists. Instead of clans within *one* tribe, we have many different tribes that do not share a common vision for religious life and formation programmes. Even within the *same* congregation or community there can be several different tribes represented, each claiming that it alone is authentically interpreting the principles of religious life and their congregation's mission.

Communication across the boundaries of these religious life tribes may be poor, as is commonly the case between ethnic groups at any time in human society. Each tribe, says anthropologist Edward Hall, usually takes the position of 'thinking and feeling that anyone whose behavior is not predictable or is peculiar in any way is slightly out of his [*sic*] mind, improperly brought up, irresponsible, psychopathic, politically motivated to a point beyond redemption, or just plain inferior'.[17] This rather blunt but generally accurate statement of tribal ethnocentrism describes the strong prejudice that *my* tribe is the centre of everything, and all other groups or tribes are to be rated with reference to its superiority.

Unfortunately, the way some religious tribes or their representatives at times view other groups with hostility and self-righteous intolerance is not unlike Hall's description. Theologies that divide them are so different that serious communication between them and consensus about issues pertaining to religious life or congregational identity, for example formation programmes, seem impossible. Sometimes religious tribes agree to co-exist with apparent harmony; a truce is maintained because they agree at least tacitly not to raise their significant differences over the meaning of religious life. They deny or suppress differences lest exhausting tensions erupt openly. Dialogue, which demands an openness to the other and to the possibility of change, is difficult in these circumstances, even impossible. Communication is reduced to superficial issues that will not re-open deep divisive wounds from bitter past interactions.

Reasons for tribalism in religious life today

The answer to why the tribal unity of the pre-Vatican II world broke up into different tribal groups and different theologies of formation has been explained by what has gone before. The following is a summary of influences that contributed to the development of this tribalism. Anyone concerned about refounding religious life formation must be aware of them.

1. In Chapter 1 we saw that the founding myth of religious life evolved when people began to gather together to live the radical values of the.gospel, to devote themselves totally to the person of Christ and his kingdom. The major movements (monastic, conventual and apostolic) were *prophetic reactions* to abuses or corruption of power within the Church and society at large. Prophetic action is at the very foundation of religious life.[18] In Chapter 2 it was seen that myths are value-impregnated beliefs, born in sacred time and space, that people live by and live for. Myths are primarily unconscious, powerful in their influence, and difficult for people to articulate objectively except in story form or by describing the life histories of their culture's heroes and heroines. Myths provide feelings of certainty, direction and trust.

Over time, however, myths may drift away from their original message without people being aware of what is taking place. This in fact happened to the founding story of religious life. In recent centuries religious life lost a great deal of its dramatic prophetic emphasis within the Church and the world; the institutional Church domesticated its prophetic dynamism. Three pivotal assumptions, contrary to its original. founding story, had become so integral to the daily living of religious that the degree of myth drift[19] in religious life had become dramatic: the world is fundamentally evil and to be avoided; religious are the spiritual elite of the Church; and their task is to be uncritically supportive of the ecclesiastical and pastoral *status quo*.[20]

In consequence of the myth drift the vows, which had developed to be at the service of the mission, frequently became the mission itself. If religious, for example, received permission from a superior for a car then the vow of poverty was being perfectly kept. Whether or not the car was needed for the mission was not important. In the original founding myth of religious life the vows were not seen as the essence of religious life. The core of religious life is rather the radical commitment to Jesus and his ministry; the vows logically follow as a consequence of this commitment.

2. Vatican II challenged these aberrant assumptions, and the distorted religious life myth they had come to sustain, when it expressed the belief that the world is capable of redemption and the Church must interact with it through a process of exchange/dialogue (i.e. inculturation) and that furthermore, all people – not only religious – were called to, and capable of, holiness.[21] Religious, like all Christians, could no longer remove themselves from the concerns of the world, nor could they ever again consider themselves the spiritual elite of the Church.

The Council challenged religious to rediscover the prophetic heart of their ministry when it directed them back to the person of Christ, the founding experience of their own congregations and the apostolic needs of the world. The Council understandably could not neatly formulate the authentic founding myth of religious life. It would require much time (even decades) and effort on the part of religious and others to come to this clarity. Religious had to ask themselves, as they had not done for generations, questions like: What does it mean to be prophetic? Are our ministries really prophetic? How do religious in the contemporary world become prophetic?

3. However, a basic anthropological axiom is: *any interference with, or process of deconstruction of, a founding myth of a group – even when justified (as occurred at Vatican II) and intellectually assented to by the people involved – is catastrophic and chaos-evoking at the level of identity, belonging and feeling.* A satisfying, purified and interiorized myth is never recreated quickly out of the turmoil or chaos. Many groups never succeed in this task. They flee from the challenge by nostalgically retreating to the comforting securities of the old myth, or they remain paralysed in confusion, forming reactionary tribal groups. Only a few can be expected to struggle in the darkness of uncertainty to articulate and live the purified founding myth.

The reactions of religious congregations to the challenge given them by Vatican II show they are not exceptions, like the Church in general, to this sobering reality. I believe that many existing communities are dying simply because the challenge is too great; they lack the inner energy and people of refounding calibre to use the chaos constructively and their tribal lives today reflect this ongoing failure to adjust positively to the demands of the Council. Formators will need to discern in faith if their own communities are capable of revitalization, a point we return to in subsequent chapters.

Contemporary tribal groups in religious life

With the aid of the preceding models of the Church, it is possible to identify several tribal types in today's religious life. In practice each tribe will be made up of what are equivalently clans, that is groups which diverge in part from the tribe but not enough to make them a distinctive tribe in their own right. Within each religious community there may be representatives of several different tribes; rarely all or most members of a community or congregation will belong to one particular tribal category. Each tribal group has its own preferred criteria for the selection of candidates and their formation, so there is bound to be conflict when a community contains people of different tribal orientation.

1. The pre-Vatican II tribe
Pre-Vatican II religious life, as it was lived over several centuries, largely approximated to the strong group/strong grid culture. It was a tribal life governed by rigid hierarchical structures, detailed regulations regarding

every aspect of daily living, separation from the world including one's family of origin, formal community prayers and inflexible liturgical regulations. Public spontaneous or shared prayers were not permitted. The culture's heroes and heroines were the people who most perfectly conformed to the system and its values, the axiom being: 'Keep the rule and the rule will keep you.' It was a world tuned to crush all initiative, spontaneity and creativity for mission. It fostered a culture of dependency, that is, the perfect religious submitted without question to the wishes of superiors who were seen to be the representatives of God in the community.

The religious life tribe was equivalently a *sect* within the Church, especially in its relations with laity. A sect is an ideological collectivity, hostile or indifferent to the secular world, claiming to possess a monopoly on truth or salvation and demanding of its adherents total loyalty or commitment; errant members are usually harshly punished.[22] In formation an individual's identity must be removed and replaced by that of the group. All these qualities of sect life – including the formation process – were to be found to varying degrees within tribal religious life of the pre-Vatican II Church. Laity, for example, as non-members were commonly thought to be incapable of having the gnostic-like knowledge of God possessed by religious; religious were viewed as being 'half-way between earth and heaven'. When individuals withdrew from religious life, especially after profession, they were often branded in the Catholic culture as 'spoilt-religious', people who 'failed to persevere'. The fear of this marginalization forced many religious to remain within the tribe living thoroughly unhappy lives in consequence.

I rarely meet 'pure type' representatives of this tribal model in the Western world today, but they remain relatively common in parts of the Third World.

The following tribal model is substantially similar in many respects to the pre-Vatican II type but there have been some adaptations in it to the realities of the contemporary Church and society.

2. The restorationist tribe

One quality common to many sects is their restorationist emphasis, that is, they are formed in protest against, and usually separating from, another religious or tribal group. They assert that they represent a return to beliefs, moral standards and ritual practices of an earlier orthodox period. This seems to be the case with many newly established or 'reformed' religious communities today. They attempt to re-live the alleged purity of pre-Vatican II religious life, with the sect-like qualities and formation structures previously described, but commonly with minor modifications, such as simpler religious habits. However, even congregations originally established for active ministry re-adopt a monastic spirituality and community structures which downplay ministerial service and prophetic challenging of unjust structures in the Church and society.[23]

With fundamentalist zeal they vehemently proclaim their support of papal authority, though they selectively ignore ecclesial documents on social justice. Those who differ from them are branded as unorthodox and disloyal to the traditions of the Church.[24] However, they differ in at least one significant way from the previous model in that, though taking a world-rejecting stand theologically, they nonetheless often use contemporary mass media techniques with considerable skill to communicate their message to the Church and society.

3. The accommodationist tribe

Acculturation is a term describing assimilation by one culture of various characteristics of another culture to the point where the first culture experiences significant identity changes. Accommodationist religious tribes are groups and individuals who have so acculturated to the secular cultures that they are indistinguishable in significant ways from these cultures. An unacceptable syncretism has taken place. In Western societies this means that they are highly individualistic, and materialistic with little or no accountability to their congregation in matters of finance, community life and ministry. Elsewhere I have described this tribal life as therapeutic, me-istic or narcissistic; the congregation exists primarily to satisfy the individual needs of its members.[25]

Paradoxically, despite the emphasis on individualism, group bonding can be very strong among members of this tribal type. Tight cohesion comes, not from commitment to work together in dialogue and mutuality for a common mission, but simply in defence of their individualism. Members join forces to stop anyone who dares to challenge them to live the community values of authentic religious life, even manipulating the founding charism to support their actions. Within the tribe there are clan-type associations of a very fragile nature; that is, people form alliances with one another to maintain or improve their level of personal satisfaction or independence, but they move on whenever new groupings emerge that can better satisfy their self-fulfilment aspirations. The tasks of the official community or congregational leaders are confined to unthreatening duties such as organizing recreational or social events, attending necessary group and individual rituals such as funerals and profession anniversaries, and arranging insurance and transport facilities for members.

In brief, this tribal model is akin to a social club which members join not for the sake of the common good of the club itself, but primarily for the satisfaction of their individual needs. If any pressure is placed on them to participate in a common project, they either leave or excuse themselves 'to attend to rather more urgent apostolic business elsewhere', justifying their individualism with grandiose references to gospel values and/or the congregational founding experience. The congregational leader is equivalently a club captain.

Candidates may join accommodationist religious communities primarily to satisfy personal needs such as a sense of belonging in the midst of a harsh and tumultuous world. Such people have little or no desire to be concerned about the prophetic role of religious in the world; they especially like to speak about community life in terms of what it must do to satisfy their personal needs. Unwary congregational recruiters and formators develop formation programmes that satisfy the therapeutic needs of candidates, vainly hoping that this approach will eventually convert these candidates into dynamic prophetic evangelizers! In fact, authentic religious life cannot possibly develop in this self-centred ethos.

4. The tribe of depression

One reaction to chaos is to become paralysed by the experience, that is, to become so overwhelmed by the loss of the predictable as to lose hope in the future. People suffer the symptoms of chronic grief, for example anger, lethargy, fatalism, denial, scapegoating others and envy of the success of others. They cannot or do not want to move forward. I sense that many religious in the Western world now belong to this tribal grouping. They lack all energy for creative mission and destructively frustrate people in their midst who show such innovative zeal. At times they may come together and even agree on a mission statement or participate in lengthy discussions on the need to restructure their communities and administrations, but nothing of any substance happens since there is no collective commitment to act on their resolutions. The group depression then becomes worse. Issues such as the recruitment of candidates or formation programmes do not really concern them, because deep down they have given up any hope of a future.

5. The protest tribe

Religious of protest tribes, alive with the mission of the Lord and their own congregation, bind themselves together with like-minded people in faith-based communities after the style of those described in the Acts of the Apostles. Inspired by Vatican II values, they recognize the need to co-operate to better serve the faith/justice mission of Christ, but with an awareness that this interdependence is strengthened by shared faith and prayer. These are prophetic people characteristic of founding and refounding communities, attracting the anger and condemnation of accommodationist and restorationist tribe members. The accommodationists in particular see in protest religious what they should be themselves but refuse to be. At least unconsciously, accommodationists seek to marginalize protest religious to avoid being reminded of what they themselves should be.[26]

Protest tribes require of their recruits from the beginning an ability and a willingness to acquire a high level of human and spiritual maturity. Without this maturity they will be unable to contribute evangelically to, or survive in, a world of tumultuous change; they will be excessively demanding of support from other members of the group, draining away energy that should be directed apostolically outwards to the needs of the world. Formation programmes are structured to foster this apostolic maturity and they are regularly evaluated with this aim in mind; recruits must learn to function apostolically with a minimal degree of structural support. Protest tribes do not expect large numbers of recruits because of the high level of maturity demanded of candidates and the rigorous nature of their training programmes.

New religious movements and religious life formation

Earlier in this chapter in describing the restorationist Church, reference was made to new sect-like movements within the Church. More needs to be said about them in view of case studies like the following.[27]

Case Study: Troubled leaders

Recently a temporarily professed religious asked his superiors for permission to join the Neo-Catechumenate movement. He said: 'This organization really impresses me with its evangelical zeal, strong sense of community and faith in the Lord. By being with them I can only become a better religious.' The superiors (and formators) agreed, but after a few months they found that the religious was increasingly unavailable for community projects and less interested in the spirituality and formation requirements of the congregation. At the same time he became intolerant of those who questioned the movement's methods of evangelization. When these issues were pointed out to him, he replied: 'To be true to the movement's goals I must give all that I have. After all, that is what commitment to the Lord means in religious life. I am just fulfilling what the Lord wants of all Christians and especially religious. Moreover, this movement has the full backing of the Pope himself, so we must do what he says.'

This incident raises a serious question for today's recruiters, superiors and formation staffs. Is the membership of movements like the Neo-Catechumenate (which is commonly called 'the Way') compatible with the requirements for authentic contemporary religious life as described above under the heading 'Protest tribe'? I believe that a religious cannot in fact belong to both because he/she cannot be totally committed to two distinct groups whose primary goals are in opposition. A recent Vatican document on community in religious congregations expresses considerable caution about these movements: '(Those) whose principal membership goes to the movement and who become psychologically distanced from their own institute become a problem. They live in a state of inner division: they dwell within their communities, but they live in accordance with the pastoral plans and guidelines of the movement.' The document then states categorically that 'Candidates for the religious life . . . (must) place themselves . . . under the authority of the superiors (of the institute) . . . . They cannot simultaneously be dependent upon someone apart from the institute.'[28]

In addition to splitting loyalties for religious, these movements have a narrow pre-Vatican II view of the mission of the Church. Movements such as the Way downplay the importance of inculturation or the faith/justice apostolate, but an authentic religious must unconditionally support inculturation. Consequently, religious superiors (and formators) have an obligation to set limits to the involvement by members of their communities in the Way and other such movements, in order to safeguard the charisms of religious life and the congregation. The following section explains why new religious movements have developed in the Church and looks in some detail at the Way. The reservations in my analysis of the Way's organization, formation and pastoral methods can be used by readers to assess other contemporary new religious movements within the Church. I believe that formators need to be wary of accepting candidates who wish to maintain any significant links with these new religious movements.

Understanding new religious movements

Particularly over the last two to three decades a wide variety of new religious movements (NRMs for short) has emerged both within and outside the mainline Christian Churches. History shows that movements of this kind arise at times of socioeconomic/political upheaval or cultural chaos. They emerge as initial and inevitably simplistic efforts to provide a new social integration in response to conditions of acute social anomie or normlessness.[29] For example, the cultural revolution of the 1960s in the West affected every aspect of life; no political, religious, social or artistic institution remained unaffected by the revolution's radical evaluations. People were left emotionally and culturally exhausted, without a sense of identity or belonging, because the old securities had disintegrated under the speed and depth of its attack. The NRMs, such as the Unification Church (Moonies) and Scientology, offered disoriented people ready-made, clear-cut meaning systems and direction in life.

As we have seen, Vatican II's demolition of the Church's ghetto culture coincided with this countercultural or postmodernist chaos, so many Catholics were left struggling to cope with the after-shocks of *two* revolutions at the same time, namely the cultural and the conciliar revolutions. Little wonder that NRMs within the Church, for example the charismatic movement, Opus Dei and the Neo-Catechumenate, had such an immediate appeal.

Church history shows that, when movements form by way of reaction to disruptive forces of rapid change within the Church or the wider society, they run the risk of developing sect-like qualities and becoming elitist, claiming to have the total truth, so that salvation is possible only by belonging to the movement. Though they tend to be lay organizations, priests may be accepted as necessary, but they must submit to lay authority in matters other than the sacramental role. Individuals must earn their membership of a sect by performing acceptable actions or by undergoing a dramatic conversion or re-birthing experience. Sects may accept, at least in theory, a democratic form of government, but in practice the power of the group to control individuals, directly or through its leaders, commonly becomes authoritarian. Total loyalty is demanded of adherents to the group; errant members are harshly dealt with, even through formal expulsion, if rules are broken. Sects generally are fundamentalist in orientation – that is, they reject *dialogue* with the contemporary world or non-believers: the Holy Spirit cannot possibly be saying anything to us in a world that is intrinsically evil. When fundamentalists react to the 'polluting evils' of modernity, they assert that the world and/or the parent Church has gone wrong and that their task is to bring it back to an assumed golden age of a former period, even if this means using moral and/or physical violence to achieve it. Sect members, believing they have the fullness of the truth, are intolerant of people who dare to think differently; they indignantly condemn anyone questioning their assumptions of righteousness.[30]

Origins and critique of 'the Way'

The Neo-Catechumenate or 'the Way', I believe, shows the sect-like features just described. It originated in the early 1970s, emerging out of the personal religious conversion of an artist and musician, Kiko Arguello, and a small group of companions in the Palomeras slums of Madrid. The movement aims theoretically to recreate the lengthy period of training and teaching that catechumens underwent in the early Church. This necessitates an intimate knowledge of biblical texts in its followers, a powerful experience of the Church as a small accepting community, the revitalization of the Easter Vigil as the central Christian feast, and participation in Sunday evening Eucharist and sacraments with a degree of commitment exceeding what is expected in an average parish.

The Way sees the Church as ideally consisting of small communities with members being held together by strong communitarian bonds; lay catechists have a central position and members are expected to give generously of their time and income to the group's activities. They may be required to go as missionaries of the Way to any part of the world at any time decided by the movement's authorities. The Way is not concerned with any particular social or political programmes. Their task, they claim, is to proclaim the Word of God *verbally*, not to become actively involved in any way in social justice issues. Gordon Urquhart comments:

> [The] Neocatechumenate takes the most extreme position. Although it sees its mission as 'saving the world', and describes its members as 'leaven' and 'salt of the earth', in fact its world-rejecting stance is so extreme that little interaction with the wider society is possible. The emphasis is on the spiritual life and detachment from all worldly cares, which are considered 'idols'. All attempts to change or influence society are actively discouraged as presumptuous.[31]

Given its world-rejecting approach, the Way sees no need to dialogue with cultures. Consequently no cultural knowledge of the area chosen to be evangelized is necessary; all that is needed is zeal and dependence on the power of the Holy Spirit.[32]

While the Way may do much good for many of its followers, it is, in my experience and that of others, gravely deficient at the theological and pastoral levels for a number of reasons. *First*, the Way in practice commonly exemplifies many of the features previously listed for sects. For example, it demands total and unquestioning commitment from its members and submission to the authority of its organizers; it is elitist and frequently divisive within parishes by demanding excessive time from members who are priests and/or religious and acting without reference to existing parish structures.

Second, the Way rejects the gospel's call, repeated in Vatican II and subsequent ecclesial documents, to struggle for justice in society. *Third*, the Way rejects the notion of inculturation. Yet, as with the call to struggle for social justice, we are not free to choose or reject inculturation. It is a gospel imperative. As John Paul II says: 'the Church's dialogue with the cultures of our time (is) a vital area, one in which the destiny of the world . . . is at stake'.[33] In their enthusiasm to preach the good news, the Way's followers adopt a Eurocentric model of the Church and evangelization. This is precisely the oppressive situation that Peter and Paul condemned at the Council of Jerusalem (Acts 15:1–35). The rituals and catechetical material of the Way's evangelizers are pre-packaged in Europe and they are then imposed on other cultures.[34] Furthermore, there are no concerted attempts among the Way's evangelizers to prepare themselves for work in cultures different from their own. Simple trust in the Holy Spirit is no substitute for the serious cultural openness and respect for diversity, discernment and pastoral competence that Paul VI considers essential for inculturation.[35] The Way also exemplifies fundamentalist qualities: its followers are not prepared to dialogue with people who question their pastoral assumptions and methods; they have the truth, so dialogue is unnecessary.

Religious life commitment versus 'the Way': divided loyalties

A religious is one who is called by God for a mission of faith/justice service. He/she is to respond freely and totally to gospel values by witnessing within a Church-approved community whose members are striving to be formed by Christ and in his vision. By 'Church-approved community' we mean that the Church acknowledges the gospel authenticity of the founding insight; members commit themselves *exclusively* to live out that insight under the legitimate authority of the group, not that of another congregation or group. Anything that interferes with this exclusive commitment to the charisms of religious life and the congregation, no matter how good it might be in itself – such as, for example, a particular form of spirituality, a type of community life – is contrary to the original offering made by the religious to Jesus Christ, his Church and his/her congregation.

Therefore, should a religious or candidate for religious life become a member of the Way without restriction, I believe he/she has equivalently opted out of the congregation and should be asked to leave, because the Way demands *unconditional* loyalty to its vision and authority structures. The fact is that a religious cannot simultaneously be committed to two organizations, each demanding of its followers total commitment. It would be tantamount to attempting to be a Dominican and a Jesuit at the same time!

From the standpoint of mission and spirituality, religious must struggle to be prophetically at the cutting edge of the gospel and cultures. That is their primary task. They exist, especially through their individual and corporate example, to challenge the world and the Church to be true to the values and vision of Christ. This prophetic stand means that they must be specialists in inculturating the gospel. Since the catechetical methods and assumptions of the Way fundamentally conflict with inculturation, religious cannot be unconditionally involved in the Way. Authentic religious life, contrary to the sect-like Way, stands for universality and a critical openness to the world.

In brief, a religious congregation, if it is to be true to its charism must not become a sect, nor can it support sect-like activities in other groups. Neither can a congregation act authentically unless it is committed to the faith/justice mission of Christ to which inculturation is integral. The Way does not accept this apostolic vision and openness. Whenever a New Religious Movement (e.g. the Neo-Catechumenate) in the Church does not adhere to the values of Vatican II no religious nor candidate for religious life can belong to it.

Summary

The primary task of religious is to challenge both the world and the Church to be true to Christ's mission and his kingdom values. Since

Vatican II, people have openly different ways of defining the Church; some reject the fundamental directives of Vatican II. The differences are mirrored in contemporary religious life and in the variety of approaches to formation: some religious withdraw from Christ's mission to evangelize a world of cultures, others adopt cultural values in conflict with authentic religious life.

Formation programmes and the selection of candidates should never be based on aberrant reactions to the Council's call to reform religious life. As religious are committed by profession to help build the Church according to Vatican II values, formation programmes must be established with this vision primarily in mind. Whenever religious accept models of the Church not sanctioned by the Council, and base formation programmes on them, they are not true to the mission of Christ. Candidates should not be accepted into religious communities if they wish to maintain significant links with sect-like religious movements in the Church which contradict basic principles of Vatican II.

Congregational leaders and formators, therefore, need to rediscover in the midst of the contemporary chaos the essentials of religious life and build appropriate selection systems and formation programmes. This process of refounding religious life formation is a difficult and complex one, as will be explained in the following chapter.

Notes

1. R. P. McBrien, *Ministry: A Theological Pastoral Handbook* (San Francisco: Harper and Row, 1987), p. 66.
2. The following analysis of restorationism is a brief summary of my book, *Refounding the Church: Dissent for Leadership* (London: Geoffrey Chapman, 1993), pp. 1–97.
3. Cited by K. Rahner, *Free Speech in the Church* (London: Sheed and Ward, 1959), p. 5.
4. Cited by L. Swidler, 'Democracy, dissent, and dialogue' in H. Küng and L. Swidler (eds), *The Church in Anguish* (San Francisco: Harper and Row, 1987), pp. 312–13.
5. See analysis by E. Hall, *The Silent Language* (New York: Doubleday, 1959), passim.
6. See W. G. Dotty, *Mythography: The Study of Myths and Rituals* (Tuscaloosa, AL: University of Alabama Press, 1986), p. 25 and passim.
7. See Arbuckle, *Refounding the Church*, op. cit., pp. 39–43.
8. J. W. O'Malley, 'Developments, reforms, and two great reformations: towards a historical assessment of Vatican II', *Theological Studies*, vol. 44, no. 3 (1983), pp. 403–4.
9. See M. Douglas, *Natural Symbols: Explorations in Cosmology* (New York: Pantheon Books, 1970) and *Purity and Danger: An Analysis of the Concepts of Pollution and Taboo* (London: Routledge and Kegan Paul, 1966), passim; also G. A. Arbuckle, 'Innovation in religious life', *Human Development*, vol. 16, no. 3 (1985), pp. 45–9 and *Refounding the Church*, op. cit., pp. 80–94.
10. See comments by R. Tarnas, *The Passion of the Western Mind: Understanding the*

    Ideas That Have Shaped Our World View (New York: Ballantine Books, 1991), pp. 162–4.

11. For a critique of the Neo-Catechumenate, Communion and Liberation and Focolare see G. Urquhart, *The Pope's Armada* (London: Bantam Press, 1995), passim.

12. R. Wuthnow, *Sharing the Journey: Support Groups and America's Quest for Community* (New York: The Free Press, 1994), p. 365.

13. C. Handy, *Gods of Management: The Changing Work of Organizations* (Sydney: Random House, 1995), p. 244.

14. See C. C. Murphy, *An Introduction to Christian Feminism* (Dublin: Dominican Publications, 1994), pp. 50–8.

15. See explanation in Arbuckle, *Refounding the Church*, op. cit., pp. 91–2.

16. R. Linton, *The Study of Man: An Introduction* (New York: Appleton-Century-Crofts, 1936), p. 231.

17. E. Hall, *Beyond Culture* (New York: Doubleday/Anchor, 1976), p. 43.

18. See Document *Instrumentum Laboris* for Synod of Bishops, *Consecrated Life and Its Role in the Church and the World* (Vatican: Vatican Press, 1994), para. 64.

19. For a fuller explanation of myth drift see G. A. Arbuckle, *Earthing the Gospel: An Inculturation Handbook for Pastoral Workers* (London: Geoffrey Chapman, 1990), pp. 40–1.

20. See G. A. Arbuckle, *Out of Chaos: Refounding Religious Congregations* (London: Geoffrey Chapman, 1988), pp. 68–77.

21. See 'Dogmatic Constitution on the Church' in W. Abbott (ed.), *The Documents of Vatican II* (London: Geoffrey Chapman, 1966), paras 40–41.

22. See J. A. Beckford, *The Trumpet of Prophecy: A Sociological Study of Jehovah's Witnesses* (Oxford: Basil Blackwell, 1975), pp. 122–3.

23. See P. Wittberg, *The Rise and Fall of Catholic Religious Orders: A Social Movement Perspective* (New York: SUNY, 1994), p. 270.

24. See Arbuckle, *Earthing the Gospel*, op. cit., pp. 126–7.

25. See Arbuckle, *Refounding the Church*, op. cit., pp. 168–74. In this book I describe different kinds of religious communities as ascetic, relationship oriented, therapeutic and mission oriented. Jon Sobrino from his experience sees very similar types of communities in religious life. See his book *The True Church and the Poor* (Maryknoll, NY: Orbis Books, 1984), passim. See comments by Johannes Fullenbach on the similarity: 'Religious life in the year 2000', *Theological Digest*, vol. 42, no. 1 (1995), pp. 19–23.

26. See G. A. Arbuckle, 'Obstacles to pastoral creativity', *Human Development*, vol. 16, no. 1 (1995), pp. 15–20.

27. The following section is an updating of an article I originally published in *Religious Life Review*, vol. 33, no. 164 (1994), pp. 2–7.

28. Congregation for Institutes of Consecrated Life and Societies of Apostolic Life, *Fraternal Life in Community* (Vatican: Vatican Press, 1994), para. 62.

29. See Arbuckle, *Earthing the Gospel*, op. cit., pp. 113–29.

30. See B. R. Wilson, *Sects and Society* (London: Heinemann, 1961), pp. 1–11.

31. Urquhart, op. cit., p. 270.

32. See A. Orensanz, 'Spanish Catholicism in transition' in T. M. Gannon (ed.), *World Catholicism in Transition* (New York: Macmillan, 1988), p. 141.

33. John Paul II cited by A. Shorter, *Toward a Theology of Inculturation* (London: Geoffrey Chapman, 1988), p. 230.

34. See Urquhart, op. cit., p. 287.

35. See Paul VI, Apostolic Letter: *On Evangelization* (Vatican: Sacred Congregation for Evangelization, 1975), para. 20.

4 The refounding of religious life formation

Formation must be human, ongoing, inculturated, open to ecclesial communion and mission, and in touch with real life and the conditions of the poor. Its orientation must be a vital process centred on the person of Christ.

(*Instrumentum Laboris*, 1994)[1]

This chapter explains:

- the meaning of refounding;

- the processes and assumptions required for the refounding of formation in religious life;

- several models of initial formation;

- reasons why the pilgrimage model is ideal for contemporary formation.

Religious life formation is in a state of chaos, as the previous chapter explains. Yet a fact of human experience, reinforced by faith in God, is that chaos, the radical breakdown of the predictable, can be a most positive experience personally and organizationally. Like the Israelites of old, we can use chaos to free ourselves from irrelevant formation attitudes and structures to make a radically new beginning based on the mission of Christ, the Church, the founding experience of our congregation and the needs of the world. It is not a question of modifying old methods, which is *renewal*, but of going back to first principles and building structures based on them. In brief, the challenge is to *refound* formation.

Contemporary management literature is constantly inventing new terms or recycling old ones to articulate how leaders of businesses can in a competitive environment achieve productivity improvements, for example by 're-engineering', 'restructuring', 'reframing', 'downsizing', 'relayering'. Now we introduce the term 'refounding'; readers can be forgiven if they feel confused by all this jargon. However, by clarifying some of these expressions it is possible to sharpen understanding of the unique nature of *refounding.* I will define several terms from management studies and then explain more deeply the meaning of refounding.

Reframing connotes the process of changing the way people and organizations *think* about themselves; *restructuring* refers not to the mind of an organization, but to the necessity of altering the parts of the organizational body that hamper growth. *Renewal* in corporate language implies the process whereby people are moved to develop new skills that will lead to the regeneration of the group, but the term does not connote any need to radically restructure the organization.[2] *Re-engineering*, however, means 'the fundamental rethinking and radical redesign of business processes to achieve dramatic improvements in critical . . . measures of performance, such as cost, quality, service, and speed'.[3] The texts that explain these popular terms have several key things in common: they are all about improving the financial profitability of companies; the reality of culture and the complexity of culture change is rarely referred to. It is assumed that organizations are like machines, made up of parts that can be changed with little or no injury to the people involved.[4] They at least implicitly adopt the traditional or mechanistic definition of culture, that is, culture is 'what we do around here, not what we feel about what we do'. As was explained in Chapter 2, this definition is seriously limited. Hence, it is unwise to use these terms with reference to planning in religious congregations or the Church in general without first critically assessing their limitations and ideological presuppositions.

Of the above terms it is 're-engineering' that comes closest to our understanding of refounding. It speaks of radical redesign, that is, creatively getting to the roots of issues, not making superficial changes. It is about *dramatic* change, not 'about making marginal or incremental improvements but about achieving quantum leaps in performances'.[5] The term 'refounding' certainly shares this sense of going to roots of problems, of radically rethinking the way we do things and of quantum leap creativity, but there is a fundamental difference. Ultimately, refounding is a journey in faith with Jesus Christ to bring his message of salvation to the very roots of contemporary pastoral problems. As a process of change it draws on the insights of management studies and social anthropology, but above all, on sacred scripture.

Refounding

I will explain the process of refounding through a series of brief axioms drawing on material already published[6] and adding further clarifications where necessary. Before proceeding, however, readers may find it useful to return to Chapter 2 and re-read the sections on the nature of culture and cultural analysis.

Axiom 1: Chaos: potential for creativity

An experience of chaos – that is, the radical breakdown of the personally or culturally predictable – contains potential for immense creativity. One has the chance then to rediscover, and be re-energized by, one's roots.

Chaos is a freeing or subversive experience for it breaks the crust of custom or habit, allowing the imagination to dream of alternative or radically different ways of doing things. When people own their chaos, admitting to their powerlessness, they return to the sacred time of the founding of the group. There they can ask fundamental questions about their origins, about what is essential to the original founding vision and is to be kept, and what is accidental and to be allowed to go. An example from the experience of the giant corporate cultures of IBM and AT&T in the United States illustrates this basic axiom. Through government anti-trust action AT&T had to be broken apart, but not IBM. The latter rejoiced. AT&T's organizational culture went into chaos, but not IBM's, yet it is AT&T that has triumphed. It used chaos to radically rethink its purpose for existence and moved dramatically to rebuild itself. Its stock rose 222 per cent, winning at the same time awards for quality, but IBM lost two-thirds of its market share.[7]

Axiom 2: Refounding: initial definition

Refounding requires the return to the sacred time of the founding experience of one's culture or organizational roots. By locking-in on the energy of the founding story we can be moved to take radical creative steps to apply the founding experience to today's most urgent needs.

Case study: The regenerative potential of chaos

Many years ago, on my first visit to Japan, I became utterly lost in a subway station in Tokyo. Every sign was in Japanese. Panic struck me and I became angry about everything Japanese. There should be a law, I said to myself irrationally, to force all Japanese to write their signs in English. In a miserable state of mind I accidentally turned to a shop window behind me, and by an extraordinary coincidence I noticed blankets made in my homeland, New Zealand, on sale there. In the corner of each blanket there was a small stylized kiwi (a flightless bird which is the national symbol of New Zealand). At the sight of this symbol everything kind, gentle and orderly came flooding into my memory. Then came memories of great heroes and heroines, people who had travelled last century thousands of miles through dangerous seas for months on end and established from the wilderness one of the finest farming industries of the world. These courageous and innovative people form the creation story of my country: when the world is in chaos there is nothing a New Zealander cannot do! In imitation of our founders we are tough, innovative and resilient people.[8] Suddenly, I felt an immense surge of energy within me. Who am I to be overcome by this situation! I am a New Zealander! In imitation of my forebears I will find a creative way out of my lostness. And I did. I put aside embarrassment by standing on a small raised platform holding up a sheet of paper with the word 'Help' in large letters. Gone was my paralysis, my self-pity and demands that the Japanese change their language for people like me. I had become Arbuckle REFOUNDED. Finally an English-speaking Japanese came to my aid.

This simple example encapsulates a profound truth: chaos, by challenging people to return to their founding story, provides the chance, not for superficial change, but for the most profound and radical transformation. This radical transformation is called *refounding*. In the above case study, the experience of chaos provided me with the chance to rediscover and re-own what it means to be a New Zealander. I locked-in on the creative energy of the founding people and their successors.

Axiom 3: Cultures as well as individuals experience chaos

As individuals experience chaos as a normal dynamic in their journey of life, so also do cultures of all kinds.

Cultures, like individuals, decline in vigour, undergo times of uncertainty or chaos, and can rediscover in the chaos energy for creative action. The United Kingdom at the time of the Battle of Britain was threatened with total disaster as never before in history, but Winston Churchill energized the people by inspiring them to re-identify and re-own the founding story of the nation, a nation built by hardy, creative and justice-loving people. Britain then entered into a refounding phase. In the period of the Great Depression in the United States, a time of widespread socioeconomic chaos, there emerged Franklin Delano Roosevelt and the creative New Deal from rediscovery of the dignity of the human person inherent in the founding story of the nation. To be true to this founding story, Roosevelt argued, the nation had to detach itself from excessive individualism and embrace a collaborative approach to solving problems of unemployment and poverty. Under Roosevelt the nation was truly *refounded*.

Axiom 4: Change: a three-stage process

Cultural and personal change involves three dynamically related, cyclically repeated stages: the separation stages, the liminal or chaos-evoking stage, and the re-entry stage. Progress through these stages is generally extremely slow, filled with uncertainties and dangers; we are constantly tempted to escape from the learning experience.

The first stage of change is initial unease or malaise. In my Tokyo example at the beginning of my journey from the security of the English-speaking community into the subway system I was apprehensive, fearful that I might become lost. The second stage, the liminal phase or chaos, is sometimes called the reflection stage. It is a phase of profound ambiguity that must be accepted with respect, awe and patience. It is that moment between old patterns of reality and new ways of looking at reality. For me this was knowing I was lost in the subway. This is a very dangerous stage, because we can avoid facing its fundamental questions about identity and purpose. We can blame others for the chaos and dream of instant and impossible solutions to it. Or we can own the enormity of the trauma and the psychic pain of loneliness and fear, in order to get in touch with what is essential in our personal or cultural founding myth. In brief, there is a point of choice in the chaos of the liminal stage: to retreat nostalgically to past securities, stand still, paralysed by the chaos and dreaming of miracles to overcome it, or to move forward with risk and hope into an uncertain future (see Figure 4.1).

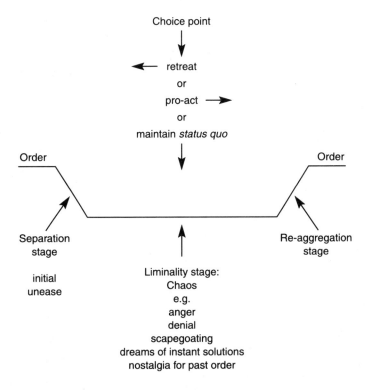

Figure 4.1 Stages of change

The third stage, in many ways the most difficult, is the re-entry or re-aggregation stage, that is, ongoing movement out of chaos to establish a new personal or cultural integration. It is still easy in the re-entry stage to give up the struggle, to fall back into self-pity, nostalgia, denial, cynicism, to give way to fantasies of unreal quick-fix solutions to the chaos, or to be overwhelmed by the fear of the unknown. If one's vision is unclear, if one is not in touch with the vision of the founding experience of one's group, then one may give up the struggle in the darkness. The reality is that we will never see the full fruits of our journey, yet we must begin and continue in hope. This axiom will be more fully explained in the next chapter.

Axiom 5: Order is preferred to chaos

Although experiences of chaos are the normal ways we are stimulated to change, we so much prefer the security of order and predictability that the significant change opportunities of the chaos stage are commonly ignored.

Culture is a shared defence against the anxiety of chaos. From experience we know that individually and corporately we so dread the pain of chaos that we commonly resist it with all our might. As Margaret Wheatley comments: 'We are not comfortable with chaos, even in our thoughts, and we want to move out of confusion as quickly as possible.'[9] Recall the reactions of the Israelites when confronted with the chaos of the desert. They leave Egypt with enthusiasm inspired by the leadership of Moses, but then they feel overwhelmed by the starkness of the desert. They blame Moses and want to return to Egypt; better the order of an oppression one knows, than the chaos of uncertainty: 'To Moses they said: "Was it for lack of graves in Egypt, that you had to lead us out to die in the desert? What was the point of bringing us out of Egypt? . . . We prefer to work for the Egyptians than to die in the desert"' (Exod 14:11–12).

Axiom 6: The primary purpose of refounding

By refounding we mean the collaborative process of returning to the original founding experience of the group, in order to identify and re-own its primary purpose/vision, and to be energized by it to create radically new responses directed at the causes of contemporary problems.

This axiom requires two clarifications. The primary purpose of a group, that is, its mission, is determined by its founding experience or myth, but this creation myth must be carefully distinguished from another type of myth, namely the *instrumental* myth. The instrumental myth tells people how the mission is to be carried out at a particular time and place: it can change – and sometimes must change – without interfering with the richness of the founding experience. For example, founders of many congregations last century insisted that their followers educate the poor. At that time building schools was seen as the only way to do it. Today people are open to other ways of educating than through the traditional school system. To refound teaching communities, therefore, people must return to the original vision and see whether radically new ways are necessary to implement it. This means changing the instrumental myth.

The second clarification concerns the distinction between renewal and refounding. An example illustrates the difference. Renewal projects aim to improve *existing* methods, say, of poverty relief, by speeding up food supplies to the poor through more efficient transport systems. Refounding, however, *begins* with rediscovery of the myth of human dignity. Having re-owned this foundational insight we are inspired with the energy to invent, through quantum leap innovative actions, entirely new structures, and programmes that attack the fundamental causes of poverty, for example the corruption of officials and the paucity of educational facilities.

Axiom 7: Refounding: three kinds of people are needed

For refounding to occur the collaboration by three kinds of people is required: authority position persons, refounding and renewal persons.

Authority position persons, such as managers, trustees, boards of directors, congregational leaders, are a group's official gatekeepers to change, that is, by their position they can prevent or foster change. Capable authority position persons recognize a difference between creativity and innovation. Creativity is the thinking process by which people give birth to ideas; innovation is the actual application of ideas towards doing things better. As Simon Majaro says, 'creative ideas can be wild, outlandish and impractical', but innovations 'must be practical, realistic and results-oriented'. People become frightened by 'crazy ideas' and want to abandon them and jump as quickly as possible to 'down-to-earth innovation', but many of the most successful innovations in history have come from ideas that were considered outlandish and impractical. Research has shown that, on average, 60 ideas are needed before a single innovation is put into practice. Majaro comments: 'A plethora of ideas is necessary before one can be identified as deserving of implementation. While creativity represents the. *quantity* of input, innovation is the *quality* of output. One without the other is like a child without a parent.'[10] Therefore, a primary task of authority position persons is to build a proactive organization, that is, a culture in which people generate ideas and know that they will be given serious consideration and may possibly lead to innovative action. Responsible leaders also keep calling their organizations to own chaos when it occurs, to let go the irrelevant and to be open to the new. And they accept the fact that creativity and innovation is a very disorderly process, involving the personalities, emotions and pecularities of people. Creative action never works neatly. It involves much darkness, courage, trial, error and evaluation.

Refounding people, with their above-average gifts of imagination, intuition, creativity, innovation, collaborative skills, courage and hope, are *dreamers who do,* contemplatives who act, that is, they are able to relive at depth the founding experience of the group and in a collaborative way take innovative, quantum leaps into the present world. Passionately committed to the refounding vision, they are not lightly dissuaded from action. The person who invented the personal computer made such a quantum leap in theory and action. Such persons are rarely easy to be with, simply because they challenge a group's or an individual's comfortable *status quo,* but an organization which domesticates these responsible dissenters achieves peace, but loses its future.[11]

Renewal people with 'nuts and bolts' skills and willing commitment to a group's mission are indispensable collaborators in the refounding process. In summary, refounding is not a cult of individualism, nor the exaltation of a hierarchical, self-centred status system. Rather, its priority is the collaboration of people with skills and commitment for the sake of a common vision and mission.

Axiom 8: Biblical chaos has a positive aspect

Biblical chaos is not something negative. It is frequently described in a variety of fear-evoking terms, such as fierce storms, exile, desert, wilderness, grave illness, death, confusion, darkness, emptiness, void, yet at the same time with connotations of immense creative potential. Chaos provides space for God's creative power to enter into our lives; with our co-operation, dramatically new and vigorous life beyond our wildest dreams will emerge. For the Israelite and the Christian, refounding is a faith journey of owning up in the midst of chaos to our utter powerlessness without God in our lives; from this comes the energy to use the experience of chaos constructively for the building of the faith community.

The Israelite creation myth is this:[12] Yahweh has a special love for the chosen people; the Israelites must return this love to God, especially through worship and justice to the poor and marginalized. When the Israelites forget this message, they are overwhelmed by chaos. The exile into Babylon is a horribly painful experience of a liminality begetting massive chaos. With the destruction of the three pivotal symbols of their culture, thought to be eternal witnesses to God's abiding presence – the kingship, the temple and Jerusalem – the people move into depression, anger, sadness, scapegoating, numbness and pain beyond description: 'By the waters of Babylon we sat and wept at the memory of Zion. . . .

How could we sing a song of Yahweh on alien soil?' (Ps 137:1, 4). Walter Brueggemann writes that

> It is impossible to overstate the depth of trauma produced (in the Israelites) by the events of the exile. . . . There is no doubt that this was a most profound theological crisis for Israel as well. Along with a deep sense of guilt . . . Israel was left with deep theological wonderment: Is Yahweh any longer powerful? (Isa 50:2; 59:1) Is Yahweh no longer faithful? (Lam 5:20; Isa 49:14) Is there indeed any future for this community known by the name of Yahweh?[13]

Yet once they retell how they were founded as a people in the Exodus, admit the depth of their pain and their total dependence on Yahweh, new creative ministries of worship and justice emerge: 'You heard me on the day when I called, and you gave new strength to my heart' (Ps 138:3).

Throughout the Israelite history Yahweh uses prophets as his co-refounders of the covenant. They call the people back to their God-centred founding and then to quantum leap pastoral innovation to assist the poor and voiceless. In the Hebrew scriptures God frequently allows chaos to develop, as a necessary preface for a creative faith response from his/her chosen people: 'Look, today I have set you over the nations and kingdoms, to uproot and to knock down, to destroy and to overthrow, to build and to plant' (Jer 1:10). In chaos they discard what is not essential to the founding myth and consequently discover a new and vigorous life of creative justice and peace.

For Christians the creation story or myth of their faith is the life, death and resurrection of Jesus Christ, and the transforming power of the Holy Spirit: 'You have been buried with him by your baptism; by which, too, you have been raised up with him through your belief in the power of God who raised him from the dead' (Col 2:12). By identifying with this creation event, we become one with the mission and energy of Christ himself – a mission to be constantly in a process of refounding as persons and as believing communities, that is, of being radically innovative in responding to the pastoral needs of the world.

At many points of Christ's life we see the fertile potential of chaos if it is constructively owned. Ponder the mysterious chaos of Jesus in Gethsemane, an integral step in the salvation story. Jesus enters into the liminal space of the garden, a stage of intense confusion, pain, fear and anguish: 'In his anguish he prayed even more earnestly and his sweat fell to the ground like great drops of blood' (Luke 22:44). He is confronted with a choice: escape the chaos and its lessons, remain paralysed with fear in the midst of the chaos, or move forward with hope into an uncertain and painful future. In fact, three times he unsuccessfully tries to retreat from the chaos experience, attempting to revive the security of past friendship with his closest disciples. They are 'busily' asleep. Then, having failed to escape the chaos and in the midst of incredible inner darkness, tempted to paralysis by the intensity of his fear, Jesus prays with a vigorous trust and hope to the Father to be spared the suffering. But he prays with detachment: 'let your will be done, not mine' (Luke 22:42). Now notice Jesus beginning the re-entry stage. Having acknowledged his total dependence on the Father, Jesus experiences a quantum leap of energy and creativity, in vivid contrast to his previous paralysing fears and escape efforts. It has its source in the Father. Jesus is met by the guards sent to arrest him and takes an initiative, a small physical movement, profound in its implications for the salvation of the world: 'Jesus came forward and said "Who are you looking for?" They answered, "Jesus the Nazarene." He said, "I AM HE"' (John 18:4–5). There is an energetic, proactive self-confidence here that is not in the liminal stage. Jesus now personally assumes a creative role as victim and priest of the sacrifice. Fear remains, but it is under control.

This is the model Jesus sets in the founding of the Church. It is therefore the pattern for the refounding of all our ministries, formation included.

Axiom 9: Refounding involves two simultaneous rituals

Refounding necessitates two simultaneous rituals: the ritual of grieving, that is, of letting go the irrelevant, and the ritual of initiation, allowing new life to enter.

> 'Cease to dwell on days gone by and to brood over past history. Here and now I will do a new thing; this moment it will break from the bud. Can you not perceive it?'
>
> (Isa 43:18–19)

Grief is the mixture of sadness, sorrow, denial, depression, guilt and confusion that accompanies significant loss. Cultures, nations, organizations – not only individuals – all experience grief. One has but to recall the worldwide expressions of grief in response to the tragedy of the terrorist bombing in Oklahoma City in 1995. And all change involves loss, and therefore grief. We may assent intellectually to change, but at the feeling level where culture primarily resides, the assent to change is far slower and more problematic. In fact our feelings instinctively resist change because it means that we must experience a period of uncertainty, even chaos, before the new is confidently named and embraced. Grieving is the public expression of loss within the protected boundaries of sacred ritual space in which feelings can be freely expressed without condemnation or judgement. Unless individuals and cultures utilize this ritual of mourning, which acknowledges loss and allows it to be let go of, grief will haunt them, stopping them from moving forward into new life. Suppressed grief suffocates creativity, holding people back from re-imagining the new and the future.[14]

The Hebrew prophets are skilled grief leaders. They refuse to be seduced into the denial of the grief of the people, no matter the personal cost to themselves. 'Do not prophesy the truth to us', the Israelites shout, 'tell us flattering things; have illusory visions, turn aside from the way, leave the path, take the Holy One out of sight' (Isa 30:10–11). On the contrary, the prophets passionately call the people to acknowledge their losses and the need to let go their attachment to them. Moses was such a leader par excellence. In the midst of the chaos of the Exodus not only did he give sacred space to the people in which to grieve, but as a wise grief leader he continued to re-articulate the visionary newness of the time ahead of them: 'Yahweh is bringing you into a fine country, a land of streams and springs . . . . Be careful not to forget Yahweh' (Deut 8:7, 11). And wherever the Israelites admitted to their anger and their complete dependence on Yahweh they experienced signals of the newness beyond their wildest dreams; they found not a God of anger but one of 'tenderness and compassion' (Exod 34:6).

It is the same dynamic in the New Testament. On many occasions Jesus calls his disciples to let go the past. For example, at the transfiguration, just when Peter wants to hold on to the revered Moses and Elijah, symbols of the covenant that is dying, they disappear: 'when they looked round, they saw no one with them any more but only Jesus' (Mark 9:8). The lesson is that: the new covenant cannot emerge unless they disengage themselves from the old. It is a message that must be repeated over and over again, for the disciples are slow to learn. Just prior to his passion Jesus repeats the admonition, but they are still reluctant to hear it: 'now I am going to one who sent me. Not one of you asks "Where are you going?" Yet you are sad of heart because I have told you this . . . . (It) is for your own good that I am going, because unless I go, the Paraclete will not come to you; but if I go, I will send him to you' (John 16:6–7). But even by the time of Christ's ascension the lesson has still not been interiorized. The Acts recalls that the disciples remain 'looking into the sky' (Acts 1:11), so the angel becomes a grief leader: 'Why are you Galileans standing here . . . ? This Jesus who has been taken up from you into heaven will come back in the same way as you have seen him go to heaven' (ibid.). For a new beginning we must say goodbye to the past – the initiation into the new presupposes the art of grieving.

Axiom 10: Refounding demands ongoing conversion

Refounding is a risk-filled journey of faith and hope, whereby we enter into the heart of the paschal mystery itself to unite ourselves with Christ and his mission, thus being energized to be ongoingly creative in bringing the kingdom message to the world of our times. As it is a journey demanding personal and group conversion, it is a slow and hesitant process, the outcome of which is ultimately in the hands of God.

This axiom repeats a fundamental principle of refounding: we must plan for the future using all the human resources available to us, including the latest managerial insights,[15] but ultimately refounding is a faith journey with Christ requiring continuous radical conversion. The newness we dream of may not be what God wants; conversion means being open to all possibilities, even the destruction of the very group we belong to and love dearly. The admonition of Moses to the Israelites remains always true: 'Beware of thinking to yourself, "My own strength and the might of my own hand have given me the power to act like this." Remember Yahweh your God; he was the one who gave you the strength to act effectively like this . . . ' (Deut 8:17–18). Conversion is a slow and unsure process. It took generations of chaotic experiences for the Israelites as a *culture* to abandon their attachments to Egypt and their belief in their own power to control their destiny: 'God led (you) a roundabout way through the desert of the Sea of Reeds (Exod 13:18) . . . to humble you, to test you and know your inmost heart . . . . He humbled you, he made you feel hunger . . . . Learn from this that Yahweh your God was training you as a man trains a child' (Deut 8:2, 3, 5).

In the New Testament the conversion of Peter and Paul testifies to the slowness of *personal refounding*. It is a thoroughly rocky journey. Simon Peter, with a burst of initial enthusiasm, 'left everything and followed him' (Luke 5:11), yet we quickly find Peter not understanding the words and intentions of Jesus (John 13:6–11), sinking because he lacks faith (Matt 14:28–31), being vigorously rebuked as 'Satan' (Mark 8:33) and finally denying Jesus after his arrest (Mark 14:66–72). Through all this, Jesus is trusting, waiting for Peter's conversion to become more deeply rooted in his heart and actions. Finally that trust is rewarded: 'and the Lord turned and looked straight at Peter . . . . And he went outside and wept bitterly' (Luke 22:61–62). Paul's journey of personal refounding is equally instructive. During the ten years after his dramatic conversion on the way to Damascus and prior to his first successful mission to Cyprus and Asia Minor, people find him a disturbing influence and are quite happy to see him go: 'The churches throughout Judaea, Galilee and Samaria were now left in peace' (Acts 9:31). He preaches conversion, but his instinctive way of speaking and acting is still that of the pre-conversion evangelist. Paul thinks he can convert people without the help of God. He has yet to allow a spirit of detachment and trust in the Lord to affect his faculties and senses. The Lord allows the negative reactions of the local churches he visits, a chaos experience of failure and rejection, to catalyse Paul into a deeper conversion – a personal ongoing *refounding*. Slowly Paul discovers detachment at last; it is the Lord who converts, not the eloquence of Paul (1 Cor 3:5, 18). Now we have a humbler Paul, one who discovers the power of newness in his personal chaos: 'I am most happy, then, to be proud of my weaknesses, in order to feel the protection of Christ's power over me. For when I am weak, then I am strong' (2 Cor 12:9–10).[16]

Axiom 11: Refounding requires support structures

Since the process of refounding involves a break with past securities and a journey into the unknown, there is bound to be resistance, sometimes of considerable, even paralysing, power. For the sake of the mission this resistance may need to be bypassed so that it does not de-energize people from the task.

Elsewhere[17] I explain that Christ himself directed his disciples to avoid situations, institutions and people that persistently obstruct the preaching of the kingdom. They are to bypass these obstacles and take the good news to people who are willing to listen: 'And if anyone does not welcome you or listen to what you have to say, as you walk out of the house or town shake the dust from your feet' (Matt 10:14). I term this pastoral principle 'the new belongs elsewhere'. For example, authority position people will need to apply this directive, as we will see in Chapter 6, when unauthorized persons unnecessarily interfere with the formation process. Structures must be established to allow formators to exercise their authority without being bothered by unfounded, de-energizing criticism and unwarranted interference from other members of a province.

Refounding formation: processes and assumptions

Let me restate the thesis of this book. Vatican II led us to challenge the distortions of the founding myth of religious life and formation processes that had evolved over the preceding three hundred years. This has resulted in chaos, the space between old ways of thinking and acting, and the birth of the new. The refounding is painful, demanding patience, creativity, innovation, faith and much hope. To build it, we must re-identify and re-own the original founding experiences of religious life and our own congregation, and that means returning first to the mystery of Christ's life and mission. Only then are we in a position to build new methods of forming religious in the contemporary world. To assist formators in this task I suggest below four processes and several guiding assumptions.

Processes

First, to return to the founding experience of Christ forming the community of believing disciples, those in charge of formation must ask themselves questions like:

— what was the vision and mission given by the Father to Jesus?

— what were the *faith shocks*[18] of Jesus, that is his experiences of grief, as he perceived the gaps between the behaviour of people around him and the kingdom values of love, justice and peace?

— how did Jesus react to these faith shocks?

Ultimately there can be no authentic formation programme that is not based on this founding experience of our faith.

Second, the following question must be asked about religious life: what must distinguish all active religious congregations from monastic communities?

Third, the fundamental and instrumental myths of the congregation must be identified, that is, what is essential to the founding story must be separated from accidents of history. Questions like the following are to be asked:

— what was the heart of the faith experience of the founder as he/she reflected on the chasm separating people's lives and the kingdom values?

— what did he/she do about this gap?

— how can would-be followers re-experience the faith shocks of the founder, so that they can identify with the heart of the founding story and leave aside what is historically unimportant?

Fourth, once the authentic founding myths of our faith and congregation have been identified, the next stage is to formulate a model of formation that will foster the interiorization of these founding myths by candidates.

Guiding assumptions

The following assumptions should guide the development of an appropriate model for formation:

1. The primary formator is God; through the Spirit God reveals the mystery of his/her abiding love for each person, and challenges in the deepest recesses of our being.

2. The candidate has a primary responsibility to respond to the call offered by God. Formators must accept candidates only if there is good reason to believe they are prepared to enter the formation process with an open and listening heart.

3. The formation process begins where the candidate is – spiritually, emotionally, affectively and intellectually; while the formation pro-gramme must be based on a clear goal, namely holistic integration for the sake of the mission of Christ, the methods of leading candidates into this must not be pre-set or inflexible.

The words *holistic integration* require explanation. One of the obsessions of pre-Vatican II formation programmes was intelligence understood as 'cleverness', mental agility and intellectual or logical strength. Little recognition was given to affective and creative abilities. In fact, they were rigorously discouraged. A formation programme that is refounding will, however, recognize six types of intelligence.[19] *Emotional* intelligence connotes an awareness of one's own feelings, sensitivity to the feelings of others, the ability to deal with emotional questions openly and to empathize with the feelings of others. *Intuitive* intelligence means imaginative ability, understanding of the need for recreation, respect for gut feelings about things, willingness to take risks and openness to change. *Physical* intelligence is a feeling for a sensible and balanced diet, recognition of need for physical exercise, practical skills. *Intellectual* intelligence is the ability to reason, use abstract ideas, analyse and solve problems. *Spiritual* intelligence is a dynamic faith commitment to the person and mission of Jesus Christ. *Congregational* intelligence is a knowledge and love of the founding experience of the congregation. Although a candidate will be gifted in some types more than others, nonetheless each candidate must be encouraged to develop as far as is possible all six in order to be an integrated person in the service of the mission of the congregation.

Personal effectiveness as a religious draws on all these types of intelligence. However, *spiritual* intelligence energizes people to develop and integrate the other intelligences in the service of Christ and the world. The *intellectual* must not be overvalued at the expense of the others. In contrast to pre-Vatican II formation, however, the *intuitive* intelligence needs vigorous encouragement, because the Church requires religious who are creative and innovative in worship and evangelization. For this candidates need to be exposed to art in all forms, for example music, poetry, drama, painting. An appreciation and love of art can dispose people to be open to a sense of mystery and to be creative. Clement McNaspy comments that 'Art, to be sure, is not the same as aestheticism. But a balanced spirituality requires that the affective and emotive side of human nature be incorporated into one's prayer and worship. Platonically to ignore or suppress or diminish this dimension of experience . . . is to run the risk of serious imbalance in one's religious attitudes.'[20]

4. Formation is an *ongoing* process of discovering God's love in Christ, demanding of candidates that they continue to struggle to be open to human and spiritual development, finding and letting go of all that hinders them in this journey.

5. Candidates must learn to recognize that the test of the authenticity of their response to God's love will be their own love of others, especially those with whom they live, and the most abandoned. Candidates must not be accepted for profession if they wish to use religious life as a way to improve their social, economic or intellectual status.

Comment: Formation in the Third World

Religious life, if authentically lived, is a prophetic protest against whatever in social or ecclesiastical life is contrary to the kingdom values. As Aloysius Pieris writes: 'the obedience we vow is obedience to God who calls us *in the poor* and calls us *to be poor*; a God who calls us to speak *for the poor* and struggle *with the poor*'.[21] However, historically joining a religious congregation was not uncommonly a way to social mobility and power both in the Church and society. Virginity and celibacy were often lived out in institutions that were in no way poor; the vows of obedience and poverty were apostolically ineffective. Pieris rightly notes that religious in the Third World are in danger of falling again into this grave error. Candidates can be attracted into religious life, not as a prophetic service to their people, but as a desirable way to achieve status and power over people, including the poor.

I hear comments like: 'The Lord truly loves us; the more we die in the West the more vocations we receive in the Third World.' 'We do not need refounding, because we are receiving so many vocations.' It is my impression from working in and visiting parts of the Third World over many years that there is insufficient critical screening of candidates and that their formation is commonly based on the institutional or pre-Vatican II model to be critiqued below. Congregational leaders can lose their objectivity when faced with large numbers seeking admission to their communities, seeing this as a sign of God's special blessing as their communities face death in the First World. Pieris is correct: 'The vocation boom in the third world must, therefore, be critically assessed'[22] in order that the vows truly serve their prophetic purpose. If the proper screening and formation structures are not in place, then religious communities in the Third World will merely continue to repeat the tragic mistakes of their forebears in Western societies. The refounding of formation is as urgent in the Third World as it is in the first, no matter how many recruits apply to enter congregations.

6. The mission of Christ is to a world in rapid change. Therefore, candidates must be prepared not only to understand the nature of change intellectually and pastorally, but to give experiential proof:

— that they are able to maintain an integrated human/faith balance in the midst of tumultuous change;

— that they are willing and able to live the form of community life required by their founding charism;

— that they have the willingness and capacity to work collaboratively in prophetic ministries with others, including members of the opposite sex.

7. Formation demands skilled mediators to accompany candidates in their journey of discovering Christ and his will in their lives; in order to take up their role, formators must have the freedom to use their authority without undue outside interference.

8. The mission of the Church has priority, not the survival of a particular province or congregation, that is, criteria for entrance into formation and profession are determined by the purpose for which religious life in general and every religious congregation exist: to challenge society and the Church to be true to the kingdom values. These standards must not drop just to guarantee the numbers or survival of a province or a congregation.

Case study: The disease of 'province-itis'

One province of religious sisters has struggled to maintain an ill-staffed and inadequate formation programme for many years for one or two candidates. The neighbouring province has a well-qualified formation team and several candidates, but the first province resists all efforts to unite with the second province's programme. The main reason given is: 'If we move to the other province it will be too hurtful for our professed members; their morale will drop because our inability to support our own programme will be seen as a sign of our death.'

Provinces are only administrative units of a congregation, existing to be of service to its mission. Therefore, when a province begins to interfere with the effectiveness of a congregation's mission, it ceases to have a reason to exist. If candidates cannot be adequately trained within their own province, they must be directed to wherever the best facilities exist. In this case study, candidates are unjustly deprived of an adequate formation simply to maintain among professed members the charade that all is still well in the province. Inevitably a province will feel grief over its numerical decline and possible death, but this grief must be dealt with openly and honestly. The longer the fear of dying remains unaddressed the more a province is unable to re-imagine not only alternative formation programmes, but any kind of other ministerial option.[23]

9. Religious are called to prophetic ministry. Hence, candidates who enter a clerical religious congregation must be clearly told that they join not to be priests as such but prophetic agents of the gospel. They are to exercise their priesthood as the service to the prophetic mission of the congregation.

Case study: A confused formator

A formator in charge of a Third World training centre of an international clerical religious congregation was asked to describe his role. He said: 'My principal task is to form candidates for the priesthood. The students enter with this in mind. Our country needs more and more priests and the best thing our congregation can do is to respond to this need. As regards religious life and the particular emphasis of our congregation, the students can discover what all this means in novitiate and after ordination. I know the novice master does not accept this thinking. He needs to be more practical. He wants to send away candidates that will make fine priests because he says they have no vocation to religious life. Fortunately, the provincial insists they remain as novices. All is well when they come back to our training centre.'

This formator and his provincial are seriously mistaken. Religious life values are not to be secondary to the priesthood in his congregation. Rather these values are to be the primary focus of *everything* throughout the training programme. The novice director is placed in an impossible situation.

Defining formation

Given the preceding assumptions I would define formation as follows:

- Formation for prophetic mission is a process whereby a person in and through community assumes responsibility for his/her growth in Christ, in the service of the Church and society, according to the founding experience of his/her particular congregation.

- It is a process of liberation by which, under skilled guides, a person frees himself/herself from constraints of:
  - a personal order (sin, pride, ignorance of Christ as the centre of life, ignorance of academic/pastoral skills necessary to be part of Christ's mission today);
  - a social or cultural order (undue cultural pressures, prejudices).

Assessing culture models of formation

Over time several models of formation have emerged and they can be assessed in light of the above processes, guiding assumptions and definition explained in the previous section.

1. The conformity/institutional model

The overall aim of this model, which was popular following the Council of Trent, is the formation of individuals to fit unquestioningly into pre-set, unchanging roles of ministry in the Church, for example the apostolates of nursing and teaching. The emphasis of training is primarily to cultivate in candidates at least external conformity to the customs of the religious life culture. This behaviour pattern is characteristic of a *strong group/strong grid* culture and the pre-Vatican II Church as defined in the previous chapter.

The model assumes that the world is static and problems predictable. Hence, there is no need to change the training methods or to foster in candidates any creative qualities. Candidates receive information from above and must not question it in any way. As long as candidates can prove they have the knowledge given them and conform to detailed rules they are considered acceptable to the group and its mission. The fear of punishment, even for the inculpable breaking of minute regulations, is used to inculcate external conformity in candidates. Accidents, for example the breaking of a plate, indicate that candidates have not yet reached perfection expected of them! For the perfect even accidents do not happen! Since it is not considered necessary for staff to develop formative personal relationships with candidates at any depth, this model is popular when there are large numbers of candidates to be trained. For this reason it remains an attractive model of formation within Third World countries when candidates are numerous.

This is a totally inadequate model of formation. It respects neither the dignity of the person nor the mission of active religious life. For example, candidates are trained neither to be creative for mission nor to be free autonomous persons; interior personal conversion to Christ and his mission is downplayed. The overstress on the keeping of minute rules, under threat of punishment beyond the seriousness of any infringement, gives candidates a false sense of what is truly sinful. In this model there is no need for skilled guides; tradition alone, as concretized in detailed rules and customs handed down from generation to generation, is seen as the major shaper of behaviour. Staff are chosen chiefly for their known ability to accept and maintain the *status quo*. Teaching gifts are not necessary, because all that is needed is to provide candidates with information already set out in manuals and then to check that it has been adequately received. The principle behind this form of teaching has been described as the 'mug and jug' theory of learning; the recipient of a lecture is likened to an empty mug expecting to be filled with information from the jug, the source of information. Students are not expected to examine their emotional response to the material given them. They could be taught through lectures about the pastoral care of dying patients and their anguished relatives, but they would never have the chance to examine the ways in which their own fears of death could influence the quality of their being with people.[24] Students with good memories can shine in this system.

As regards the popularity of the model in Third World local churches today, it is argued in its support that it often reflects the cultures of origin of candidates, namely strong group/strong grid cultures. The institutional approach is, it is said, an example of 'inculturating formation'. This is an untheological understanding of inculturation. The formation process must in fact aim to break down the excessive emphasis on group cohesion in this type of culture, to foster a healthy individuality in candidates and a capacity in them to challenge customs according to gospel values.

2. The apprenticeship model

Apprenticeship is a method of passing on trade skills and of maintaining a supply of craftspeople. It normally involves at least two people – one possessing specialized skills and one who wishes to acquire and develop those skills for himself/herself. Apprenticeship thus consists of a social relationship. Historically, this has been an important model of secular education; it remains so today in the Third World and also in Western societies (though far less so than in the past).[25]

While there is a place for this model in religious life for the acquisition of particular skills, it should not become the dominant one simply because in a complex and changing world it places considerable and often impossible burdens on one teacher. A temptation in today's congregations, where candidates and formators are few, is to expect an already busy religious to be responsible for the apprentice. In practice, the teacher commonly becomes so absorbed in pastoral duties that little or no time is left to supervise the apprentice. There is also the danger that the apprentice becomes overly dependent on one person, imitating that person without developing necessary qualities of independence and creativity.

3. The personalist model[26]

In this model the stress is primarily on the candidate and his/her psychological needs, not the mission. Although the psychological well-being of an individual is of critical importance in the formation process, so that he/she becomes liberated from personal blocks to apostolic life, there is a real danger that an overemphasis on this point will turn the process into a therapeutic or narcissistic one. This has already been critiqued in Chapter 3. Candidates can become so absorbed in their own personal problems and their need for healing that their focus on Christ's mission to the world is lost. Moreover, the emotional demands on integrated members of the formation community by those who are less so can become overwhelming, so that energy for mission outside the community is needlessly weakened. Healthy members may seek formation communities more adapted to the needs of mission or leave entirely.

This model of formation can attract candidates with above average needs for affirmation and healing, but also formators who themselves have an excessive need for support from the community. The criticism does not mean that candidates should not when necessary seek professional psychological counselling, but there must be well-founded hope that this counselling will contribute to integration *within* a reasonable time.

4. The ecclesial model

The formation process here is based on the principles and steps of the Rite of Christian Initiation of Adults, stressing the interaction between the candidates and the community in which they live. At first sight this model looks perfect for the formation of religious, but in practice it has serious deficiences. It assumes what is impossible, namely, that most communities have the time *and* professional expertise for the hands-on approach that this formation needs. According to this model, for example, candidates could be placed within communities whose primary purpose is not formation, but something more directly apostolic such as the servicing of a parish. Jane Ferdon rightly notes that this model could be valuable for postulancy or pre-candidacy programmes, but not for the entire formation process. But even in these two programmes, skilled guides must be available at times to assist candidates; they do not have to be part of the community and can be brought in at appropriate times.[27]

5. The contemplative model

This model focuses primarily on the candidate's spiritual relationship with God. Unlike the therapeutic model, the emphasis is not directly on oneself, but on how to develop a more intimate relationship with God. The process stresses, for example, a solid intellectual and spiritual training, as well as a deep appreciation of the masters of the spiritual life. Rightly understood, this model contains the positive aspects of all the other models considered here, but in practice there is always the danger that issues will be over-spiritualized to the neglect of human and cultural problems at the personal and group levels. One's spirituality, especially for active religious, must be mission-based, that is, candidates must learn to relate their spirituality in an integrated way to the exercise of their ministry (see assumption 8 above).

6. The social justice model

In this model candidates are trained to respond *primarily* to social justice issues, hence emphasis is on social analysis, direct involvement in programmes among the poor and marginalized, and the need to challenge unjust economic, political and ecclesial structures.

Even though candidates must be trained to see that the pursuit of social justice is a constituent element in the mission of the Church, the social justice model should rarely be used as the *primary* focus in formation. Such an emphasis would expect candidates to specialize in ministry far too early in their lives as religious. The social justice apostolate is an extremely demanding one, requiring of people well-developed and balanced spiritual and human qualities. Otherwise, the risk of burn-out is too great. In practice, when social justice is made the major focus in formation, individual candidates and their communities may be tempted to use their involvement in justice issues as an escape from having to face personal and community problems. The apostolate requires specialist guides, and these are not readily available at the initial formation level.

Case study: Culture shock overload

Candidates from First World provinces of a male religious congregation were customarily sent immediately after novitiate to a Third World country for social justice exposure programmes. Over a period of ten years most candidates left the congregation or returned to undergo psychological counselling. A study showed that far too much was expected of the candidates over a short period of time: they were expected to integrate their novitiate learning while at the same time learning a foreign language, adjusting to vastly different foods, a culture of poverty and extreme violence. At no time did they have available to them adequately trained supervisors to guide them through this totally foreign environment.

---

7. The blossom model

In this model residential staff members see their primary role as one of creating for candidates a warm, loving and supportive environment. Staff members do not call candidates to be accountable to any clearly defined criteria or structures to measure their growth. Nor are candidates challenged to integrate their studies, pastoral experiences and prayer life for fear that they would become discouraged and feel offended. It is assumed that, provided the formation culture is loving enough, candidates will themselves recognize the need to confront key problems of development in their lives.

This is a dangerously flawed model. Candidates are insulated from the world of suffering, hard work and a necessary degree of tension. They grow overly dependent on frequent affirmation, which itself becomes a real obstacle to self-starting innovative action on their part. And, as in the therapeutic model above, integrated personalities feel suffocated by this culture and either regress in their behaviour or leave. Henri Nouwen correctly comments:

> Students want to be criticized, reprimanded and even punished . . . .
> But the authority by which this happens should be based not on subjective feelings and ideas . . . but on a critical, competent and object-ive understanding of the students' behavior. Conflicts, frictions and differences don't have to be avoided. They are part of formation. But only when the faculty claims its own authority and insists on it, will the student be able to identify himself, evaluate his own experiments in life and take a firm stand where he feels solid ground.[28]

8. The *laissez-faire* model

According to this model, candidates run the entire programme, deciding the curriculum and structures of life. Community life barely, if ever, exists, as the model fosters individualism and lack of accountability to clearly stated goals. The formation staff withdraw from all significant involvement.

After a time candidates become increasingly confused and angered by the lack of direction, challenge and interest on the part of the officially appointed staff and congregational leaders. This model was especially popular in the late 1960s and 1970s. During this time formators became confused about the nature of formation and its purpose, because of the combined impact on formation programmes of Vatican II and the world-wide student revolt against existing institutions which affected even religious life formation. Formators felt inadequate for the task, opting for this model as a way out of their malaise. Nouwen, writing in 1969, felt that depression in the seminaries (and I believe in religious formation communities also) was very much due to the inability of formators to clarify their role and establish correct structures:

> We are taking away structures . . . . But it is certain that all are looking for a structure, clear, explicit and articulated, in which they can test themselves and be tested by others in order to allow the necessary decisions for their future life . . . . The principle is that all formation has as its primary task to offer a meaningful structure which allows for a creative use of the students' energies. Structure is the key word of the formation and the criterion of any educational guideline. Structure allowing one to judge which feelings to trust and which feelings to distrust . . . . Structure providing unity to the many seemingly dis-connected emotions and ideas of the student . . . [29]

When a congregation places its survival as *the* priority in planning, then it is tempted to encourage the *laissez-faire*, the therapeutic or blossom model for fear that the few candidates it has will be tempted to leave. It is a dangerously short-sighted policy and unjust to the candidates and the people they eventually hope to serve.

9. The pilgrimage model[30]

This model, which reflects the *weak group/weak grid* culture type as explained in the previous chapter, is the one most in tune with the previously described processes and assumptions for the authentic refounding of formation. It is based, unlike previous models, primarily on the mission of Christ to the contemporary postmodernist world of rapid change; it assumes radically new structures must be developed to best prepare candidates for this mission.

The model aims to form religious to work collaboratively in teams, to cope with rapid change in society and to maintain – without the need for *undue* affirmation – innovative pastoral ability. They will be religious trained to share their faith journeys with others, especially members of their own religious communities, as a source of energy for their personal lives and ministry. The model assumes that people are not prepared *for* ministry, but rather *in* ministry, that is, the formation process is experientially based. Candidates are involved in the ministry of the Lord to themselves, to one another and at times to others outside the immediate formation community. Their experiences in these levels of ministry form the foundation for significant learning under the supervision of skilled staff. The aim is to establish a collaborative interaction between formators and candidates; they have different, but complementary, roles.

The term 'pilgrimage' is used of this model for the following reasons:

- There is an initiatory quality to a pilgrimage; a 'pilgrim is an initiand, entering into a new, deeper level of existence' than he/she has known before.[31] In the formation process candidates are initiates who are being called by God to enter into an ever-deepening experience of faith and conversion, at a level never before reached by them.

- Pilgrimages are not only initiatory events, they are also grieving rituals in which pilgrims must, with the grace of God, let go of all that holds them back from achieving their goal. So also formation candidates. They are invited by God, for the sake of Christ's mission to the world, to learn the art of letting go attachments both good and bad that keep them from a deepening awareness of God's presence within themselves, their community, the sacraments and the world in which they live.

- Pilgrimages are commonly group movements in which pilgrims of different rank and status must learn to relate supportively at a level of deep faith and love with one another. So also in the formation process, candidates must learn to interrelate with mature human/spiritual intimacy in the midst of inevitable frictions and conflicts.

- Pilgrimages develop explicit or implicit structures that create space for community prayer and privacy for personal reflection. Similarly with formation programmes.

- Pilgrims know *where* they are going, but there is always uncertainty, even stress-evoking experiences, about *how* to get there. Authentic pilgrims cannot remain on their journey if they do not recognize the need for God's gifts of hope and faith; the normal human securities of predictable order rarely exist. So also candidates for religious life.

- Pilgrims, because the way is uncertain, must pause at times to evaluate seriously their progress. In light of what they find, they may need to plan their journey anew, even radically change direction and structures. They must ask themselves questions such as: 'Why are we on this pilgrimage? Have we lost sight of the true purpose of the pilgrimage? Are we carrying unnecessary baggage? Are there other more suitable routes that should be taken in light of the purpose of the pilgrimage? Are the guides skilled enough for their task?' So also in the formation process there are times when candidates must ask themselves profound questions about the purpose of their pilgrimage, for example whether or not God is calling them to this particular journey in religious life. Periodic evaluations, and the planning of new strategies, are essential for candidates, their guides and their communities.

- Pilgrimages need skilled guides, that is people who have made the journey before; so also the formation process.

- Pilgrimages, as in the formation of candidates for religious life, are holistic experiences, that is, they seek to inspire in pilgrims an emotional, spiritual, intellectual and physical integration.

- The pilgrimage or journey model is a fundamental paradigm of the conversion process in the scriptures. The biblical God is not a distant divinity 'frozen into an immobile and inaccessible splendour . . . . He is a pilgrim God — alive, creative, resourceful. If God is the first Pilgrim, then faith consists essentially in imitating, in following, in walking in God's footsteps: it receives from God both its dynamism and its direction.'[32] The paschal mystery of our salvation for Christ is a pilgrimage and he calls us to commit ourselves to the same journey with all its radical demands. The pilgrimage is thus the most perfect model on which to base the planning and process of initial formation: 'Thomas said, "Lord, we do not know where we are going, so how can we know the way?" Jesus said: "I am the Way; I am Truth and Life. No one can come to the Father except through me"' (John 14:5–6).

- The pilgrimage model of formation has noble roots in the history of the Church. The earliest Christian pilgrimages to Rome and Jerusalem were considered times of very special graces, freely undertaken by people yearning to come closer to Christ and his saints. Only later, in the Middle Ages, did a compulsory penitential quality emerge as a dominant theme, even as punishment for secular offences. However, it was taken for granted that in all pilgrimages there would be hardships, dangers and bodily privations that would bring pilgrims a deeper union with Christ in his journey to Calvary.[33]

The pilgrimage model faded in importance as an image of the Church in post-Reformation times because the institutional Church now emphasized 'a static ontology of grace, clearly defined structures of the supernatural organism, and an ahistorical approach to spiritual life as a primarily interior relation to God'.[34] Vatican II, with its call to Christians to enter into dialogue with a changing world, again returned to the ancient pilgrimage theme: we are a pilgrim people 'led by the Holy Spirit in (our) journey to the kingdom of (our) Father';[35] as we move through the ages, like pilgrims in a foreign land, 'nothing genuinely human fails to raise an echo in (our) hearts'.[36] The formation process as a pilgrimage returns therefore to the ancient tradition of pilgrimages, before the obligatory requirement was introduced, and to the notion of the Church itself as a pilgrim.

Summary

It is for their faith that our ancestors are acknowledged . . . recognising that they were only *strangers and nomads on earth*.

(Heb 11:2, 13)

Refounding is not a managerial technique, nor is it a quick fix for congregations to revitalize themselves. It is a faith-filled collaborative journey of ongoing conversion, whereby we struggle to re-own the mission of Christ to the world by re-identifying with his journey through death into resurrection. This reuniting with Christ's pilgrimage offers us the energy to be radically creative and innovative in bringing kingdom values to the very roots of contemporary issues.

Formation is today in chaos. It but mirrors the confusion in the Church and religious life since Vatican II. Yet this chaos is a God-given opportunity for us to refound our formation processes and structures fundamentally. The creativity necessary to refound initial formation requires, as all significant inventiveness, the experience of the irregularity and instability of chaos to shatter old preconceptions and patterns of thinking and behaviour, so making way for the new. Since Vatican II, many models of formation have been invented, some religious have even tried to restore the pre-Vatican II training system, but all except the pilgrimage type are inadequate. The latter has deep biblical and historical roots. Its formation process, as the following chapter explains in practical ways, invites candidates to join with God the first Pilgrim in a journey of personal and group transformation.

Notes

1. Document *Instrumentum Laboris* for the Synod of Bishops, *The Consecrated Life and Its Role in the Church and in the World* (Vatican: Vatican Press, 1994), para. 91.
2. See F. J. Gouillart and J. N. Kelly, *Transforming the Organization* (New York: McGraw-Hill, 1995), p. 7.
3. See M. Hammer and J. Champy, *Reengineering the Corporation: A Manifesto for Business Revolution* (New York: HarperBusiness, 1993), p. 32.
4. Peter Senge in his best-selling management book, *The Fifth Discipline: The Art and Practice of the Learning Organization* (New York: Doubleday, 1990), does not refer to culture at any point.
5. Hammer and Champy, op. cit., p. 33.
6. For example, see G. A. Arbuckle, *Out of Chaos: Refounding Religious Congregations* (London: Geoffrey Chapman, 1988); *Refounding the Church: Dissent for Leadership* (London: Geoffrey Chapman, 1993).
7. See M. Kelly, 'Taming the demons of change: when chaos turns out to be an angel in disguise', *Business Ethics* (July/August 1993), p. 7.
8. See G. A. Arbuckle, *Earthing the Gospel: An Inculturation Handbook for Pastoral Workers* (London: Geoffrey Chapman, 1990), pp. 26–7.
9. M. J. Wheatley, *Leadership and the New Science: Learning About Organization from an Orderly Universe* (San Francisco: Berrett-Koehler, 1994), p. 149.
10. S. Majaro, 'Creativity in the search for strategy' in S. Crainer (ed.), *The Financial Times Handbook of Management* (London: Pitman, 1995), p. 165.
11. See Arbuckle, *Out of Chaos*, op. cit., pp. 88–111.
12. Ibid., pp. 46–62.
13. W. Brueggemann, 'Crisis-evoked, crisis-resolving speech', *Biblical Theology Bulletin*, vol. 24, no. 3 (1994), p. 99.
14. See G. A. Arbuckle, *Grieving for Change: A Spirituality for Refounding Gospel Communities* (London: Geoffrey Chapman, 1991), passim.
15. D. Murphy totally misinterprets the meaning of refounding, for he assumes it is merely a managerial technique. See his book *The Death and Rebirth of Religious Life* (Sydney: E. J. Dwyer, 1995), pp. 207–13.
16. See Arbuckle, *Earthing the Gospel*, op. cit., pp. 109–10.
17. See Arbuckle, *Refounding the Church*, op. cit., pp. 149–55.
18. For a fuller explanation of 'faith shocks' see ibid., p. 147.
19. I am adapting the insights of D. Postle, *The Mind Gymnasium* (London: Macmillan, 1989), passim and P. Whitaker, *Managing Change in Schools* (Buckingham: Open University Press, 1993), pp. 35–6.
20. C. McNaspy, 'Art in Jesuit life', *Studies in the Spirituality of Jesuits* (April 1973), pp. 104–5.
21. A. Pieris, 'The religious vow and the Reign of God', *The Way Supplement*, no. 5 (1989), p. 9.

22. Ibid., p. 12.
23. See G. A. Arbuckle, 'Beyond frontiers: the supranational challenge of the Gospel', *Review for Religious*, vol. 46, no. 3 (1987), pp. 351–70.
24. See T. Hobbs in T. Hobbs (ed.), *Experiential Learning: Practical Guidelines* (London: Routledge, 1992), p. xiv.
25. See M. W. Coy (ed.), *Apprenticeship: From Theory to Method and Back Again* (Albany: State University of New York, 1989), p. 1 and passim.
26. For information and critiques of this and several of the following models I draw on the instructive articles by J. Ferdon, 'Religious formation: a contemplative realignment', *Review for Religious*, vol. 48, no. 5 (1989), pp. 698–710; B. H. Lescher, 'Religious formation: beyond the healing paradigm', ibid., vol. 42, no. 6 (1983), pp. 853–8.
27. See Ferdon, op. cit., pp. 702–3.
28. H. J. Nouwen, *Intimacy* (Notre Dame, IN: Fides/Claretian, 1969), pp. 80, 81, 99.
29. Ibid., p. 100.
30. See G. A. Arbuckle, 'Seminary formation as a pilgrimage', *Human Development*, vol. 7, no. 1 (1986), pp. 27–33.
31. V. Turner and E. Turner, *Image and Pilgrimage in Christian Culture* (Oxford: Basil Blackwell, 1978), p. 8.
32. John of Taizé, *A New Testament: The Way of the Lord* (Washington, DC: Pastoral Press, 1990), p. 10.
33. See J. Eade and M. J. Sallnow (eds), *Contesting the Sacred: The Anthropology of Christian Pilgrimage* (London: Routledge, 1991), pp. 21–9.
34. R. Byrne, 'Journey: growth and development in spiritual life' in M. Downey (ed.), *The New Dictionary of Catholic Spirituality* (Collegeville, MN: Liturgical Press, 1993), p. 565.
35. 'The Church in the Modern World' in W. Abbott (ed.), *The Documents of Vatican II* (London: Geoffrey Chapman, 1966), para. 1.
36. Ibid.

5 Novitiate as a pilgrimage/rite of passage

Beginning with Abraham . . . the divine call turns human beings into sojourners, into pilgrims on a journey into the unknown, guided only by trust in an often elusive God. The image of the pilgrimage depicts well the open-ended character of salvation history, its creative aspect. . . . In consenting to the call . . . believers do not give up their freedom; they acquire it to the full.

(John of Taizé)[1]

Ritual is transformative, ceremony confirmatory.

(V. Turner)[2]

This chapter explains:

- the anthropological nature of initiation as a rite of passage;

- various initiation rites in the scriptures;

- novitiate as an initiation rite.

Since pilgrimages are *rites (or rituals) of passage* we can learn much which is applicable to formation, through a deeper appreciation of the dynamics of rites of passage. *Rites of passage* is a term first used by anthropologist Arnold van Gennep[3] early this century to describe particular life-crisis rituals, such as those accompanying birth, marriage, initiation into adulthood or entrance into political or religious offices. Such rituals mark the passage of individuals or groups from one social status to another in the course of life.

Processual rituals: three stages

Van Gennep found that all processual rituals have three stages: rituals of separation; rituals of transition, marginality or liminality; and re-aggregation rituals (that is, rituals of entry into, waiting in and leaving

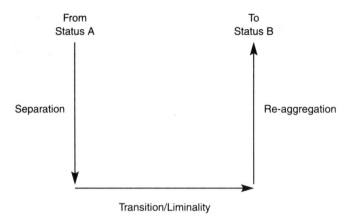

Figure 5.1 A rite of passage

the intermediate no-person's land) (see Figure 5.1). The three stages are not equally emphasized in all rituals of passage; for example the element of separation is more important in death rituals, that of re-aggregation in marriage, transition in initiation rites.

The threefold pattern is particularly clear in *initiation* rituals because the symbolism of death and rebirth gives orderly sequence to the rituals. The rituals of separation articulate a symbolic death, removing the neophyte from a former social status before he/she achieves a new status in the marginal stage. The initiate is actually 'reborn' back into the community through rituals of re-aggregation. Van Gennep notes that the liminal stage is especially long in initiation rituals. Initiates in this phase are considered outside normal society and, without social status in the daily life of the wider group, they are frequently tempted to flee back to the comfort of the old way of life. The stage is a lengthy one because the letting go of attachment to former status, that is the grieving dimension of the ritual, and the 'birthing of the new', which is the actual initiation into the new status, are slow, hesitant and painful. These stages, including a dramatically brief separation phase, are illustrated in the next case study and will be explained more fully in the pages that follow.

Case study: An initiation ritual

The initiation ritual for boys in the northern part of the island of Bougainville, Papua New Guinea, consists of three stages. The *first* is very brief and dramatic. The men of the village take the boys from their mothers amidst much ritual crying and hide them in the jungle. Now begins the *second* stage. During this period the novices avoid all contact with females, let their hair grow, observe numerous food taboos and live a slow and highly regulated life, one that is vastly different from anything they have been used to in the past. After a year, some of the men of the village put on

114

ancestor masks and show themselves to the women at a distance. Other men tell the women the figures are supernatural beings who have come to devour the novices. The masked men then descend on the boys, gesticulating over them, and take them off into a hut full of masks. Here a pantomime of death and resurrection is performed. The men place special conical hats on the 'resurrected' novices to hide the hair that has grown long during their seclusion. After a number of minor rituals, the boys return to the village.

Stage *three* is also lengthy. For about four or five years the youths, though no longer secluded, are subjected to numerous restrictions. They never remove their head-dress and they live in a closely knit bachelor association. A few years later, the novices, in the jungle, remove their hats and show their long hair to the assembled men. After this they again live together as a group. Still later, the novices spend a short period of seclusion in the jungle, after which they again enter the village and climb trees to show all the villagers their long hair. Various minor rituals follow, including the burning of the hats and the cutting of the hair. This completed, the novices are at last considered adults; the status of childhood is now ended for good.[4]

Initiation rituals: Turner's insights

Anthropologist Victor Turner further refined van Gennep's insights by analysing more deeply with great fruitfulness the experiential implications of liminality, that is, the second stage. He distinguishes two types of cultures. First, there is *societas*, a type of culture in which there is role differentiation, structure, segmentation and a hierarchical system of institutionalized positions. Most people live most of their lives in cultures like this. The second type is called *liminal* or *liminality*, that is, a type of culture which is undifferentiated, homogeneous, in which individuals meet each other integrally or as one human being to another, not segmented into status and roles. He argues that life is a process where individuals or groups of people pass from *societas* through *liminality* to *societas*. The word *liminal* can be confusing since it has two connotations: first, a point in a process for neophytes where 'they are betwixt and between the positions assigned and arrayed by law, custom, convention and ceremonial',[5] and second, a category of people, sometimes called *liminars*, *threshold* or *protest* people, who commit themselves to this transitional stage as a way of life. By their lifestyle liminars stand for fundamental values that people of the *societas* are ignoring; civil and religious prophetic persons belong to this category.

Liminality: ritual levelling for transformation

Following Gennep, Turner recognizes that the first stage in initiation rituals is short and dramatic. In the case study above, tearing away young boys from their grieving mothers is symbolically a most dramatic and even traumatic rupture with the past status of childhood. The forceful seclusion of the initiates in the jungle evokes the feeling that something crucial and radically new is about to happen to them. The stage is brief, but powerful in its symbolism and effects.

Turner highlights the ritual levelling at the liminal stage. Neophytes in rituals preparing to move from childhood to adulthood are without roles or status as though, in relation to the society from which they have come or to the society into which they are to be incorporated later, they are anonymous, dead, non-persons, deprived of all social roles other than just being initiates. Their state is 'frequently . . . likened to being in the womb, to invisibility, to darkness . . . to the wilderness'.[6] 'They have no status, property, insignia, secular clothing, rank, kinship position, nothing to demarcate them structurally from their fellows.'[7] The purpose of this ritual stripping of former status is to dispose neophytes to develop deep interrelationships with one another and an openness to the mythology and values that form the foundation of the culture of adulthood: 'The neophyte in liminality must be a *tabula rasa*, a blank slate, on which is inscribed the knowledge and wisdom of the group, in those respects that pertain to the new status.'[8]

In the stage of liminality neophytes are expected to experience a uniquely intense and friendly companionship that Turner terms *communitas*. *Communitas* is either normative or spontaneous.[9] Normative *communitas* is integral to initiation rites, that is, circumstances are deliberately structured to evoke deep bonding or oneness in initiates, but it does not necessarily happen. Initiates, as they live so closely together and are removed from their former status, are subject to all kinds of interpersonal tensions and for this reason another term for liminality is *chaos*. Initiates cannot experience *communitas* if they are unwilling to struggle through chaos for the conversion of their inner selves, that is, to move from an 'I' to a 'we' ethos. Spontaneous *communitas* may or may not occur in the ritual process; it is an unplanned experience of bonding, for example the sense of radical oneness that people feel when confronted with a natural disaster or the sight of a beautiful sunset.

Turner speaks of 'root paradigms' in ritual. A *root paradigm* is made up of symbols in a group's creation myth that are considered crucial to the particular culture and its ongoing existence.[10] In initiation rituals the common root paradigm is death/resurrection. In the above case study, there must be death to the childish, mother-centred ways, and resurrection for service to others in the wider society of the adult world. Throughout the liminality, particularly in the early part, there is frequent stress on this need for initiates to die to the past: the boys are to be 'converted by the mystical efficacy of ritual into purified members of a male moral community, able to begin to take their part in the jural, political, and ritual affairs'[11] of the wider society.

In traditional cultures the symbolic objects or actions used to foster the interiorization of this death/resurrection transformation in initiates are often highly dramatic and fear-evoking. The symbols are often of tribal ancestors, gods, evil spirits or cultural monsters. Turner comments:

> During the liminal period, neophytes are alternatively forced and encouraged to think about their society, their cosmos, and the powers that generate and sustain them . . . . [The] communication of *sacra* both teaches the neophytes how to think about their cultural milieu and gives them ultimate standards of reference . . . . [The] monsters are manufactured to teach neophytes to distinguish clearly between the different factors of reality, as it is conceived in their culture.[12]

The previous case study from Papua New Guinea illustrates this insight There, as in so many other parts of the world, ancestors hold a pivotal position: they can be helpful or hurtful beings, they can cause harm or bring good. To highlight this, ancestor masks are presented to the novices in startling ways, so dramatic that the neophytes will never ever forget the experience and the learning associated with it. In addition to the expressive presentation of symbols relating to the cultural foundations of the tribe, neophytes undergo a series of ordeals, humiliations or testings. The purpose is threefold: to hasten the removal of attachments to the past, to make them more receptive to their learning experiences, and to strengthen them to face up to their future responsibilities.[13]

Turner writes often of 'anti-structure symbols' when describing initiation rituals. The term needs clarification in order to yield a richer understanding of initiation rituals. Anti-structure symbols connote behaviour patterns that are contrary to the conduct previously accepted of the initiates when still children, or, to what they are to enact as adults. For example, in the case study the neophytes' seclusion in the jungle, the taboo on women, testing through physical suffering, and the threatening presentation of cultural objects are anti-structure symbols. The purpose of anti-structure symbols is always the same, namely to challenge neophytes to reflect deeply on, and to interiorize, the founding mythology, values and power that hold the adult culture together. As Turner says, 'Liminality may be partly described as a stage of reflection',[14] or, put in another way, 'Liminality here breaks, as it were, the cake of custom and enfranchises speculation'.[15] The anti-structure symbols provide physical, psychological, moral and spiritual shocks to evoke in initiates critical reflection on foundational symbols. Put another way, the initiation guides deliberately foster chaos in the liminal stage through various interventions, but it is carefully monitored lest it become excessive and damage the learning experience. The guides also recognize that conversion can remain superficial in their initiates, so they are vigilant and use manufactured or spontaneous events throughout the lengthy liminality to teach and to test the depth of their learning.

Liminality in 'modern' cultures: liminoid

Liminality periods lead initiates into experiential contact with the creation mythology of the culture they are to enter as adults. This is apt to generate a tension within them, as they reflect on the drama and quality of this mythology on the one hand and, on the other, the imperfect living of it by adults. They want to reform the world. 'Initiation', notes Turner, 'is to rouse initiative as much as it is to produce conformity to custom. Accepted schemata and paradigms must be broken if initiates are to cope with novelty and danger. They have to learn how to generate viable schemata under environmental challenge.'[16] In tribal societies (*strong group/strong grid* cultures, as explained in Chapter 3), however, the potentiality for creativity is strongly controlled, because the identity and life of the group depends on the maintenance of the *status quo*. The adults want the graduating novices to be creative in a *renewal* way, but they definitely do not desire a radical process of refounding to take over. That is, they expect graduating novices to inject revitalizing life into existing institutions, but they will not sanction revolutionary ideas and action that would undermine these institutions. Hence, in societies which foster conformity to traditions, creativity is permitted only within clearly defined limits.

However, in post-industrial societies, or in cultures that are open to radical change, people are free to enter an initiation process and to discover in the transition stage the energy to challenge institutions, not just to the level of renewal, but also to refounding if they so wish. *Liminality* in these societies is called by Turner *liminoid*, because of these two distinguishing qualities.[17] *Liminoid* is leisure in the fully human sense: 'leisure can be conceived of as a betwixt-and-between, a neither-this-nor-that between two spells of work or between occupational and familiar and civic activity'.[18] Leisure is the time when people without the pressure of ordinary work experience the desire and freedom to be contemplatives, pilgrims, poets, artists, dreamers, revolutionary thinkers, inventors, sportspersons, sculptors, comedians. In leisure people have the space to come into contact with deep metaphysical realities, founding myths, mysteries of space, nature and the universe. Such reflection in liminoid space can generate a subversive reflection on the values and structures of the culture from which one has temporarily removed oneself in leisure and this reflection can beget, not just renewal, but the revolutionary action of refounding. Little wonder that dictators control or suppress liminoid phenomena such as pilgrimages, comedy or satirical shows, political cartoons and rallies, various religious/theological, political or academic conventions. Likewise, restorationists in the Church try to prevent liminoid phenomena such as theological conferences in which liberation or feminist theologians reflect on the Church in light of gospel values.[19]

Re-aggregation

In the case study of an initiation ritual in Papua New Guinea described above, the liminal period is lengthy, but the third phase of the ritual is significantly longer. This is the period in which the initiates actually insert themselves into the adult world. Although in other tribal societies this stage may not be so long, it is still generally longer than its predecessor. Anthropologist Mary Douglas gives a reason for the length of this phase: 'It is consistent with the ideas about form and formlessness to treat initiands coming out of seclusion as though they were themselves charged with power, hot, dangerous, requiring insulation and a time for cooling down.'[20] As initiates approach integration into the adult world of roles, expectations and structures, they need time to adjust, to experiment under wise guidance with the new-found enthusiasm discovered in the liminality/*communitas* stage. In the case study we see the initiates over a period of years being exposed to ordinary village life, then pulled back to seclusion for evaluation sessions. They move back into the anti-structure, anti-ordinary space to have the time and freedom to detect to what extent they are integrating the values and myths of adulthood.

Tribal societies from centuries of experience know that neophytes will become discouraged without a 'cooling off' period, wounded by their failures to interiorize the mythology presented in its purest form in liminality, cynical about the behavioural inconsistencies they perceive among adults. They need to experience once more the comradeship of *communitas* and the chance to share and evaluate with ritual guides their exposure experiences in the village setting as quasi-adults. Humbled by the failures or buoyed up by the successes of their experiments, the initiates are ready to listen to deeper theoretical instruction and learning. This is an important time, because for a good period of the liminality stage, the stress is on experiential knowledge, rather than abstract or learning skills.

Rituals of initiation: biblical reflections

> Yahweh said to Abraham: 'Leave your country, your kindred and your father's house for a country which I shall show you . . .' So Abraham went as Yahweh told him.
>
> (Gen 12:1, 4)

Initiation in the Hebrew scriptures

The tripartite pattern of initiation – separation, liminality, re-aggregation – is evident in many descriptions of pilgrimages or journeyings in both

Testaments. For the Israelites the Exodus is the archetypal experience of initiation. It is through this ritual that they formally become a people of Yahweh. There is a separation phase, that is, the journeying out of Egypt, which is a mixture of joy and grieving, as has been explained earlier; then there is the liminality stage in the desert, followed by the entrance into the promised land – the re-aggregation phase. In the desert there are the anti-structure symbols of suffering, darkness and death, and there are trials aplenty as they wander 'through a land of drought, of shadow dark as death' (Jer 2:6).

Yahweh allows the Israelites to be tempted and when they fall they think they can survive without him: they said to Aaron 'Get to work, make us a god to go at our head' (Exod 32:1). Their reliance on other gods and their own strength ends in bickering and fighting among themselves, weariness and total loss of direction, but Yahweh is waiting for them to admit to their self-made chaos. Now is the chance to teach them a lesson: 'For thus says Yahweh . . . he is God, who shaped the earth and made it . . . he did not create it to be chaos, he formed it to be lived in . . . I did not say, "Offspring of Jacob, search for me in the chaos!"' (Isa 45:18–19). Yahweh invites them to acknowledge and embrace the chaos of their failings, but not to linger too long over what they have done. They must face the future in hope and wait to experience his action of newness in their lives.[21] When they do so, they experience a *communitas* with God and one another beyond all human comprehension: 'Yahweh preceded them, by day in a pillar of cloud to show them the way, and by night in a pillar of fire to give them light . . . . The pillar of cloud never left its place ahead . . . during the day, nor the pillar of fire during the night' (Exod 13:21–22). They find out 'As tenderly as a father treats his children, so Yahweh treats those who fear him' (Ps 103:13). Generation after generation when in the depths of chaos will recall and be energized by this hope-filled *communitas* experience: 'Sojourners in gloom and shadow as dark as death . . . for defying the orders of Yahweh . . . he rescued them from their plight, he brought them out from gloom . . . . Who is wise? Such a one should take this to heart, and come to understand Yahweh's faithful love' (Ps 107:10, 11, 14, 43).

The re-aggregation stage of the ritual is depicted in the Book of Joshua. Here is traced the history of the Israelites from the death of Moses to that of his successor, Joshua; the book recounts their entry into the promised land and its partition among the twelve tribes. Their proclaimed loyalty to Yahweh, marking the end of the liminoid experience of the desert, is quickly tested in the re-aggregation stage. They fail the test by disobeying Yahweh. They must learn *anew* that there is but one God and that whenever they cease to offer Yahweh total loyalty they must expect chaos: 'you will not be able to stand up to your enemies, until you have rid yourselves of that object which has been put under the curse of destruction' (Josh 7:13). So from bitter experience they re-learn the fundamental lesson of the liminoid stage: 'If you desert Yahweh and serve the foreigners' gods, he will turn and maltreat you anew and, in spite of having been good to you in the past, will destroy you' (Josh 24:20). The people declare they have re-learnt this basic message by re-identifying and re-owning their tribal learning in the liminoid experience of the desert: 'Yahweh our God was the one who brought us and our ancestors from Egypt . . . who worked wonders before our eyes . . . . We too shall serve Yahweh, for he is our God' (Josh 24:17–18).

Initiation rituals in the New Testament

1. *Jesus: from protected 'child' to anointed prophet*
The threefold ritual pattern is strikingly evident in the initiation of Jesus himself into his public ministry as the greatest of all prophets. Mark McVann highlights the three stages in the evangelist Matthew.[22]

Separation (3:23 – 4:1)
There are two steps in this stage: the first is Jesus moving alone away from familiar Galilee to the Jordan to be baptized; the second break with the past is his passing 'into the desert to be put to the test by the devil' (4:1). Each step removes him further from *societas*, that is, from his normal surroundings and kinsfolk.

Liminoid/*communitas* (4:2–11)
Significantly, Jesus travels into the desert, the sacred Israelite paradigm of marginality, trials and the experiential discovery of human weakness and the power of God – in brief, chaos. Jesus fasts, dramatically symbolizing the letting go of his former identity and disposing him to receive a new one. Now Jesus is confronted by the devil as the 'cultural monster' whose temptations are the catalyst of much learning and self-growth. In response to each temptation Jesus expresses his solidarity – *communitas* – with Moses, and symbolically with all the prophets who followed him through the centuries down to John the Baptist. Jesus comes through the tests: 'Absolute loyalty to God, solidarity with the prophets, an ability to see through the devil's tricks and recognizing and driving away evil are all essential characteristics of the authentic prophet. Matthew's audience sees that Jesus has full and flawless possession of these faculties.'[23]

Re-aggregation (4:11; 4:12–25)
There are two scenes in this stage. The first is the appearance of the angels who 'looked after him' (4:11), representing 'the virtually unmediated presence of God', symbolizing 'God's certification of Jesus' status as prophet, just as the Voice from heaven at the baptism declares that Jesus is God's Son'.[24] In the second scene (4:12–25), Jesus takes up his role as the Son of God and prophet: he proclaims his mission, as foretold by the prophet Isaiah, summons his first disciples, preaches and heals the sick. He not only has divine approbation as a prophet, but the people now publicly endorse it. He is the fully anointed prophet.

2. The initiation of Jesus as saviour

Again the threefold ritual pattern is clear in Matthew's account of the passion and resurrection.

Separation (26:1–35)

There are several steps in this stage, each one marking a further movement of Jesus away from the predictable order (*societas*) he had established as a preacher of the kingdom: the anointing in anticipation of his burial (6–13); the drama of the last supper (17–19; 26–29); the distressing actual and anticipated loss of friends – Judas and Peter (14–16; 20–25; 30–35). One senses in the narrative an ever-deepening sadness in Jesus as he begins the pilgrimage of withdrawing from a world of loving crowds and supportive friends, and an exciting ministry of preaching and healing.

Liminoid/*communitas* (26:36–56)

There are many scenes, each one a further experience for Jesus of deepening marginality. It begins with the trial of the agony in the garden. Jesus wrestles with the fear of facing death; there is a harrowing inner struggle, for he does not want to die. And there is the yearning to revive the bonding or *communitas* relationship with his three closest disciples but in this he fails. Having subordinated his will to God's, he lets the relationship go and in its place discovers an invigorating new *communitas* experience with the Father (26:36–46). As is customary in initiation rituals at this liminoid phase, Jesus is presented with sacred cultural symbols, but they represent opposing views of what is considered traditionally authentic. Jesus must make a choice: the monstrous powers of the Sanhedrin and the civil authority represented by Pilate, *or* the role of the suffering servant as portrayed in the messianic psalms and prophecies (26:57–68; 27:1–31). Fundamentally the option in the chaos is God *or* the world. As in his earlier initiation as the anointed prophet, Jesus passes the test, expresses his total loyalty to God and continues his pilgrimage.

The crucifixion and death of Jesus and his burial conclude this stage, in which Jesus experiences marginality to an extreme degree (27:32–56): mocked, stripped of his clothes, crucified between two rogues, with a few remaining friends 'watching at a distance' (27:55). Yet in the midst of this darkness, the humanly, impossibly new begins to break through. Jesus recites the lamentation Psalm 22 which, though it recounts the sadness of total disaster, also expresses its opposite, that is, hope in the saving power of God. In the chaos of his dying, Jesus is already being initiated into the new life of hope that comes only from a God in whom he has total trust:

> My God, my God, why have you forsaken me?. . .
> For he has not despised nor disregarded the poverty of
> the poor, has not turned away his face . . .
> The whole wide world will remember and return to Yahweh.
> (Ps 22:24, 27)

As in the desert, Jesus triumphs over evil, proving himself fit for the greatest of all actions lovingly longed for by all the prophets of old: 'No one can have greater love than to lay down his life for his friends' (John 15:13).

Re-aggregation (27:62–66; 28:1–20)

Jesus joins his disciples, but as the resurrected one – the one who has vanquished death and is about to join his Father. Because he has become the resurrected saviour through an initiation ritual, Jesus now has the Father's authority to pass on the mission of preaching to others: 'All authority in heaven and earth has been given to me. Go, therefore, make disciples of all nations . . . ' (28:18–19).

3. The Emmaus pilgrimage: initiation for two disciples

In this incident recounted by Luke, the tripartite pattern of initiation is again depicted, along with customary grieving.

Separation (24:13–15)

Two former followers of Jesus are moving away from Jerusalem, escaping from the place in which their hopes of Jesus as a political revolutionary have been irrevocably crushed. They cannot take any more! Deeply disappointed, they have had enough!

Liminoid/*communitas* (16–32)

Jesus the skilful grief and initiation leader joins them, but they fail to recognize him. Their inability to identify Jesus is caused more by spiritual blindness on their part than by anything unusual about Jesus' appearance. This fact adds to the drama of the event, for it highlights their need for conversion. Jesus invites them to express their feelings: '"What are these things that you are discussing as you walk along?" They stopped, their faces downcast' (24:17). All their anger and sadness tumble out at great speed. They had wanted Jesus to be a political revolutionary to expel force-fully their Roman oppressors (24:21). Jesus listens patiently to them before he begins-to challenge them. He presents them with several key sacred symbols of Israelite cultural history: Moses, the prophets, and the messianic texts (24:25–27). Now they must make a choice: continue to run away dreaming of a 'monstrous', military-minded saviour *or* accept what has been said and move forward out of chaos into the future in faith and hope. They choose Christ and experience *communitas* with him that words cannot fully express: 'Then they said to each other, "Did not our hearts burn within us as he talked to us on the road and explained the scriptures to us"' (24:32).

Re-aggregation (24:33–35)

They testified to the radicality of their conversion by returning immediately to Jerusalem to share their experience with the faith community there.

Refounding the novitiate process as an initiation ritual

Prior to an analysis of the novitiate process as an initiation ritual, the following assumptions need to be stated. I believe they are among the non-negotiables for an authentic novitiate in contemporary religious life.

Prerequisites

1. Free choice to enter
The Code of Canon Law states that 'only those who . . . have a suitable disposition, and have sufficient maturity to undertake the life which is proper to the institute'[25] are to be admitted into the novitiate. The novitiate is not a place to help novices grow up. If people request admission to a novitiate process, they must have the human, academic and psychological maturity to make a *free* petition. Given the unstable global postmodern culture in which we now live, the level of maturity needed by applicants in both the First and Third Worlds is markedly higher than that expected in the pre-Vatican II Church.

2. Must want religious life
The applicant must *want* religious life, that is, he/she must want to enter an initiation process because there are good grounds to believe, in the estimation of the individual and the responsible congregational superiors, that the Lord is calling them to such a life. Paul Molinari in writing on the pre-novitiate stage rightly reminds us that it is the Lord who calls: 'Look, I stand at the door and knock; if anyone hears my voice and opens the door, I will come in and eat with him, and he with me' (Rev 3:20).[26] The process of discernment is slow, requiring prayer and recourse to human expertise such as appropriate psychological testing.

3. Knowledge of faith needed
In the post-Vatican II Church and world it can no longer be assumed that candidates have the requisite knowledge of faith and practice to make an informed request to enter the novitiate. Good will is no substitute for knowledge, hence the need to provide would-be initiates with the necessary catechesis during the pre-novitiate stage. It is also a fact that 'Many candidates are affected by emotional immaturity, a prolonged adolescence, and a certain imbalance due to family problems or the negative influence of society',[27] an added reason for requiring of candidates professional psychological testing.[28] There is the real danger that people seek to enter religious life as a way to solve or escape personal emotional problems. Since that is not the primary purpose of religious life formation, they should not be accepted.

4. Qualities for refounding needed

Religious 'must be the first to undertake the task of the new evangelization',[29] showing apostolic boldness in their efforts to bring kingdom values into the contemporary world and Church. This call to be in the forefront of refounding the Church is at the very heart of the religious vocation. As religious life begins with novitiate,[30] if there is no *well*-founded hope that applicants possess the qualities to collaborate in a refounding process they should not be admitted. Prior to Vatican II the emphasis in the liminality stage of the novitiate was to mould candidates into being *uncreative* evangelizers, exemplary upholders of the ecclesiastical and pastoral *status quo*. Today in the liminoid the emphasis is the opposite, hence the need to refound the contemporary novitiate process and to establish rigorous screening procedures. As the gifts expected of candidates are uncommon in society in general we can never again expect large numbers of suitable people to apply to enter religious life.

In brief, the mission of religious life in today's postmodern world and that of the particular congregation determine the capacities required of a candidate. Acceptance of a candidate signifies that the applicant has not only the human and spiritual maturity to make a free decision to enter, but that he/she, together with the responsible congregational superiors, believes that God is calling them to take part in the formation process.

Case study: Consequences of inadequate preparation

A novice director in the Third World wrote to her provincial: 'I wish to resign from this post. For several years now I have complained about the poor screening and preparation of candidates for novitiate. I am spending most of my time counselling novices to leave. Given their lack of maturity and unwillingness to enter the process of the novitiate, they should not have been admitted in the first place. They make it difficult for those few who genuinely desire to do a good novitiate. Those who I do believe have a vocation to religious life most commonly begin novitiate in the eighth or ninth month . . . . The reason? They enter novitiate without having decided whether or not God is calling them to be novices for religious life. They resist the process for months. When they finally give themselves to the task, the novitiate is almost over. All those months were of little or no value to them. Because I have frequently raised these issues with you, but no action has been taken, I am bound in conscience to resign. If I continue any longer in this post I will be guilty of colluding in an unjust situation. We are dealing with people's lives and the well-being of the Church itself.'

The provincial refuses to accept the purpose of novitiate and the need for the appropriate qualities in applicants. The novice director rightly has no option but to resign.

5. *Exclusion of distractions*

The novitiate is the most sacred experience in the life of a religious. It is not a time for anything that does not directly relate to the primary task of novitiate: 'Whatever may be the special aim of the institute, the *principal* purpose of the novitiate is to initiate the novice into the essential and primary requirements of religious life.'[31]

6. *Necessity of a peer group*

Peer group interaction is essential for *communitas* to develop in the novitiate process. Wilkie Au comments:

> In my experience, peer formation is an important aspect of religious socialization. As novices experience together the different aspects of religious life and share their faith and religious experiences with each other, they are supported and 'edified'. . . . Spiritual conversation among novices regarding the story of their vocation, their experience in prayer and ministry, their struggles with the vows and with community living can provide much needed support and insight.[32]

When vocations are few this is a difficult requirement and we are tempted to ignore it. I agree with Au when he states the goals of *communitas* or socialization 'are very difficult to achieve with just two or three novices absorbed into a regular apostolic house'.[33] Hence, there is need for inter-congregational formation, but it should not be a substitute for periods where candidates are under the direct guidance of their own congregational formators. National and international novitiates for the same congregation are other options. An international novitiate not only allows for peer group interaction, but it also highlights the international nature of the congregation. If there is to be an international novitiate, however, candidates must be fluent in the group's common language *before* they enter. Novitiate is not a time to be learning languages or struggling to understand what is being said. Novitiate begins from the *first* day; candidates must have the qualities on that day necessary to realize the principal task of the novitiate.

7. *Qualified staff*

If a congregation has candidates but no formation staff trained for refounding and available full time, it should not offer a novitiate. A congregation that is serious about its mission and future will find and train appropriate people for the task.

8. *Two years duration*

I do not believe that the goal of religious life initiation can be achieved today in one year, still the customary time in many congregations. It should cover a period of two years. The conditions of the postmodern world and the Church, as explained in this book, require enough time for the candidate to 'taste the presence of the Lord', feel the powerful attracting force of the congregation's charism and be tested in ministry. In former times, when the Church approximated a stable tribal culture, the one-year novitiate may have been sufficient, but definitely not now.

Novitiate as initiation: stages[34]

The three stages of novitiate as an initiation are shown in Figure 5.2.

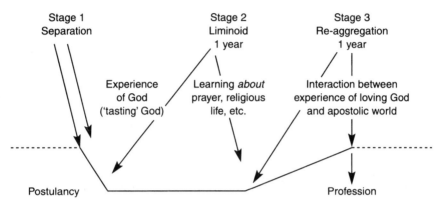

Figure 5.2 The three stages of novitiate as an initiation rite

Stage 1: Separation

The anthropology of initiation shows that the first stage should be dramatic. The symbolism of anti-structure must be clear and unambiguous, that is, the symbolism must communicate to the candidate that in order to respond to the call of Jesus Christ there needs to be a withdrawal from the world of 'ordinary living' (*societas*) with its roles and interests, its emphasis on the need for constant change and its distractions. To follow the radical demands of the gospel message, one must be prepared to leave 'father, mother, wife, children, brothers, sisters, yes and his own life too' (Luke 14:26) for the sake of the Lord. This is the stage, in other words, where the dynamics of the ritual of grieving will be emphasized.

The symbolism of letting go attachments as a requirement for becoming a novice will involve the separation of the novitiate from other apostolates of the congregation, including postnovitiate programmes. If the primary task of the novitiate is to be realized, novices require the uncluttered space of a secluded site for at least the early months, in order that they may be able to hear the Lord speaking to them. I do not see that this stage of separation can normally be achieved in the heart of a busy city. A move to some remote site, even for a short period, would of itself provide the needed symbolism. In the gospels we see this dramatic break with 'normal living' (*societas*) when Jesus takes his disciples to a *lonely* place where they can be by themselves (Mark 6:31; Luke 9:10).

A novice director comments

A Marist novice director[35] comments on his experience of these stages. He describes the first stage of the novitiate:

> We began this (stage) with a ritual on the day of arrival. After the evening meal, the novices returned to the front gate (a symbol of *societas*) and walked to the front door where they were met by the formation staff. Each novice asked to enter the Marist house to be formed in the values of the gospel and the charism. Each novice was then embraced and welcomed into the house. We moved to the chapel in which we set up symbols of the faith and the charism. I outlined the Marist story which they were asking to be formed in. Together they prayed to be formed in the spirit and mission of the congregation and we, the formation team, pledged our commitment to them in this task. The next four weeks were occupied in living out this phase of *separation*, for example sharing our stories, working together around the house, praying together. We gave plenty of time to our meals together as a community. My desire was that they would begin to experience the bond of the 'common table' in contrast to our culture which celebrates individualism and the fast-food syndrome. No television. *Solitude time* was set at an hour each day to be spent alone and in silence for spiritual exercises – a crucial experience for the development of internal and external silence . . .

Stage 2: Liminoid

In light of the theory above, I believe that this second stage should last several months, even a year, and that there should be no interruption for significant formative apostolic experiences for at least nine months. If Jesus is to speak to the candidates in private and reveal the secrets of the kingdom (Mark 4:11; Matt 13:11) 'there is need for a protracted period of relative withdrawal and of quiet solitude, sufficient to enable the person to be at the side of the Lord to contemplate the One so loved'.[36] Since the cultural background of many candidates today is one of ever-intensifying noise and pre-packaged leisure activities, the emphasis on seclusion and periods of silence in a novitiate will provide powerful anti-structure symbols in which novices have the space to 'taste' the presence of God. In their *communitas* experience with God they become open to a radical conversion to Jesus, his mission and his Church.

Research into tribal initiation rituals points to the importance of experiencing foundational values, not just learning about them. Thus, in tribal initiation rituals, tribal objects representing the group's founding mythology are presented to the candidates in dramatic and stark ways. The melodramatic nature of their staging aims to shock the candidates into realizing the importance of the values of their tribal culture. In these early stages of the novitiate liminoid, the scriptures are also to be opened to candidates, not as books for learning and analysis on a formal level, but as ways to *experience* the power, mercy and love of God. This is the opportune time to introduce novices to faith sharing. This is the chance for an individual, in the presence of others, to articulate a personal faith experience. It involves several steps:

— reflecting on biblical texts;

— asking key questions of oneself:

    how does this text impact on my experience?

    how does it relate to where I am in my pilgrimage with Jesus?

— offering oneself, trusting in the power and inspiration of the Holy Spirit;

— sharing with a few others the insights received;

— respecting the silence of others;

— holding in confidence the group's sharing.

The novice director will help novices to see that faith sharing is not a time for discussion, theological critique or debate, or for the offering of advice. No one should be forced to speak.

I think that in the early period of liminoid it is also suitable to expose the novices to well-written and historically exact studies of the lives of the Church's saints and the congregation's cultural heroes/heroines. People such as St Francis of Assisi and other founders of congregations experienced the presence and the call of the Lord, becoming symbols of radical commitment to gospel values and prophetic innovators within the Church and society. They became *liminoid*, *anti-structure* or *protest* persons, that is, people whose lives were in vivid and dramatic contrast to what was acceptable in the world of their times.[37] In this they are 'ancestral models' to novices, symbolizing that conversion to Jesus is possible and is radical in its demands.

Now is the decisive time for the candidates to grasp more deeply in their pilgrimage the fundamental root paradigm for the novitiate – the death/resurrection paradigm. If there is to be a continuing response to the call of the Lord to closer intimacy, the 'price' must be paid; there must be death to self, death to false worldly attractions. The anti-structure (that is, anti-*societas*) symbols of the novitiate, for example geographical isolation or separation, increased spells of external silence, and periods in which the initiates are bored and lonely, proclaim to them that a *communitas* centred on Jesus and a bondedness amongst themselves will require mortification, a growing self-control and ongoing death to self. The noises and allures of the world must be put aside if the Lord is to be heard and listened to.

All initiation rituals necessarily involve testing events in one form or another, for example: the pain of separation from the comfort of one's immediate family, the dramatic rupture with one's past style of living, the restrictions of community living, the uncertainty of what will happen next in the process, the loneliness and monotony of isolation. There is no need to invent trials; they will inevitably arise in the course of the novitiate and can be used as learning experiences. Growth occurs most often in moments of crisis and chaos in life; each individual's exodus to the promised land of oneness with Jesus must pass through the tribulations of the desert. There can be no escaping this dynamic, if one is struggling to love Christ above all things. The wise director knows this. He/she uses these built-in opportunities of pain to help candidates test their progress in purification and ability to take up their role as pilgrims with the suffering Servant. The director must not mother the candidates or in any way create a therapeutic or blossom type ethos; that would deny to the novices the learning potential of these unpleasant or agonizing experiences. Rather, these opportunities are God-allowed and to be used to help novices uncover the reasons for any negative or inconsistent behaviour patterns.

The novice director has a vital role in facilitating the process of the liminoid and in helping the candidate to experience the power of Christ's call. Prudence is needed to know when to wait or intervene. Sometimes the director finds himself/herself acting on hunches born of his/her own experience of walking with Jesus the Pilgrim. I agree with Paul Molinari's comment: 'It is essential, therefore, that the novices be in contact with a "spiritual guide", that is, a man or woman of God whose primary concern is not theory or "book learning", but one whose life and learning have been integrated, and who has come to know the ways of God by experience.'[38]

After about two or three months the novices should be exposed to the sacred experience of the congregation's founding in ways that resemble their exposure to the scriptures, that is, not as a question of learning texts, but of meditatively reflecting on the life, writings of the founders and the congregational constitutions. Questions like the following can be asked novices:

— What do you feel the founder is saying to you personally through what you are reading?

— How do you think you might have reacted, if you had been one of the founder's companions?

— What is prophetic in the founding experience? Do you see any relevance in the founding experience for today's world?

— How did the founder cope with personal trials?

Only later in the liminoid stage should there be an emphasis on such things as *learning about* the religious life, the theology of vows, and relevant sections of canon law.

Further comments by a novice director[39]

> I signalled the second phase (*liminoid*) in various ways. I increased the
> *solitude* time by another half hour (eventually it increased to two and
> three-quarter hours each weekday); we began our reflections on the
> charism and history of the congregation; I presented each novice with
> a copy of the constitutions . . . . We set about learning and *experiencing*
> the Marist story, charism and mission . . . . And I gradually prepared
> them for the spiritual exercises of St Ignatius Loyola. After a period of
> time we felt they were ready for the month's exercises, which I believe
> is the best process to experience conversion, discipleship, vocational
> discernment and mission. They provide a radical experience of Jesus,
> the Father, Mary and the saints, the Kingdom of God and Christ's
> mission to the world . . . . Rather than talking or reading about these
> things, the exercises provide an *experience* of them . . . .

The novice director emphasizes the primacy of experience at this stage.
His use of the spiritual exercises of St Ignatius Loyola is in line with this
approach. The exercises provide novices with a skilled instrument to help
them discover God's will for themselves: how can they become, through
wise and faith-filled decisions, more intimately allied with the will of
God for the world and Church? Ignatius wants retreatants to choose what
best leads to the glory of God. The exercises are perfectly attuned to the
theme of refounding, the heart of which is the struggle to be constantly
searching for the best ways to bring kingdom values to contemporary
cultures.

Stage 3: Incorporation or re-aggregation[40]

I assume that the novitiate liminoid stage should last about a year and
the third stage should also cover a similar period. The aim of this stage
is summarized as follows:

> Besides gradual preparation for apostolic activities, they (i.e., the
> experimental periods outside the novitiate) can also have as their purpose
> to bring the novice into contact with certain concrete aspects of poverty
> or of labour, to contribute to character formation, a better knowledge of
> human nature, the strengthening of the will, the development of personal
> responsibility and, lastly, to provide occasions for effort at union with
> God in the context of active life.[41]

Molinari sees these apostolic periods as the chance

> to call forth from their hearts an even greater generosity, and refine
> further the quality of the relationship with Christ. The object here
> will be to help them to test the sincerity of their attachment to Christ,
> to become more aware of what it means to be with him in sharing his
> attitudes and concern for people . . . . It can only be realized by exposing
> them to situations and circumstances where the capacity for love can
> express itself in new and much more demanding ways.[42]

If we take the root paradigm as death/resurrection, then this is the stage in which the novice must become familiar with the resurrection values. Here the candidate has the chance to discover, from his/her own experience of themselves, and with others, the comforting virtue of hope in the midst of distress, forgiveness and mercy in the thick of guilt and sin. The initiation aspect of the ritual process as the opportunity to encounter the new life of the resurrection, rather than the emphasis on what the novice must be detached from, now comes into marked prominence. It is also the chance for neophytes to come to know through first-hand experience more of the apostolates and personnel of the congregation.

This exposure period must be evaluated with the help of experienced guides. During this stage, however, the overall direction of the novices is to remain the responsibility of the novice director.[43] It is imperative that the director, who knows the candidates from the first stage, be involved to help them evaluate their experiences. This is a director's full-time and specialist task. If the evaluation role is left to others, then the unity of the formative or pilgrimage process is lost. Other people cannot be expected to know the ways in which the candidates have been interacting with the Master himself.

Understood in the way explained this stage cannot be seen as a chance for the congregation to fill gaps in communities or pastoral teams, nor should it be seen as an opportunity for novices to break away from the monotony of the novitiate setting. On the contrary, this is a crucial formative period, with a dynamic based on the particular needs of novices at this point, the realities of the culture they are to enter and directives of Jesus himself. Recall the insight of Douglas given previously: 'Initiands coming out of seclusion . . . (are) hot, dangerous, requiring insulation and a time for cooling down.' If novices fail to have a 'cooling down' period provided by formative and evaluated sessions of pastoral involvement, then liminoid learning is in jeopardy. Candidates may feel either that the ideals can never be realized by anyone or, if they can be by some, they cannot be achieved by themselves personally. Discouragement, guilt and cynicism become real possibilities. Some, having accepted that the ideals cannot be acquired by themselves, may develop a 'coasting or nesting mentality', that is, an outward show of being good religious, but lacking passionate commitment to the kingdom and inner sincerity. Others will want to extend the liminoid stage to avoid the 'unclean' world where they feel God can no longer be reached in prayer. The re-aggregation stage, under right supervision, will surface these reactions and learning can continue. A fundamental insight of Ignatius Loyola explained in Chapter 1 applies here: religious committed to ministry must ultimately be assessed in it. To stop the novitiate and assessment of novices at the liminoid phase is to miss this fundamental point.

The question is asked: can formal studies be undertaken in this period of the novitiate? Again I feel that anthropological research into initiation rituals helps here. In tribal life initiates are introduced to the *total* life of the village in order to be challenged in a *multi-dimensional* experiential way. Formal theological or academic studies, for example for the priest-hood or other ministry, provide what is in fact a *one-dimensional* intellectual challenge or experience for novices. It is too limited. During the third stage, therefore, initiates should not be allowed to undertake purely academic or ministry studies for long periods. In multi-dimensional apostolic exposure, candidates have to face people in often very human, even depressing, situations. Such periods will test the candidates in ways that formal study cannot do.

The evangelist Luke recounts two occasions in which Jesus clearly uses the third stage to instruct his followers. The first is with his inner circle: 'He called the Twelve together and gave them power and authority over all the devils and to cure diseases, and he sent them out to proclaim the kingdom of God and to heal' (Luke 9:1–2). Jesus gives them a list of guidelines to follow in their ministry and reminds them of the liminoid detachment they have experienced through their closeness to him over several months. Now, without his presence, they must on their own test in the rough-and-tumble of a busy world the depth of their personal conversion: 'Take nothing for the journey: neither staff, nor haversack, nor bread, nor money; and do not have a spare tunic' (Luke 9:3). After their pastoral exposure he sits with them to evaluate their experience: 'On their return the apostles gave him an account of all they had done' (Luke 9:10).

The second incident is the missioning of the 72 disciples: 'After this the Lord appointed seventy-two others and sent them out ahead of him in pairs, to all the towns and places he himself would be visiting' (Luke 10:1). Jesus reiterates his pastoral guidelines for evangelization. The disciples returned from their missionary exposure 'rejoicing', bubbling with enthusiasm over their successes: '"Lord", they said, "even the devils submit to us when we use your name"' (Luke 10:17). Jesus rejoices with them. But no doubt he also uses the occasion to remind them, as the wise instructor, that their apostolic success comes ultimately not from their power but his own: 'Look, I have given you power to tread down serpents and scorpions' (Luke 10:19).

A novice director comments on re-aggregation[44]

Something I noticed as the liminoid period was drawing to a close – resistance. The novices wanted to stay 'on the mountain top'. They suggested that I was being hasty and mistaken by challenging them to move on. They argued that they needed more time and solitude to process the richness of the experience so far. I told them we were religious for mission to the world, not contemplatives in a monastery. For us, Nazareth must lead always to Pentecost, otherwise we are unfaithful to our founder.

From now on (in the re-aggregation stage) there were no set solitude times. The novices had to make their own time for prayer, study etc.

(There was resistance to this.) Among the exposure programmes arranged for them was a weekly encounter with prisoners at the local prison. This was no easy task. They experienced a variety of responses: acceptance, rejection, being ignored, challenged and ridiculed, and the profound sharing of personal stories. The chaplain kept an eye on them at a distance. Sometimes they came home exhausted, sometimes elated. Each time they returned, we spent about an hour reflecting on and talking about the experiences of the day. This was done in the light of faith that acts lovingly and justly. It was about 'finding God in all things'.

The time in the prison was a difficult one for me as novice master. Was I asking too much of the novices? Was it too tough for them? I needed to keep in regular contact with the chaplain and listen carefully at communal reflection for signs of undue stress. This was a time of deep trust in God, in the novices, in the process and in my judgement.

In the process I wanted the novices to experience Christ's mission to the world as a pilgrimage, to imitate his own journey. We had several pilgrimages, one of a few days and the other 21 days. The latter was to the site where the faith in New Zealand was first planted and where our early Marist missionaries laboured. (Today it is also the centre of a new evangelization effort by Marists based on refounding principles – GAA.) The local people welcomed us, fed us, shared their faith with us and showed us the sacred places of this part of the country. We also participated in the life of the Marist community there. For me, the spiritual exercises and this lengthy pilgrimage were the two corner-stones around which the novitiate process functioned. They were the key liminoid and re-aggregation learning experiences.

These comments contain a wealth of wisdom. The director's objective is clear and he will not be tempted away from it: namely, to provide a structure to allow the novices to test the depth of their conversion to Jesus. They have intellectually assented, as future members of an apostolic congregation, to the need to become contemplatives *in action*, yet they resist at first the chance to test themselves. A less perceptive director would be impressed by their desire to remain on the mountain top. The pastoral exposure programmes, in which the novices are the recipients of all kinds of human reactions to their work, are regularly evaluated. The pilgrimages with their personal and group inconveniences are also pivotal in his planning for the re-aggregation stage. The major pilgrimage, however, is to the founding site of the Church in New Zealand where the novices learn first-hand from people their feelings of the history of this event, for example the faith of the early evangelizers and their converts in the midst of considerable poverty and hostility. The novices also experience a pastoral effort to refound the Church in that area by members of the congregation they are to join. They listen to the hopes and challenges of its initiators and people they serve.

Summary

An initiation process consists of three sharply defined stages: separation, liminoid and re-aggregation. It is simultaneously dangerous and empowering. It is dangerous because an initiate's feeling of predictability is temporarily lost, and instead he/she experiences radically new ways of looking at life. Initiation pushes the initiate to the margins and, as Douglas observes, 'all margins are dangerous. If they are pulled this way or that the shape of fundamental experience is altered.'[45] The initiate does not not know the outcome of the experience. This is exactly why an initiation ritual is also empowering. The initiate becomes more powerful by daring to move beyond the margins of his/her former status and beginning to build for himself/herself new possibilities of being and acting.

Since a religious novitiate is an initiation ritual, formators are able to draw on the rich insights of anthropology and scripture in planning its structure. The process and qualifications for entrance into novitiate are determined by the mission of religious life itself: to prophetically challenge the Church and the world with the kingdom values. Religious are called to be at the heart of the refounding of the Church's mission to the world of today, hence the radical conversion of novices to Christ the Prophet is the primary aim of the novitiate's stages, especially stages two and three. As in all initiation rituals, this reorientation process will evoke joy, a bonding with Christ and with one another (*communitas*), but also fear and pain; the overall paradigm is death/resurrection. The second stage (liminoid) requires lengthy seclusion. It is not a return to monastic formation, because in the third or re-aggregation stage novices are exposed to the realities of the world through evaluated pastoral experiences. These pastoral exposures provide candidates with the chance to test the depth of their refounding intimacy with the Master, as well as to discover something more of the congregation's way of living. The necessity and nature of this third stage has been in the past the most poorly understood.

For entrance into novitiate candidates require a high level of human and spiritual maturity. No one should be admitted if he/she lacks the required qualities. The spirituality of the initiation process, which is itself a pilgrimage, finds its roots deep in scripture, for example the Exodus and Christ's initiation into his role as the anointed Prophet.

Notes

1. John of Taizé, *A New Testament: The Way of the Lord* (Washington, DC: Pastoral Press, 1990), p. 9.
2. V. Turner, *The Forest of Symbols: Aspects of Ndembu Ritual* (Ithaca, NY: Cornell University Press, 1967), p. 95.
3. See A. van Gennep, *The Rites of Passage*, trans. M. Vizedom and G. Caffee (Chicago: University of Chicago Press, 1960).

4. For other examples see M. Eliade, *Birth and Rebirth: The Religious Meanings of Initiation in Human Culture* (New York: Harper); J. Alves, 'Transgressions and transformations: initiation rites among urban Portuguese boys', *American Anthropologist*, vol. 95, no. 4 (1993), pp. 894–920; A. Iteanu, *La Ronde des échanges. De la circulation aux valeurs chez les Orakaiva* (Cambridge: Cambridge University Press, 1983); G. H. Herdt (ed.), *Rituals of Manhood: Male Initiation Rites in Papua New Guinea* (Berkeley: University of California Press, 1981); L. C. Mahdi *et al.* (eds), *Betwixt and Between: Patterns of Masculine and Feminine Initiation* (La Salle, IL: Open Court, 1987); J. S. Fontaine, *Initiation: Ritual Drama and Secret Knowledge Across the World* (Harmondsworth: Penguin, 1985); M. N. Fried and M. H. Fried, *Transitions: Four Rituals in Eight Cultures* (New York: W. W. Norton, 1980); E. McClafferty, 'Rites of passage on an American high school swim team' in C. P. Kottak (ed.), *Researching American Culture* (Ann Arbor: University of Michigan Press, 1982), pp. 199–209.
5. See V. Turner, *The Ritual Process: Structure and Anti-Structure* (New York: Aldine, 1969), p. 95. For commentaries on Turner's insights see R. L. Grimes, *Beginnings in Ritual Studies* (Lanham, MD: University Press of America, 1982); W. G. Doty, *Mythography: The Study of Myths and Rituals* (Tuscaloosa, AL: University of Alabama Press, 1986); T. F. Driver, *The Magic of Ritual* (New York: HarperCollins, 1991); B. Morris, *Anthropological Studies of Religion* (Cambridge: Cambridge University Press, 1987); K. M. Ashley, *Victor Turner and the Construction of Cultural Criticism* (Bloomington, IN: Indiana University Press, 1990).
6. Turner, *The Ritual Process*, op. cit., p. 95.
7. Turner, *The Forest of Symbols*, op. cit., p. 99.
8. Turner, *The Ritual Process*, op. cit., p. 103.
9. See V. Turner, *Dramas, Fields and Metaphors: Symbolic Action in Human Society* (New York: Cornell University Press, 1974), p. 232.
10. See Turner, *The Ritual Process*, op. cit., pp. 67–8.
11. Turner, *The Forest of Symbols*, op. cit., pp. 265–6.
12. Ibid., pp. 105, 106, 108.
13. Turner, *The Ritual Process*, op. cit., p. 103.
14. Turner, *The Forest of Symbols*, op. cit., p. 105.
15. Turner, *The Ritual Process*, op. cit., p. 106.
16. Turner, *Dramas, Fields and Metaphors*, op. cit., p. 256.
17. See V. Turner, *From Ritual to Theatre: The Human Seriousness of Play* (New York: Performing Arts Journal Publications, 1982), pp. 32–3, 52–5.
18. Ibid., p. 36.
19. See G. A. Arbuckle, *Refounding the Church: Dissent for Leadership* (London: Geoffrey Chapman, 1993), pp. 1–97.
20. M. Douglas, *Purity and Danger: An Analysis of Concepts of Pollution and Taboo* (Harmondsworth: Penguin, 1966), p. 117.
21. See W. Brueggemann, *Interpretation and Obedience: From Faithful Reading to Faithful Loving* (Minneapolis: Fortress Press, 1991), pp. 317–18.
22. See M. McVann, 'One of the prophets: Matthew's testing narrative as a rite of passage', *Biblical Theological Bulletin*, vol. 23, no. 1 (1993), pp. 14–20 and 'Rituals of status transformation in Luke–Acts: the case of Jesus the prophet' in J. H. Neyrey (ed.), *The Social World of Luke–Acts: Models for Interpretation* (Peabody, MA: Hendrickson, 1991), pp. 333–60. Wayne A. Meeks describes baptism in the Pauline communities as a three-stage process of an initiation ritual: see his book *The First Urban Christians: The Social World of the Apostle Paul* (New Haven: Yale University Press, 1983), pp. 150–7.

23. McVann, 'One of the prophets', op. cit., p. 18.
24. Ibid., p. 19.
25. Can. 642.
26. P. Molinari, 'The initial stages of formation', *The Way Supplement*, no. 41 (1981), pp. 45–6.
27. Document *Instrumentum Laboris* for the Synod of Bishops, *The Consecrated Life and Its Role in the Church and the World* (Vatican: Vatican Press, 1994), para. 90.
28. Ibid., para. 89.
29. See ibid., para. 96.
30. See Congregation for Religious, *Instruction on Renewal of Religious Life* (Vatican Libreria Editrice Vaticana, 1969), paras 13–14.
31. Ibid., para. 13. The *Code of Canon Law* states: 'The period of novitiate . . . is to be set aside exclusively for the work of formation. The novices are therefore not to be engaged in studies or duties which do not directly serve this formation' (Can. 651).
32. W. Au, 'Understanding the novitiate process', *Review for Religious*, vol. 47, no. 5 (1988), pp. 680–1.
33. Ibid., p. 680.
34. Wilkie Au, a former Jesuit novice director, comments on the validity of the novitiate process as explained here: 'In my opinion, (the) three-stage approach provides a rich and comprehensive understanding of the novitiate process, as well as a sound basis for determining the question of separation and contact that would be helpful for novices . . . . The model is useful because it enables the novitiate to effectively bond new members to the religious group, which is the goal of religious socialization'. Ibid., p. 673.
35. Allan Jones (Marist Fathers/Brothers, New Zealand province).
36. Molinari, op. cit., p. 54.
37. See Turner, *The Ritual Process*, op. cit., pp. 140–1.
38. Molinari, op. cit., p. 56.
39. Jones, op. cit.
40. I feel that Thomas A. Krosnicki, in his instructive article 'Christian Initiation of Adults and the formation of religious', wrongly gives the impression that novitiate is synonymous only with the liminoid stage. See *Review for Religious*, vol. 41, no. 6 (1982), p. 875.
41. Congregation for Religious, *Instruction on the Renewal of Religious Life*, op. cit., para. 25.
42. Molinari, op. cit., pp. 58–9.
43. See *Code of Canon Law*, Can. 650.
44. Jones, op. cit.
45. Douglas, op. cit., p. 256.

6 Refounding communities for postnovitiate formation

In the Church as communion – an image of the Trinity – (religious life) is presented as a visible, prophetic reminder of the communion which the whole Church must already be living.

(Instrumentum Laboris, 1994)[1]

A religious community is not a family, neither is it an ethnic, professional, or social group; it is certainly not built on affinity and friendship. A religious community is a group of people who have been called to the same vocation and who . . . live their calling by faith.

(M. Azevedo)[2]

This chapter explains:

- reactions of religious in the postnovitiate stage to receiving communities;

- a Vatican document (1994) on community life;

- the nature of an intentional community;

- the reasons why the postnovitiate community must be an intentional one and that its establishment is an act of refounding;

- criteria for evaluating personal growth at the postnovitiate stage.

The task of the novitiate is to initiate candidates into religious life in accordance with the founding experience of a particular congregation. The primary task of the postnovitiate period is twofold: to continue deepening the commitment of candidates to religious life values, and to foster their 'professional preparation for ministry or actual involvement in ministry'.[3] Since the purpose of this period is unlike that of the novitiate, so will its structures and processes differ, but as for the novitiate, all candidates will require community life that is ongoingly formative and staffed by qualified personnel.

Receiving communities: statement of problem

Is it possible to provide the appropriate community life and staff for newly professed religious in today's religious congregations? Since the early 1980s I have frequently asked religious belonging to this post-novitiate stage in many parts of the world to describe the quality of their community life. The great majority, assigned to live with finally professed members of their congregation actively involved in ministry or/and retired, complained that their community life was a spiritually negative and apostolically de-energizing experience. The following are representative comments from these candidates in the First and Third Worlds. Readers may wish to spend time evaluating them in light of the material in previous chapters before continuing.

1. 'My community, in which the majority are professed members, is depressed. You see it in their faces, their voices and conversations. Nothing enthuses them. It is a deadly experience to come back each day from my ministry training to face this group. They told me in novitiate to expect this type of thing, but it is worse than anything they could have told us. I spoke to the provincial about it, but she said: "Keep trying. It is good for the soul." I am beginning to think it is not! Surely the mission has the priority and my community life must be supportive for this.'

2. 'All that I learnt in novitiate and practised by way of consultation in decision-making is rejected here.'

3. 'There is no peer group support.'

4. 'Community prayers, if we have them, are too formal and rushed.'

5. 'No one is interested in faith sharing.'

6. 'As I am the first newly professed member for many years people in the community keep saying to me: "Good to have you. You are our refounding person!" This is ridiculous! They see me as the great hope of the future. They place on my shoulders the future of the entire province . . . . There is no arguing with them.'

7. 'I would very much like – and need – an intentional community. It was placed before us at novitiate as the only way to go in refounding. I believe this, but no one is showing any interest in it in my community.'

8. 'There are people in the community who say that we must direct our religious life to the Transcendent. Forget about justice. Direct ourselves to the Holy. This is abhorrent to me and I do not believe it is according to Vatican II. Surely our ministry is about the bringing of Christ into the world of our time. My holiness depends on this struggle. It is a balance, we discovered in novitiate, between the Transcendent and the Incarnation. Yet I cannot get support for this and wonder about staying.'

9. 'There is a weariness in the community. It is not that they are old, but few seem interested in finding new ways to preach the gospel. It is a depressed atmosphere.'

139

10. 'We have no trained formation staff to guide us. Good sisters have been given us, but they lack the knowledge and expertise to really understand and direct us. We believe that the provincial administration is not sincerely interested in our formation.'

11. 'We keep hearing stories from older community members about the "good old days" in the seminary, the same old incidents recounted many times of the characters who taught them. It all seems like another planet. There is nothing stimulating in the conversations. People fear to share what really concerns them. We relate on the joking level, but now after being away from novitiate a few months I wonder if I can take this superficiality any longer. If I am to give of my best in my ministry, then I need good support based on mature relationships and shared prayer.'

12. 'I feel I am being smothered by kindness. The older ones want me to be a child again. Community for them seems to mean sitting around talking about the old days. People are so concerned about themselves. Even their smothering is possessive. They want to feel good, I think, by constantly doing things for me and they want me to keep saying how good they are for doing this.'

13. 'I have the feeling that they are envious of me – of my youth and good novitiate training. They keep saying in often subtle ways that my training was not what it should have been. It should have been tougher, like the old days. They seem keen to destroy my faith in my novitiate experience.'

14. 'I find no space for myself in the community. People seem to invade my boundaries, demanding as though by right that I should share my inmost thoughts with all and sundry.'

15. 'The community is busy, busy . . . . There is no regular prayer, but time for television. I bring this up in community meetings which we have on very rare occasions, but I get stony silence. Everybody is doing their own thing. This is not the community life I was trained for or need.'

16. 'People go out of their way to tell me "It is a good community". I think they are trying to convince themselves this is so. On the contrary, there is no in-depth reflection on mission and our ministries. There are little kingdoms here and one must not enter or challenge them.'

17. 'Our community has established some rigid rules about times for community prayer, when we can receive visitors and so forth. When my ministry training keeps me away from community prayers at times, I am subtly told I am not a good religious. Yet, our congregation is apostolic. Rules we need but not so rigid. At community meetings it is argued that we must return to structures, otherwise there cannot be adequate formation. Fine, but no one asks the purpose of the structures. It is a return to the old ways of training that the old ones talk so much about.'

18. 'I return from my ministry with the poor daily, yet I cannot get anyone to be interested in what I am doing. I am not asking for every-one to be interested, but I would like to evaluate things and share my reactions in faith sharing at times, but it is impossible.'

19. 'I have been placed in a large community in which relationships are very formal, including community prayers. All spontaneity and faith sharing are considered signs of sentimentality. I yearn for a small community, such as we had in novitiate, in which we can pray together in ways that relate to our ministerial needs. I know small communities have their own tensions, but I feel there is no other way not just to survive but to grow in our ministries.'

There is a pattern in these dismal comments. The descriptions of the receiving communities reflect several overlapping and interconnected cultures already explained in earlier chapters, for example cultures of depression, unresolved grief, envy, me-ism, restorationism. The culture of envy needs some explanation. Envy is the sadness that a person/group feels, because someone else has what that person/group wants; if the object or relationship cannot be obtained then the person/group is prepared to destroy it so that no one can enjoy it. Envy is a predictable symptom of chaos reaction and it can become so dominant in people's lives that we can speak of a culture of envy, though few will be conscious that they exhibit its symptoms.[4] Comment number 13 makes direct reference to envy, but I suspect it is an underlying reality in many other comments also. I commonly find among religious of the pre-Vatican II era a sadness as they reflect on the poverty of their own training compared with that offered contemporary religious in their congregation. It is a despondency that can turn into a destructive envy. Restorationism is evident in comments numbers 8 and 17, unresolved grief in numbers 1, 6, 9, 11, 12. There is a yearning by several for faith sharing in numbers 4, 5, 18 and for a community supportive of the candidates' ministries in numbers 1, 3, 7, 11, 16, 17, 18. I find that candidates in congregations which have very few vocations are often seen by other members as the 'great hopes for the future' and comment number 6 reflects this. This places impossible expectations on candidates, as this comment indicates.

It is against justice to expose candidates still in formation to communities which have cultures described in these comments. The provincial in comment number 1 is ignoring an unjust training situation by glibly replying to the candidate confronted with a community culture of depression: 'Keep trying. It is good for the soul.' It is not good for the soul either of the provincial or the candidate! The congregational leader is refusing to take up her role to organize a formation process suitable for today's apostolic needs. The candidate's patience is fast running out. And rightly so. The following section argues that when a community refuses, or is incapable of, entering into a refounding process for mission, postnovitiate candidates should not be assigned to them. Instead *intentional communities* need to be established in and through which candidates can continue their formation.

Religious community life: qualities needed

Community is possibly the topic most written and talked about by religious since Vatican II. I will confine myself here to only those aspects of community life that relate to the purpose of initial formation and I outline these in a series of four action-oriented axioms. Axiom 1 describes the faith foundation for community life; axiom 2 emphasizes the need for small communities; axiom 3 stresses the importance of clarifying a congregation's founding model of community; axiom 4 asserts that post-novitiate communities must be intentional in character.

Axiom 1: Faith: the foundation of community

The religious community is essentially a commitment in faith. Members having given themselves to a common mission require a high level of faith and human maturity in order to maintain this commitment.

A Vatican document of 1994 on community life, *Fraternal Life in Community*, explains well this axiom and some of its implications and I summarize points that have particular relevance. The document emphasizes throughout that faith ultimately is the only foundation of community:

> a religious community is, above all else, a mystery which must be contemplated . . . in the clear context of faith . . . . In the entire dynamic of community life, Christ, in his paschal mystery, remains the model of how to construct unity. Indeed, he is the source, the model and the measure of the command of mutual life: we must love one another as he loved us . . . . [5]

One fundamental task of initial formation, therefore, is to guide candidates into the mystery of religious community life:

> A fraternal [*sic*] and shared common life has a natural attraction for young people, but, later, perseverance in the real conditions of life can become a heavy burden. Initial formation needs, then, to bring one to an awareness of the sacrifices required for living in community, to accepting them in view of a joyful and truly fraternal [*sic*] relationship and of all the other attitudes characteristic of one who is interiorly free. When we lose ourselves for our brothers and sisters, then we find ourselves . . . . [6]

The document accepts that grace is built on nature: communities of faith cannot develop unless there is appropriate communication and intimacy. The document is quite realistic about the problems evident in so many communities: 'The lack of or weakness in communication usually leads to weakening of fraternity [*sic*]: if we know little or nothing about the lives of our brothers and sisters, they will be strangers to us, and the relationship will become anonymous . . . . Communication [then] takes place . . . around problems and issues of marginal importance but rarely is there any sharing of what is vital and central to the journey of consecration.'[7] Many candidates in the previous comments are complaining precisely about the poverty of communication they are experiencing, for example numbers 1, 4, 7, 9, 11, 12, 15, 16, 18, 19.

The document is pragmatic about inevitable tensions within community life: 'The communitarian ideal must not blind us to the fact that every Christian reality is built on human frailty . . . . The "perfect community" does not exist yet . . . . Communities cannot avoid conflicts . . .'[8] The writers speak of the need to achieve a balance 'between the demands of individuals and those of the community, between personal charisms and the community's apostolate. And this should be far from the disintegrating forces of individualism and the levelling aspects of communitarianism.'[9] This balance is always difficult to achieve in practice, but the document offers some practical advice: the mission of the Church and congregation must be constantly clarified, and people's talents for creativity must be promoted in light of it. For the sake of the evangelical mission of each community, people should struggle to develop a mutual respect for one another that accepts 'the slow journey of weaker members *without* [my italics] stifling the growth of richer personalities'.[10] If candidates for religious life do not have the communication gifts necessary for the mission of the congregation, 'good will not withstanding . . . then no matter how good the gifts may seem to be in themselves, or how desirable they may appear to some members, *they are not for this particular institute*' [my italics].[11]

Axiom 2: Small communities: bonding for apostolic action

In small communities religious seek a faith-centred intimacy, as a reaction to the loneliness and individualism that characterizes large traditional communities, and as a source of energy for mission; pre-Vatican II formation programmes did not train religious to live in small communities.

Several references in the document *Fraternal Life in Community* refer to values and challenges of small communities. Small communities have developed for two reasons: as a move away from corporate apostolates which demand that large numbers of religious live together, and as a desire on the part of religious to promote a closer bonding in faith for the sake of the mission. These communities have 'proved to be more demanding for their members'[12] than many originally expected. Many who have lived in large communities for years find it too difficult to adjust to smaller communities. Large communities made it easy for members to have a life of hidden individualism. In large institutions people could retire to the privacy of their rooms and shut out the concerns of the community without being missed. Little wonder that these same people fear the lessening of privacy and absence of rigid structures that are inevitable in small communities. In small communities there are few structures and, unlike larger communities, meals are at flexible times and are commonly prepared by members themselves.

The previous comments of postnovitiate candidates express desire for smaller communities as ways to cultivate deeper communication. They speak of *intentional communities* and their preference for a more shared faith and prayer life. Pre-Vatican II religious were not trained to share their faith with one another, in fact it was quite deliberately discouraged; one's spiritual journey was a matter of one's private relationship with God, to be shared with a spiritual director, but with no one else. Faith intimacy with one's brothers and sisters in community was thought to lead to particular friendships, something considered very dangerous indeed. The document, while praising the practice of shared faith experience, cautions against imposing it on people who are not trained for it or are unwilling to participate:

> Where it is practised with spontaneity and by common agreement, such sharing nourishes faith and hope as well as mutual respect and trust; it facilitates reconciliation and nourishes fraternal [*sic*] solidarity in prayer. . . . Differences of age, formation and character make it advisable to be prudent in requiring this of an entire community. It is well to recall that the right moment cannot be rushed.[13]

There are, says the document, people who are not at ease in community and who are the cause of disturbance in community life because, among other things, there are 'serious gaps in (their) formation'.[14] The document admits also that there are professed members in congregations who 'are clearly incapable of living community life due to problems of insufficient maturity and psychological weakness, or due to factors which are more pathological'.[15]

From the above review of the document, and in light of the comments by candidates in the postnovitiate stage, it is possible to conclude:

• People trained in the pre-Vatican II formation system are often unable to adapt to the prayer and communication styles and needs of religious educated in more recent years according to the pilgrimage model of Vatican II. However, for the sake of the mission of the congregation, the former must not be allowed to obstruct religious desiring to base their lives on the prayer and communication styles of a pilgrim people.

• Religious in active congregations should expect to live in communities that support them in their ministries to the world.

- If a congregation cannot give reasonable guarantees that appropriate community life can be provided for candidates, then it must cease all recruitment and direct those already accepted to congregations that are able to do so. It is a question of justice to would-be candidates and to the Church itself.

Axiom 3: Models of community need clarifying

Congregations must clarify the model of community that is integral to their founding vision; candidates are to be received only if they are prepared to accept the congregational model of community and to co-ordinate, and if necessary sacrifice, their personal aspirations and actions for the sake of this community model.

It is of paramount importance for congregations to reflect on their founding vision in order to discover precisely the type of community that they should be promoting. If there is vagueness regarding the type of community required by the founding experience, there will be confusion in recruitment guidelines and formation methods; people will be accepted who lack the qualities to adapt to the founding vision of community. In Chapter 1 it was pointed out that most congregations of men and women since the thirteenth and seventeenth centuries, respectively, have ministry at the heart of their founding. They did not originate, says historian John Lozano, 'from a desire to live the Gospel together, nor primarily to foster Christian communion or to learn to serve God better, but in order to render apostolic service. Indeed, often the first element to appear in the genesis of these religious families is their apostolate.'[16]

There are two significantly different models of community among active congregations and they must not be confused. As was explained in Chapter 1, in mendicant orders the primary ministry of members of a community is the community itself; ministry to the world is *indirect* in as much as community members must primarily concentrate on gospel relations among themselves. They hope that the 'one heart and one mind' quality of their lives will positively influence outsiders close by. They evangelize the world in and through the community. I call this model of community *relational*. In the apostolic model of St Ignatius Loyola, adopted by most active congregations in the last two centuries, the *primary* ministry of congregational members is their ministry to the world. The principal role of the community is to support the legitimately approved ministries of its members; community structures are far more flexible in light of this purpose than would be accepted in mendicant communities. This type of community I term the *mission* model.[17]

Case study: Confusion causes unnecessary division

The traditions of a congregation of women gave contradictory messages to its members: one tradition stressed monastic origins while another emphasized the apostolic activities of the foundress. Consequently, people had been recruited expecting monastic *or* apostolic community life and when they did not receive what they wanted, there was considerable pain and anger at all levels of the congregation, for example, people with apostolic orientations would criticize those with monastic tendencies for being insufficiently concerned about the active ministry. At successive general chapters there were heated arguments between the proponents of the two traditions, but no chapter resolved the in-built tension. Finally, groups within several provinces believing that the dominant emphasis was monastic split away from the congregation to establish their own communities.

After the formal separation took place amid considerable bitterness, the general administration belatedly sponsored an in-depth historical study of the congregation's founding experience. The research concluded that the foundress intended from the beginning to establish an apostolic congregation, but she had been forced by Rome in the eighteenth century to adopt monastic community styles. If this research had been undertaken just after Vatican II, the energy that went into internal congregational feuding could have been directed outwards to apostolic activities. I find the confusion depicted in this case study is quite common, but most communities never reach the stage of formal congregational schisms. The unresolved tension remains submerged, waiting to surface from time to time in angry recriminations from both sides.

It is possible that research cannot solve the problem of origins, in which case I believe the confusion must be publicly acknowledged and provision made for recruits to opt for either monastic or active life. People should not be forced into one or the other against their will. Today there are members of active congregations, however, who believe that they are being called to express the *apostolic* quality of their lives through contemplative prayer, even in a quasi-monastic atmosphere, as a full-time ministry. They adopt this apostolate not because their congregations are monastic in origin, but on the basis of the apostolic needs of the particular cultures in which they happen to be living.

Since ministry is the purpose of active congregations, the structures of community life must be flexible enough to support it. This is an advantage of a small community where it is possible to maintain a higher degree of flexibility than in a larger one. However, flexibility does not mean that there are no structures at all. On the contrary, to avoid excessive individualism emerging, there must be, for example, times in which the community prays, discusses, plans apostolic activities and celebrates, but

146

the community must itself decide these issues in view of its mission and regularly evaluate members' responses. The comments of postnovitiate candidates, as recorded in numbers 15, 16 and 17, reflect justified frustration; they describe communities that are either too individualistic or too rigidly structured. On the other hand, comments numbers 12 and 14 describe therapeutic or me-istic communities, in which people are so turned inwards on themselves and their personal need for affirmation that the postnovitiate candidates are in danger of being apostolically de-energized. Intentional communities, which we now describe, aim to avoid these aberrant expressions of religious community.

Refounding through intentional postnovitiate communities

Axiom 4: The need for intentional communities

Postnovitiate candidates of active congregations require intentional communities, that is, communities whose purpose is to support their members in their apostolic action; people with refounding skills are required to establish these communities and the biblically-based axiom 'the new belongs elsewhere' will normally need to be invoked.

No existing definition of the intentional community adequately covers its nature. Therefore it is preferable to provide readers with several descriptive analyses, some of which outline what intentionality is not, followed by a working definition.

Intentional community: spirituality
The following describes three models of contemporary religious communities:[18] (1) a group of people who sacrifice their personal aspirations and actions for the goals and actions of the congregation; (2) a group of people who co-ordinate their personal aspirations and activities with the goals and activities of the congregation; (3) a group who co-ordinate and if necessary, sacrifice their personal aspirations and actions for the common good of the congregation. The first statement depicts a community with a culture of dependency characteristic of many communities in the pre-Vatican II Church. In this culture individuals surrender their wills to superiors, which is simply blind obedience; whatever the superior decides is God's will, even though it is quite obviously not so. This is not a community based on gospel values because no one has the right to hand over their will to others in this manner or to expect anyone else to do so. The second statement portrays the me-istic or therapeutic religious life culture already described in Chapter 3. Individuals are expected only to

co-ordinate their aspirations and actions with those of the congregation. It destroys group cohesiveness. The moment the congregation places demands on its personnel for the common good individuals refuse to co-operate or withdraw from the community.

The third statement goes to the heart of an intentional community. Individuals do not surrender their wills either to the group or to a leader, rather they freely decide to commit themselves to the missionary ideals of the group and its strategies for collaborative action. Their model is Jesus Christ and his commitment to discover and obey the mission given him by his Father.

Intentional community: sociology

Sociologist Patricia Wittberg defines an *intentional community* as 'a group of persons living together on a more or less permanent basis, who voluntarily surrender control over some choices which are normally considered private for the sake of establishing a whole new way of life . . . . (The) group's transcendent mission or goal takes precedence over the needs of the individual members.'[19] She concludes that an intentional community 'needs to create and maintain a strong sense of corporate commitment that will draw (its members) together'.[20] In intentional communities members agree on the mission and commit themselves to whatever is necessary to achieve it.

Intentional community: psychology

Using the helpful insights of Lucy Malarkey and Dorothy Marron,[21] we can distinguish three models of communities: two dysfunctional communities at the polar extremes of a continuum, namely the 'enmeshed' and the 'disengaged', and at the centre the 'functional' or 'integrated' type. This last, with similarities to an intentional community, is the most supportive of personal and group growth in maturity for mission. Existing communities can be graded according to where they fit on the continuum; the most integrated will be close to the centre.

The enmeshed community
Enmeshed communities, with cultures similar to the *strong group/strong grid* model outlined in Chapter 2, have characteristics such as:

— members look almost exclusively to one another for emotional, spiritual, and intellectual security;

— the group's regulations extend to members' inner lives;

— over-dependence on the leader prevents individuation and differentiation;

— conflictual situations are avoided;

— rules governing behaviour and communication are rigid and inflexible; peer group pressures on individuals to conform are strong;

- there is little room for personal space, privacy, contemplation;

- the community consumes the energy of members, so that little or nothing is left for outsiders or interests beyond the community.

The disengaged community

The cultural characteristics of a *disengaged* community are similar to those found in me-istic and *strong grid/weak group* cultures:

- individual rights take precedence at all times over the common good; there is no accountability by members to the group nor is it expected;

- there is no sense of belonging to a community; the community exists to pay the bills, provide security in sickness;

- there is indifference to one another on the part of members;

- community life has no order or regularity;

- members are highly secretive;

- community prayer life barely, if at all, exists; where it does it is highly formal or, if spontaneous, it is strongly centred on the needs of individuals.

In brief, in this model community is primarily defined physically, in terms of where people happen to reside. Superiors are equivalent to house managers, making sure the bills are paid and people are able to maintain their individualism without interference from others.

The functional or intentional community

The *functional* type includes the intentional community. It has a culture that is similar to the *weak group/weak grid* type, as described in Chapter 3. In contrast to the enmeshed and disengaged types it has the following attributes:

- members work together to clarify the vision and mission of the community which are the primary source of bonding and energy for the group; formal community structures are few and are regularly evaluated by the community in light of its vision and mission;

- members are sensitive to one another's need for privacy and for common space; people feel comfortable about being together as a group and being apart;

- the community meets some of the social, emotional and intellectual needs of its members; supportive friendships within and outside the group are encouraged;

- members encourage one another to reflect on their apostolic experiences;

149

- because of the level of trust within the community, members feel at ease to challenge one another's behaviour in light of a commonly accepted vision and goals;

- there is space for both autonomy and mutuality; dialogue and open interaction are encouraged before any significant decisions are made about community affairs;

- members recognize that they cannot minister to others outside, unless they live in a community based on faith-filled interdependence and mutuality;

- the prayer rhythm of the community is a balance between the needs of the community and those of its members; members recognize that neither interdependence nor mutuality are possible unless they personally pray, are prepared to pray together and share their faith experiences.

Jean Vanier describes the delicate balance that exists in functional communities between the need for individual autonomy and group cohesion:

> A community is only a community when the majority of its members is making the transition from 'the community for myself' to 'myself for the community'. . . . This is a movement from egoism to love, from death to resurrection . . . . It means wanting others to fulfill themselves, according to God's plan . . . . A community has to be apart from society and open to it at the same time. To the extent that its values are different from those of society, it must necessarily be apart from it. If it is too open, it will never keep and deepen its own values; it will have no identity or life of its own. But if it is too enclosed, it will not grow and it will not see the true values which exist in society.[22]

Functional or intentional communities are impossible if members do not have the capacity for a high degree of human and spiritual maturity.

Intentional community: theology

Theologian Bernard Lonergan writes that community is 'an achievement of meaning' and that there are four levels of meaning or community: there is a *potential* meaning or community when people have a common field of experience; *formal* community occurs when there is a common under-standing about that experience; an *actual* community exists when people agree what should be done about this experience; a *willed* community happens when there is effective commitment by people to act on the basis of their common understanding of an experience. Individuals can work in the same apostolate and have very similar experiences, but community remains merely potential. The same individuals can come together and develop a common understanding of the nature of the challenges and problems, even agreeing about what should be done. Still, according to

Lonergan, community has yet to be realized in practice. Community is only alive when members are actually committing themselves to an agreed action. Only then does an intentional community exist.[23]

Theologians Bernard Lee and Michael Cowan write that 'An intentional Christian community is a relatively small group of persons committed to ongoing conversation and shared action along four distinguishable but interrelated dimensions'.[24] The four dimensions are: people maintain a high degree of mutuality in their relationships; they critique the world in which they live from the standpoint of gospel values; they cultivate and sustain 'lively connections with other persons, communities and movements of similar purpose', and 'They attend faithfully to the Christian character of their community's life'.[25] For them the word 'intentional' means 'deliberate' or 'consciously chosen'.[26]

Definition

In light of these analyses I suggest the following working definition of an intentional religious community: *An intentional community is a group of religious living together who feel the need to be supported in their ministries and willingly commit themselves to develop a gospel-centred intimacy to be expressed in shared faith, ongoing conversation and shared action.*

Case study: An intentional community is established

Three sisters of an apostolic congregation had been appointed to separate apostolates of a particularly demanding nature. Recognizing that they could not continue in their apostolates without a supportive community life, they obtained permission to establish an intentional community. They committed themselves to a weekly shared prayer experience, twice-weekly eucharistic celebrations, and at least four meals together weekly. In addition, they agreed to a weekly 'accountability session', that is, each member would share with the community experiences in their apostolate during the previous week. They recognized that these simple structures were essential for the community to fulfil its mission and at the same time realistic given the different time schedules of the members. At the end of one year members agreed that the informal and formal discussions on their apostolates were energizing; since their faith sharing centred on problems being experienced in their individual ministries, they no longer felt isolated in their work; they could never return to their previous impersonal and apostolically unfocused communities.

However, the establishment of the intentional community evoked considerable criticism from within the province. The members were called elitist, judgemental of other communities and unwilling to help the 'walking wounded' (dysfunctional members in the province). They replied: 'We do not see ourselves as a spiritual elite. On the contrary we come together because we have no energy for the mission unless we can share our faith and our ministerial burdens with others. If we kept to our old way of living we would be among the "walking wounded" and of benefit

151

apostolically to no one.' The congregational leader supported them and frequently explained to the province the purpose of intentional communities, inviting others to do the same.[27]

The case study is self-explanatory. The congregational leader acted according to her rightful role, because the community was a provincially approved project and the official leader had to take full responsibility for its establishment and evaluations.

An intentional community is not something that is achieved once and maintained as such without further effort. On the contrary, community is always in a state of becoming. If the spiritual foundation is weak through lack of personal and shared prayer, openness and trust, then the will to keep going in the face of tensions cannot be sustained. Paul VI touches the basic issue: 'God's call in fact orients you, in the most direct and effective manner, towards the eternal kingdom. Through the spiritual tensions which are inevitable in every truly religious life, you give splendid and striking testimony that the world cannot be transfigured and offered to God without the spirit of the beatitudes.'[28]

Intentional communities and refounding

Historically the refounding of a congregation involves the return by a group of people to its founding experience. At the time of a congregation's founding, people developed a small intentional community, its members were alive with a gospel vision and passionately committed to give it flesh. Refounding people recognize that their congregation has lost its original evangelical enthusiasm. They yearn to recapture the founding experience, so they invite others to join them in small faith communities. As Raymond Hostie concludes in his study of the origins and decline of religious congregations, this is the way refounding occurs: 'All abiding reforms have their origins in a rather small group which begins the founding again.'[29] History shows that refounding movements normally meet considerable resistance. Refounders try to escape the intense pressures of the resistance, either by withdrawing from the congregation to found a new branch, or by remaining in it protected by structures from undue interference from the obstructive forces.[30]

We now apply this experience to the refounding of the postnovitiate stage of formation. The argument for the refounding of the postnovitiate stage through the establishment of intentional communities is based on the following assumptions:

• The pre-Vatican II theology of religious life is so radically different from that of the Council that it is not possible merely to *renew* old structures

152

of formation. Formation processes must reflect this radical theological shift.

- The only way for this refounding to occur is for people to relive the intentional style of community life of the founding experience.

- The personal and cultural resistance to refounding in existing congregational communities is so deep and widespread, as is evident in the comments of postnovitiate candidates at the beginning of this chapter, that refounding cannot take place. People committed to refounding must spend so much energy on defending what they are trying to do that they have none left for the actual mission of refounding. The pastoral directive 'the new belongs elsewhere' must be invoked as explained in Chapter 4. The *elsewhere* here means that postnovitiate candidates need to develop communities *separate* from the mainstream of the congregation. People have a right to intentional community life for the sake of the mission and they must be given the structural space to exercise it.

The recently professed have been exposed to, and have owned in the intentional communities of their novitiates, the founding experience of the congregation. When postnovitiate candidates cannot find this type of community among finally professed members, the mission of the congregation demands that the newly professed form their own intentional community. Establishment and maintenance of these intentional communities will depend on the collaborative action of authority position and refounding persons. The authority position person, that is the provincial, will choose suitable formation staff and protect them from undue outside interference from other members of the province having no authority or expertise in the formation apostolate. This staff must be of refounding calibre, because they must recreate the founding experience of the congregation, adapted to contemporary theological and cultural conditions. Several provinces may need to develop combined postnovitiate intentional communities, because the numbers of trained formation staff and candidates will usually be too few in any one province today (particularly in the First World). It is possible for non-religious to be part of the postnovitiate stage, provided they are willing to participate in an intentional community.

Case study: Geographical movement required

A province of a clerical apostolic congregation in North America had run its own seminary on the same site for over a hundred years. It was situated according to pre-Vatican II values, remote from any significant centre of population, and its internal architecture, for example the chapel, reflected a monastic style of formation. The lecturing staff members were also the formators though they had no special training for this role. In the 1970s, as the numbers of candidates declined significantly, at times to less than 20, efforts were made to redesign the buildings to facilitate formation based on the values of Vatican II. Despite the changes, the seminary was still isolated, and many traditions of a pre-Vatican II formation system remained securely in place. Dissatisfaction intensified among the students. They complained that, though they were reading about the need to be open to the world and to develop faith communities, the formation programme contradicted the principles they studied. The staff, they claimed, were as remote as ever, and the seminary buildings were so institutional in design that they intimidated outsiders daring to venture up the long entrance drive.

The provincial requested that a formation consultant investigate the situation. The consultant made two significant suggestions: *first*, the seminary should move into an inner city suburb so that students could be in touch with people's problems and the world of change; *second*, the roles of seminary lecturing and formation should be split, with the students living with formators in a separate house from the lecturing staff. The consultant's reasons for these radical suggestions were based on the pastoral directive 'the new belongs elsewhere':

> Not only are the buildings remote from the reality students should be involved in, but the entire architectural complex exudes a culture that is now irrelevant; this culture of a past age is so powerful that attempts to change it are bound to fail. The formation house needs to move well away from the site and closer to a centre of population. In addition, the roles of lecturing and formation must be divided. The latter is a specialized role and it cannot be assumed that academic lecturers have the necessary qualifications. If they have been trained for formation, however, they cannot remain full-time seminary lecturers. The task of formators is demanding of time and energy. Finally, I advise as a priority that the students reside in a house set aside specifically for formation under the direction of qualified staff. The seminary lecturers need to live in a separate house so that the formation personnel can concentrate all their efforts on devising and supervising, without outside interference from members of the same congregation untrained in formation, a new culture of postnovitiate training. In today's religious congregations *everyone* claims to be an instant authority on formation. Formation staffs must be protected from such people no matter how qualified they are in their own specialized field.

Case study: A refounding attempt fails

The administration of a province of a religious clerical congregation in the Third World in the 1970s became concerned about the quality of the formation of its locally-born religious. The majority of finally professed members in the province did not believe in intentional communities nor had the ability to live in them, yet they demanded that the newly professed members live in their houses during their postnovitiate stage (and after ordination). The provincial was unsure what to do, so he asked a consultant to advise him. In summary, the consultant found that the majority of the ordained religious:

— considered priesthood more important than their commitment to religious life;

— preferred to live and work alone;

— had lost their apostolic drive;

— were largely uninterested in shared prayer.

She concluded that the vast majority of finally professed religious in the province had adopted the disengaged model of community previously described, with no desire to change to the functional or intentional type. That is, despite agreeing at province-wide assemblies to mission statements and committing themselves to develop intentional apostolic communities, they did not intend to implement them. In fact, they would oppose people who tried to do so. She advised the provincial administration 'that it would be disastrous to continue the practice of sending newly professed members to live in existing houses of the congregation for postnovitiate training'.

Acting on this advice, the provincial proposed to the provincial chapter that postnovitiate intentional communities be formed, and that, following final profession/ordination, the young religious be allowed to form their own apostolic intentional communities. These two recommendations were overwhelmingly rejected by the chapter, with people making comments like the following:

'It is insulting to us that we are not thought worthy to receive the newly professed into our communities.'

'We are people of zeal and experience, in touch with the real world, so we have the skills to train these young men for the work of evangelization.'

'Any one of us can be formators. No special skills are necessary.'

However, in the face of sustained opposition the provincial decided to act on his own authority without the chapter's support. The central congregational leadership supported him. The postnovitiate intentional communities flourished, along with those established for the finally professed and ordained locally-born religious.

When the provincial's term of office ended, the new provincial reversed his predecessor's decisions, supported by a newly elected general government of the congregation. Skilled formation staff were no longer appointed to existing postnovitiate communities. Postnovitiate candidates were sent for ministry to houses where the apostolic staffs took little or no interest in them. A representative of the new provincial administration summarized a common reaction to the change in formation policy:

'We are tough evangelizers because we have learnt the hard way. We had to survive on our own. These locals do not need to be treated in special ways. They must experience the way we were trained. Let them become like us.'

However, the consultant was proved correct. Many well-qualified candidates left the congregation, and continue to do so, both before and after ordination. Of those who have remained many have succumbed to the values of the disengaged communities in which they are living.

This case study illustrates several key arguments of this book. The provincial accepted the consultant's advice, though he was at first tempted to reject it in view of the widespread opposition to her proposals. He recognized the importance of his authority and role. *Role* is expected behaviour associated with a social position or office; *authority* is the legitimacy that one has to take up that role and act. The provincial acted with the authority given him by his congregational constitutions after the chapter refused the consultant's advice. Committed to refounding, he went to the heart of the problem. Having concluded that radical conversion was impossible for most in the province and that the rights of candidates to the best formation took precedence over the feelings of people, he provided a protected space in which intentional communities could develop. The congregational general leader, as the supervisor of formation, supported the provincial, but his successor, like the second provincial, failed miserably when confronted by criticism from members of the province.

Case study: A chapter gives primacy to formation planning

An international congregation of sisters decided at their general chapter ten years ago to close their existing eight formation houses. In their place they planned to establish four new centres in Europe, North America, South East Asia and Africa. They did this for two reasons: primarily to improve their formation services, and secondarily because the numbers of candidates were dramatically reduced in Europe and North America. The chapter agreed that it was important to stress the internationality of the congregation as a service to the local churches. Candidates were expected to spend two years of their formation in a part of the world significantly different from their country of origin. It was argued by some 'that candidates from the Third World would never be able to readjust to the poorer conditions of their countries'. Others said that candidates 'from the First World would never survive the rigours of parts of the Third World'. The chapter admitted that these reactions could happen. If they did, formation staffs could challenge candidates about their suitability to be members of the congregation. It is better, the chapter said, that these problems emerge *before* final profession than afterwards. It was decided not to use any existing formation centre because the chapter considered 'the histories of these places would hinder innovative formation planning'. The chapter authorized the general administration to liaise with provincials in order to choose suitable personnel to be trained for the formation apostolate. The final chapter recommendation was: 'that in the new formation centres candidates must be formed within intentional communities; if numbers in a formation house are too large, then candidates will form several intentional communities and the house will be redesigned accordingly'.

One does not expect such bold creative thinking from a general chapter as the emphasis on planning for internationality and intentional communities, the recognition that existing formation buildings and cultures might interfere with the new vision of formation, and the need to train formation staff. Most decisions have been implemented. Only one formation centre remains to be established.

Evaluating personal growth

Religious require a method of evaluating their growth adapted to the purpose of the postnovitiate stage of their journey. The word *evaluation* has negative connotations for many candidates in religious life. In training for ministry they are constantly being evaluated through such means as examinations, essays, assessments of preaching abilities.[31] The distaste for evaluation is also a consequence of the Church's culture, since there is no tradition of ongoing professional assessment of its ministers. Candidates wonder why they should be singled out for frequent evaluation when their seniors are exempt. Finally, evaluations are sometimes conducted by people who fail to explain to candidates the reason for assessments and the criteria on which they are based.

Candidates need to know the purpose of their evaluations, the criteria on the basis of which the assessments are to be made, and that they are to be conducted in a personal and helpful way. If these three conditions are met, then it is likely that candidates after final profession and ordination will continue to seek periodic assessments of their religious and ministerial duties. When the apostles, and later the disciples, returned from their preaching experiences Jesus pointedly called them to give an account of their work (see Luke 9:10; 10:17). He would have evaluated their ministerial experience with questions like: What did you say about the kingdom? Did the people listen to your words about the kingdom? If not, why not? Did you prepare adequately? Did your preaching styles interfere with the message? Did you put your trust too much in your own skills rather than in the power of God to work through you? Did you work together as a team? What do you feel you must do now to improve your preaching skills for the sake of the kingdom? The evaluation would always have been in terms of the values of the kingdom. So also with postnovitiate candidates. They must be helped to realize that God is calling them to preach the kingdom by example and word, and the authentic servant will be eager to know if he/she is doing this in ways that further the mission of Christ. Evaluations will also help candidates to discover whether or not God is calling them to religious life or to another vocation.

Although the formation staff should be primarily responsible for formulating the criteria of the evaluation, the candidates themselves should be invited to comment. The evaluation is to be undertaken in a spirit of dialogue, that is, assessment is a two-way process. Both staff and candidates are out to learn what God is asking of them. It will be an impersonal and patronizing experience if the staff themselves are unwilling to listen to what the Spirit is saying to them about the effectiveness of their own formation ministry. Though ultimately the formators have the task of judging the candidates, the candidates can normally be expected in the dialogue process to make the right choices about their behaviour. Formators on some occasions will have to inform candidates directly that their vocation is not in religious life. This is to be done clearly and firmly: 'proclaim the message and, welcome or unwelcome, insist on it . . . but do all with patience and with care to instruct' (2 Tim 4:2). If doubts still remain about a candidate's suitability for religious life by the end of three years, I believe he/she should be advised to withdraw, unless there is *well-founded* hope that change is possible within a reasonable time. It is gravely unjust to the candidate and the Church to profess any candidate when there are prolonged doubts about his/her suitability.

The criteria for the evaluation of candidates at postnovitiate stage, as for the novitiate assessments, should be based on the purpose of religious life and that of the congregation. We need religious who are enthusiastic and profoundly dedicated to God's work in the Church and society, intelligent, well-formed, mature, secure, stable, well-integrated personalities, able to remain idealistic in the midst of conflict, and capable of significant leadership in times of rapid and chaotic change. Without these qualities there is little hope that religious can fulfill their prophetic role in the Church and society.[32] Joel Giallanza offers a helpful set of criteria for the assessement of candidates at the postnovitiate stage.[33] Occasionally I have added to his criteria or modified some in line with the material of this book:

A. Spiritual life
1. Willingly accepts opportunities for leadership in organizing community prayer.
2. Remains faithful to a discipline of personal prayer, shared prayer, regular visits to a spiritual director and an annual retreat.

B. Personal life
1. Continues to deepen and assimilate the values of the founding experience of the congregation, shown in his/her behaviour.
2. Continues to be readily approachable in attitude and disposition to others whose views and personalities differ.
3. Clearly, honestly and respectfully expresses his/her views at community meetings, with an openness to learn from others.
4. Cultivates leisure activities and interests other than those relating to ministry or studies.
5. Cultivates a healthy lifestyle through a balance of diet and physical exercise.

6. Continues to develop the ability to adjust positively to sudden changes beyond his/her control in community and apostolic planning.

7. Continues to develop an ability to relate with appropriate intimacy to members of the opposite sex.

8. Shows that he/she is able to learn from periods of cultural dislocation, e.g. in times of exposure to significantly different cultural experiences.

C. Community life

1. Participates faithfully and actively in the life of the community (prayer, meals, meetings, leisure, household tasks).

2. Shares generously and prudently personal gifts and skills within and for the community and takes initiative in supporting the common good.

3. Relates to others with courtesy and respect.

4. Accepts accountability for decisions and behaviours.

D. Apostolic/academic life

1. Fulfils professional obligations.

2. Co-operates and co-ordinates with co-workers and supervisor(s).

3. Continues to develop initiative academically and apostolically.

4. Willingly undergoes a periodic evaluation of effectiveness in ministry by appropriate supervisor(s).

5. Continues to develop professional skills.

6. Continues to develop an informed interest in national and international affairs, particularly in matters relating to social justice.

7. Proves that he/she is developing empathy with minority and marginalized peoples; when a choice of apostolic projects is available he/she more readily opts to work with poorer groups.

8. Fosters multicultural attitudes and actions personally and in groups.

9. Shows that he/she is able to integrate relevant findings of the social sciences into ministerial activities.

Summary

Formation as pilgrims in mission begins first by listening and receiving. As the source of mission lies within the ineffable mystery of the Trinity itself, it is in the presence of this mystery that we listen. We are silent. We contemplate. In contemplation we feel the power of love that is at the heart of this mystery. And it is out of love for us that the Father sends forth the Son to be for us Life itself. We, charged with the same mission as the Son, receive the courage to be pilgrims in mission through the power of the Holy Spirit, but we want to join with others who are inspired with the same mission. This is how religious community life was founded. Founders were seized by this vision of Trinitarian oneness and sought to make it a visible reality through their lives, that is, they established an intentional community. The process of refounding seeks to recapture this original founding experience of community and adapt it to contemporary life. The newly professed in the postnovitiate stage are to be involved in this refounding and thus in intentional community life.

Notes

1. Document *Instrumentum Laboris* for the Synod of Bishops, *The Consecrated Life and Its Role in the Church and in the World* (Vatican: Vatican Press, 1994), para. 57.
2. M. Azevedo, *The Consecrated Life: Crossroads and Directions* (Maryknoll, NY: Orbis Books, 1995), p. 73.
3. J. Giallanza, 'Postnovitiate religious formation', *Human Development*, vol. 10, no. 1 (1989), p. 24.
4. See G. A. Arbuckle, 'Obstacles to pastoral creativity', *Human Development*, vol. 16, no. 1 (1995), pp. 15–20, and *Refounding the Church: Dissent for Leadership* (London: Geoffrey Chapman, 1993), pp. 139–40.
5. Congregation for Institutes of Consecrated Life, *Fraternal Life in Community* (Vatican: Vatican Press, 1994), paras 12, 21.
6. Ibid., para. 24.
7. Ibid., para. 32.
8. Ibid., para. 26.
9. Ibid., para. 39.
10. Ibid., para. 40.
11. Ibid.
12. Ibid., para. 64.
13. Ibid., para. 16.
14. Ibid., para. 38.
15. Ibid.
16. J. Lozano, *Discipleship: Towards an Understanding of Religious Life* (Chicago: Claret Center, 1980), p. 207.
17. This point is more fully explained in my book *Refounding the Church*, op. cit., pp. 158–79.
18. See G. A. Arbuckle, *Out of Chaos: Refounding Religious Congregations* (New York: Paulist Press, 1988), pp. 114–15.
19. P. Wittberg, *Creating a Future for Religious Life: A Sociological Perspective* (New York: Paulist Press, 1991), p. 11.
20. Ibid., p. 14.
21. See L. Malarkey and D. J. Marron, 'Evaluating community interaction', *Human Development*, vol. 3, no. 3 (1982), pp. 117–24. The authors adapt the insights of S. Minuchin to religious communities.
22. J. Vanier, *Community and Growth* (Sydney: Society of St Paul, 1976), pp. 22, 85.
23. See B. Lonergan, cited in *Theology Digest*, vol. 14, no. 2 (1966), p. 123.
24. B. J. Lee and M. A. Cowan, *Dangerous Memories: House Churches and Our American Story* (Kansas City: Sheed and Ward, 1986), p. 91.
25. Ibid., p. 92.
26. Ibid., p. 91.
27. For a spirituality for small faith groups see J. English, *Spiritual Intimacy and Community: An Ignatian View of the Small Faith Community* (London: Darton, Longman and Todd, 1992).

28. Paul VI, *Apostolic Exhortation on Renewal of Religious Life* (Vatican: Vatican Press, 1971), para. 50.

29. R. Hostie, *Vie et mort des ordres religieux* (Paris: Desclée de Brouwer, 1972), p. 316.

30. See Arbuckle, *Out of Chaos*, op. cit., pp. 68–9, 110–11; Wittberg, op. cit., pp. 31–5.

31. See R. Coll, *Supervision of Ministry Students* (Collegeville, MN: The Liturgical Press, 1992), pp. 86–7.

32. See W. J. Coville *et al.* (eds), *Assessment of Candidates for the Religious Life* (Washington, DC: CARA, 1968), p. 5.

33. Giallanza, op. cit., pp. 25–6.

7 Forming for multicultural/ international religious communities

[The religious community] is an evangelizer, but she begins by being evangelized herself.

(Paul VI)[1]

Internationality does not consist primarily in putting people together from different cultures, but in allowing these people to be themselves, to be free to share their cultural heritage . . . and to make the varied cultures of community members the focal points of formation.

(A. Bellagamba)[2]

This chapter explains:

- that the mission of the Church calls religious to establish multicultural/ international communities;

- the meaning of multiculturalism/internationality;

- that religious must be formed in this apostolate;

- through several evaluative case studies the meaning of multicultural/ international communities;

- requirements for the merging of formation communities.

The postmodern world is tragically divided by ideological conflicts, pathological forms of nationalism, racial violence, ethnic cleansing (that is, the creation of homogeneous populations by means of mass exile, even mass murder) and intercultural tensions. It almost destroyed itself through interracial conflict during this century. We who gasped at Hitler's genocidal policies live in a world where ecocide, that is, the destruction of virtually all living species on the earth, is a real possibility because people of different cultures rarely live side by side with respect and justice.[3] It is a universe 'groaning in travail' (Rom 8:22).

The mission of the Church is to foster, humanly, culturally, ecologically, the reconciliation of all things in the universe to Christ (Col 1:20). In

162

as much as prophetic witness is the heart of religious life, the Church rightly expects religious communities to be models of intercultural (and ecological) reconciliation.

If we judge from the constitutions and mission statements of many congregations, there is a growing theoretical awareness of this need. Thus, there are expressions such as: 'We are committed to living inter-nationality in a divided world'; 'Let us inculturate the gospel in our own communities first by being authentically multiculturalist'; 'We are called to respect the rights of people to their culture; this applies also to people of different cultures within our congregation. We commit ourselves to train our candidates in multicultural communities'; 'We commit ourselves to foster formation communities in which representatives of several ethnic groups live together in a spirit of dialogue, justice, and charity'. But are communities in fact living according to these statements, or are the words just rhetoric and escapes into fantasy?

The sociological study *The Future of Religious Orders Study in the United States* contains disturbing conclusions about the gap between the theory and reality. For example, 96 per cent of American religious are white in a country of immense ethnic diversity; minority groups are poorly repres-ented; 'unconscious racism makes penetration of minority populations into rather homogeneous orders very difficult'. The report shows that older religious in particular, while believing they are accepting of minority members, in practice are unable to adapt readily to the cultural diversity this demands.[4] My experience is that religious of dominant cultures usually do not lack good will towards minority groups in their midst, but, while using the language of multiculturalism and internationality, they imperfectly understand what these words mean and what attitudinal and behavioural changes they must make in consequence. Not uncommonly they are unconscious racists, freely using anti-minority stereotypes wide-spread in their own culture without realizing their racist meanings.

There can be no authentic contemporary formation programme if the challenges of multiculturalism and internationality are not squarely confronted. This means not just renewing past efforts, for they have so often failed, but refounding the formation process in religious congregations (which involves radical restructuring and attitudinal change) so that the two interrelated issues of multiculturalism and internationality are integral to planning and action.

Defining terms: multiculturalism/internationality

Multiculturalism is often an emotive word, 'a buzzword with almost as many meanings as there are mouths to utter it'.[5] For many conservatives in society and restorationists in the Church, the term has come to signify a very disruptive, unsettling and dangerous force. For them diversity of cultures is something to be at best tolerated. Peace and order, they claim, have existed in the past (and will continue to exist) only when a dominant group has insisted on conformity to a monocultural ethos. Extreme liberals also dislike the term. They claim it means either a bland 'melting-pot' attitude that would remove all differences, or a situation in which cultural diversity is so emphasized that any unity between cultures does not or cannot exist.[6] Theologically, however, multiculturalism is a process of inculturation whereby cultures are so transformed and remade into a 'new creation' that they interact with one another in justice and charity in the service of personal and community growth.[7]

Bhikhu Parekh provides a helpful initial working definition that avoids the extremes of conservative and liberal theorists while respecting the theological approach:

> Multiculturalism doesn't simply mean numerical plurality of different cultures, but rather a community which is creating, guaranteeing, encouraging spaces within which different communities are able to grow at their own pace. At the same time it means creating a public space in which these communities are able to interact, enrich the existing culture and create a new consensual culture in which they recognize reflections of their own identity.[8]

The definition rejects two popular definitions, namely *demographic* and *holistic* multiculturalism. The former connotes that a particular society merely contains different cultural groups; the second means that a society values cultural diversity, but gives higher priority to group-wide cohesion. The definition supports *political* multiculturalism. This is a social philosophy which acknowledges the legitimate concerns of ethnic groups within a society or an organization, and the need for these interests to be expressed in adequate politico-economic structures and processes. Political multiculturalists seek to establish structures that permit minority peoples *by right* to be fully involved in decision-making in matters that affect their lives. They foster a balance between the demands of overall group cohesion and inner cultural diversity. Political multiculturalism historically is a reaction against policies of cultural oppression. Phrases or terms such as 'the melting pot approach to immigrants', 'cultural pluralism' and 'integration' are often synonymous with covert or overt programmes to destroy minority cultures by forcing them to be assimilated into the dominant culture.[9] Critical decisions are made about minority peoples and their future without their participation.

Multiculturalism, in these three senses, normally applies to situations within the *same* country. *Internationality* is multiculturalism in any of these interpretations as applied to relationships between cultures of *separate* countries. For the remainder of this book I will be using the third meaning, namely *political* multiculturalism or internationality.

Political multiculturalism/internationality: conditions required

The conditions for political multiculturalism/internationality to develop in the Church and religious congregations are outlined in the following sections.

Commitment to a theology of multiculturalism/internationality
Vatican II reaffirms the Church's commitment to support the rights of people to their own culture. (In today's restorationist atmosphere, however, the Council's emphasis on this point, and the need to foster cultural diversity at the level of the local church, are downplayed in favour of a return to the Eurocentric or monocultural Catholicism of the centuries before Vatican II.[10])

Informed understanding of culture
The way culture is conceptualized has significant bearing on the theory and practice of multiculturalism. As was explained in Chapter 2, an early definition of culture focused on observable phenomena (such as spoken/written languages, foods, rules of rituals) rather than on how people feel about what they do. Research has shown the inadequacy of this definition on the grounds that it assumed that formal language was the main channel of communication. Between 80 and 90 per cent of information is communicated by other means, for example, nonverbal processes comprise at least gestures, facial expressions, eye contact and gaze, posture and movement, touching, dress, objects and artefacts, silence, space, time. The nonverbal processes form 'silent languages' which are powerful means of communication.[11] The early definition exaggerates ethnic groups' historical lifestyles and customs, and downplays their adaptation to the world in which they now live. On the other hand, culture defined as *a process* goes beneath the surface of what is seen, to the felt meanings people give to what they do. This definition highlights the developmental and ever-evolving survival role of a culture for people in a world of change, prejudice and discrimination.

Education in multiculturalism/internationality
The major conclusions of the Swann Report on Multicultural Education in Britain apply, not just to secular school systems, but to the Church and religious congregations:

> While we recognize that society and its institutions seldom change rapidly, nevertheless we cannot emphasise too strongly the urgency of the need for change where attitudes to the ethnic minorities are concerned. . . . The fundamental change that is necessary is the recognition that the problem facing the education system is not how to educate children of ethnic minorities, but how to educate *all* children . . . .
>
> Multicultural understanding has also to permeate all aspects of a

school's work. It is not a separate topic that can be welded on to existing practices. Only in this way can schools begin to offer anything approaching the *equality of opportunity* for all pupils which it must be the aspiration of the education system to provide.[12]

Note the emphasis: multiculturalism/internationality is to permeate *all* aspects of the educational process. It is not something to be added on to their education only if students happen to be interested in the topic.

Two levels of education are required: general and particular. *General* education for multiculturalism/internationality involves training students to become sensitive to such issues as the power and complexity of culture, and the identification of personal and cultural (including gender) prejudices/discriminations.[13]

Particular education for multiculturalism/internationality focuses on training people for living in specific multicultural/international groups, such as is proposed for religious formation communities. Training will aim to foster in religious three levels of competency: cognitive, affective and operational.[14] *Cognitive* competency is factual knowledge that a person acquires about cultural differences of members of a community. For example, when a multi-ethnic community is to be formed, its leader, with the guidance of a skilled cultural interpreter, needs to arrange an orientation programme in which all members have the chance to explain some of their fundamental cultural symbols. Explanations can avoid considerable misunderstandings and conflicts later. Some simple examples can illustrate this point:

- Vistors to Western homes from East Asia are often puzzled when their hosts keep asking them what they would like. In their own countries the host is supposed to anticipate the needs of guests.

- Japanese culture does not encourage self-disclosure among friends, but Westerners foster self-revelations even in the early stages of friendship.

- Westerners are especially concerned about individual space and like to be on their own at times. But people of folk cultures (for example, from Asia, Africa and the South Pacific) which emphasize group identity and cohesion (as described in Chapter 2) feel embarrassed when they see Westerners on their own. Out of politeness they join them, but feel rejected when their apparently lonely friends withdraw further into private space.

- Different cultural notions of time are notorious for causing inter-cultural tensions. Folk cultures place priority on relationships, not on time schedules; Westerners prefer to keep to time commitments, even to the extent of jeopardizing relationships.

People with *affective competency* have developed the emotional and motivational capacity to contribute to a multicultural/international community with all its environmental pressures and challenges. The competency involves a willingness to learn the common language of the group and to do all that is required to foster a sense of community. People with this skill keep sharpening their own human sensors of listening, empathy and feeling. Empathetic listening across the cultural barriers is the struggle to view the world as the other does, to become more sensitive not just to the feelings of the other, but to the reasons behind them. This also involves a struggle to become aware of one's own cultural values and prejudices and their influence on one's behaviour. This is not an easy task. All cultures have prejudicial stereotypes of other cultures. A stereotype is a set image that one group has of others different from themselves; it is a shorthand method of handling or grasping a complex world of people, but is faulty and often unjust. Cultural stereotypes, if left unidentified and unremoved, will obstruct ability to empathize with people of another culture.

Cultural romanticism is a particularly insidious barrier to intercultural understanding. People of a dominant culture, using a traditional definition of culture, foster romantic visions of minority peoples considered to be inferior to them. These perceptions emphasize what are thought to be the exotic or strange features of these cultures, for example dances and rituals. People of the dominant culture claim it is a pity if such cultures disappear; minority peoples are made to feel like inanimate museum pieces to be called out to entertain 'their cultural superiors' at politically correct times and then to retire to their inferior positions once the need ceases. People with affective competency will be prepared, not just to recognize within themselves prejudices of this nature, but will want to remove them.

Operational competency refers to people's ability 'to enact, or express, their cognitive and affective experiences outwardly when communicating with others'.[15] People with this competency use their cognitive and affective knowledge in practical and creative ways to the advantage of the community. They are bound to make mistakes but willingly seek to be corrected.

Openness to ongoing conversion
The pursuit of multiculturalism/internationality entails risks for all concerned. For example, people of the dominant culture will often need to let go of significant political, social and even economic power. But the fear of losing power over others, in this case over people of other cultures, can prevent or stop multiculturalism/internationality. Consequently, the gift of ongoing personal and cultural conversion is essential, for without this God-given competency there really can be no authentic multicultural/international community, as Paul inspiringly reminds us:

> That is why you must kill everything in you that is earthly . . . evil desires and especially greed, which is the same thing as worshipping a false god . . . . You have stripped off your old behaviour . . . and you

have put on a new self which progresses towards true knowledge the more it is renewed in the image of its Creator; and in that image there is no room for distinction between Greek and Jew ... or between barbarian and Scythian, slave and free .... As the chosen of God, then ... you are to be clothed in heartfelt compassion, in generosity and humility, gentleness and patience. Bear with one another; forgive each other .... Over all these clothes, put on love, the perfect bond.

(Col 3:5, 10–15)

Availability of refounding resources

Multiculturalist/internationalist projects require people of refounding leadership. Authority position persons can authorize the political legitimacy for the breakup of traditional power structures. However, those with requisite gifts for refounding are needed to create new structures, offer a vision to inspire others to join them and, despite the uncertainties and risks involved, to keep to the task of building multicultural/international communities.

Sensitivity to the stages of culture contact

When people of different cultures meet for the first time, they tend to react according to a predictable pattern. First is the fascination or 'honeymoon' stage, the enjoyment that comes from discovering such things as new and exciting foods or fascinating ways of acting. The second stage is disillusionment, when people begin to find it increasingly tiresome to communicate for long periods across cultural barriers. This can lead to friction and conflict. If people keep striving to overcome the cultural obstacles to communication, they move to the third stage, namely authentic multiculturalism/internationality.

Most people never get beyond the second stage. Fixation at the disillusionment stage is generally inevitable for at least three reasons. *First*, popular literature on cross-cultural evangelization often asserts that the evangelizer 'must totally identify with the other culture, fully divesting themselves of their culture of origin'. When this level of identification does not happen evangelizers become discouraged and disillusioned. But the directive is unrealistic. It is impossible to identify fully with the feelings of another person even one of the same culture. Efforts to divest oneself totally of one's culture are a disservice to the people one serves and to oneself. It is only from a position of personal cultural self-esteem that one is able to give and receive from others. When one is culturally insecure or confused, then one lacks confidence to interact with other people of different cultures. No single culture has all the answers to human living. Hence, the value and the need for multicultural/international communities in which cultural experiences are shared and new insights develop for the benefit of all.

Second, cross-cultural interaction can cause what Kalvero Oberg calls culture shock. This is 'the anxiety that results from losing all of our familiar signs and symbols of social intercourse'.[16] Among the symptoms of culture shock are a feeling of what Robert Taft terms 'cultural weariness', manifested by irritability, insomnia and other psychosomatic disorders, a sense of loss arising from being uprooted from one's familiar orderly surroundings, and a feeling of impotence from being unable to relate competently to an unfamiliar cultural environment.[17] When individuals suffer culture shock they react to people of other cultures *either* through arrogant ethnocentric reactions, such as racist or paternalistic comments/actions, *or* through culturally romantic attitudes/actions as described above when the one in shock, in order to cope with the intensely frustrating situation, and yearning for acceptance by people of the other culture, attempts to discard his/her own culture by belittling it and over-praising the other culture.

Third, the difficulties involved in cross-cultural communication are so many and complex at times that conflict occurs, especially at the second stage of contact. Conflict is a state of dissonance or confrontation between two forces or systems which may be expressed openly or in very subtle ways. In the context of intercultural interactions, conflict is the 'perceived and/ or actual incompatibility of values, expectations, processes, or outcomes between two or more parties from different cultures over substantive and/or relational issues'.[18] Sometimes the methods of expressing conflict will be culturally influenced and unrecognized by people of other cultures. This further exacerbates an already tense situation. Intercultural conflict commonly begins with a simple breakdown in communication, leading to misinterpretations; if left unclarified and unmanaged this initial failure in communication causes interpersonal conflict.[19]

Conflicts can be used positively to improve communication. Sometimes the group itself can reflect on the cultural roots of the conflicts, but often the group and individuals are so emotionally overwhelmed by difficulties that this requires the assistance of independent cultural interpreters or counsellors. *Cultural interpreters* are people who listen to the group and are able to explain the cultural sources of the misunderstanding or conflicts. The people are left to work things through themselves in light of the information. *Cultural counsellors* do not provide the information directly, but lead groups caught in conflict to identify for themselves the cultural causes of the tensions and discord. Both types of intervention are import-ant, though recourse to the cultural counsellor may be more effective in the long term, because people come to master for themselves the reasons for conflict.

Recognition of past cultural oppression
People who are or have been culturally oppressed are likely to be acutely sensitive to a dominant culture's symbols of coercive power. When people of minority cultures attempt to make more direct contact with a dominant system, the resulting contact of cultures is not an abstract concept, but a high order of human drama. The plot and its cross-currents, its motives and motifs, are played out by a ghostly cast of hangers-on, prejudice,

longing, fear.[20] The humiliations suffered in the past by minority peoples are not consigned to an archive. They are remembered when contact with representatives of the dominant culture is renewed, and this arouses suspicion inimical to easy intercultural communication. Westerners in particular, when they foster international formation communities in which Third World representatives are present, can forget their nations' oppressive past colonial era or the role of their congregations as agents of Eurocentric, ecclesiastical colonialism in the pre-Vatican II period. The descendants of the oppressed cultures have longer memories.

Appreciation of cultural diversity for creativity

Historically, the multicultural/international formation and apostolic teams of particular congregations have been catalysts for vigorous pastoral creativity. For example, Raymond Hostie notes that 'Cistercians, Norbertines, Dominicans, Carmelites, Jesuits and Piarists, all emerged from groups whose members belonged to three nationalities, even four or five . . . . Heterogeneity is a necessary condition for activating effective fermentation.'[21]

However, in a multicultural/international formation group, as far as possible no one culture should numerically predominate. If one cultural group is over-represented, it is likely to dominate attitudes and policies of the group. For example, community conversations may be centred on topics that particularly interest members of the dominant culture. If a culturally balanced group is impossible, the predominant cultural group needs to be sensitive to avoid obstructing the emergence of creative supranationalism. By *supranationalism* I mean the ability and the willingness of individuals or groups to identify with cultures and needs *beyond* the frontiers of their own culture in ways that are both critical and non-exclusive. This identification with cultures is not blind or uncritical, for the weaknesses as well as the strengths of cultures are recognized. The identification is not exclusive, that is, supranationalists are open to other cultures beyond those with which they are immediately concerned.[22]

Clarification: local or/and international formation?

It is commonly argued that 'Initial formation must be given in one's own country with one's own countrymen [*sic*] and formation personnel, and must be rooted in that culture';[23] and further, that international formation is acceptable only to help candidates 'transcend and thereby purify, discern, and appreciate diverse local cultures and place them in communion'.[24] The assumption in these statements, that one can know one's culture *only* by being trained within it on one's home territory, is anthropologically inaccurate.

In Chapter 2 it was argued that to know one's culture in any depth one must experience cultural dislocation; one almost needs to be placed in a significantly different cultural environment before one is normally aware that one has a culture at all! Evangelizers need to develop objectivity in order to be able to evaluate their own culture and the normal way to this is through cultural dislocation. A prolonged international experience can provide significant cultural disorientation and learning can be considerable with the right supervision. However, for internationality to be a constructive experience candidates are required to have an appropriate level of human integration. If candidates for religious life are judged unable to use an international experience in the way described here, they should not be admitted to formation in the first place.

Case studies: intercultural communication

Case studies are detailed observations of connected processes in individual and group experience, assisting us to understand complex social phenomena and to see ways in which theoretical principles and insights may be applied. I suggest that readers reflect on the following case studies, asking themselves – before assessing my own comments – how the previous theoretical clarifications apply in each instance. Some case studies are explicitly about multicultural/international *formation* communities; those that are not exemplify tensions and misunderstandings that occur also in such communities.

Case study: Romanticism destroys formation

An international clerical religious congregation founded last century in Europe had developed several formation houses in Third World countries. In a report to an international meeting on initial formation in the congregation, the superior-general wrote: 'We thank God for so many vocations from (these lands). Because (these lands) are extremely poor, the people so happy and carefree, and their cultures so unsophisticated, we have decided for now to insist neither on the same rigorous screening criteria for applicants nor on the high-level academic and religious life formation that we have in the Western world. When you meet these students from different cultures living together in our several international and multicultural formation houses in such harmony, you immediately feel their happiness and fine community spirit. They will make good religious, but we must not expect them to measure up to our professional standards for some time to come.'

The superior-general in his high praise for the cultures of the students is a cultural romanticist, even an unconscious racist. The cultures he refers to are group oriented; that is, they stress the need for public harmony at all costs, so that tensions and unresolved conflicts are kept hidden, but remain ready to explode into violence at any time. The general's inability to recognize this deprives students of their right in justice to be professionally educated for ministry. This means, for example, being trained to understand objectively the cultural forces that influence their lives and those of their people. The general also makes a racist judgement, namely, that the students from poor technological cultures are incapable of the levels of learning expected in Western formation systems. Finally, the congregation is international, but the general is setting the stage for a two-tier membership: persons with sophisticated education from Western countries, and educationally deprived persons from the Third World. This means that Third World members of the congregation will effectively be excluded from taking up leadership positions at the international level.

Case study: Fostering a laissez-faire formation programme

Another superior-general of an international congregation of women comments on her effort to establish an international formation community: 'We have made many mistakes in the past in First and Third World countries in matters relating to formation. I believe that what we are now doing is right, namely to let the locals take over and run things their way. Their cultures are so different from ours. We foreigners will have to remain nominally in charge for some time to come, but it is over to the locals to work out their own model of screening and intercultural formation processes.'

At first sight this statement makes good sense: only the locals alone can inculturate the process. However, her comments unwittingly reflect a belief in cultural relativism, a common assertion of some postmodernists (see Chapter 2). Cultural relativism assumes that 'the standards which (measure) human cognition are neither absolute nor identical in all societies. Instead, they are cultural in nature and may vary from one society to another.'[25] Cultural relativists logically conclude that truth is culturally determined, so that what is considered true in one culture is not true in another. There can be no absolute scientific or moral standards for truth transcending all cultures. Hence, for example, psychologists can have nothing to say to cultures other than their own. Anthropologist Ernest Gellner believes that cultural relativism is a form of expiation for the sins of colonialism.[26] Westerners feel, he argues, that they have imposed so much that was wrong on Third World cultures in the past that the policy must now be one of 'hands off'. The West has nothing valid to offer them; former colonial countries have truths of their own to discover by themselves.

I sense cultural relativism is affecting religious of the Western world. They recall with a sense of shame the mistakes in missionary activity made in the past, their own lack of vocations and the abundance of recruits in Third World provinces. They conclude they have nothing more to offer their former 'congregational colonies'. The superior-general in this case study assents to this thinking, at least unconsciously. Yet it is dangerous thinking. There are theological and social science truths, for example in psychology and anthropology, that transcend all cultures. To assume these truths are not to be shared with Third World formation communities in order to help them develop appropriate formation structures and criteria for assessing candidates is an act of injustice towards candidates and their local Churches.

Case study: Theory and practice clash

A congregation of brothers from Europe has worked in Asia for more than 50 years, but with no lasting success in recruiting or retaining local candidates. Several former brothers of Asian origin commented to me through an intermediary about their experience: 'The region was established from a Western world nation. After our training we were sent to communities in which most religious were from this foreign country. They were good people, but during recreation they always spoke in English, never in our language, and the topics of conversation commonly were about incidents and characters of their formation days in Europe, or the latest sporting event at home. Then from time to time they would make ethnic jokes at the expense of our own people, putting them down, and we were expected to laugh as they did. It became so painful that we complained, but we were told to think "internationally", not with provincial and nationalistic minds! It became too much so we left.'

Foreigners in this Asian region are unaware of their cultural imperialism; it is as if they had never left their homeland; their use of ethnic jokes illustrates their lack of cultural sensitivity. Ethnic jokes are common in most societies, but examination shows that the object of such jokes is to belittle members of other cultures and present one's own group as normal and superior. Ethnic jokes are unjust and can be most painful to members of minority groups, who nevertheless may be expected, if present when the jokes are told, to laugh submissively and accept the alleged expression of inferiority.[27] The foreigners are also unaware that their frequent gossiping about their experiences of their homeland in Europe is a way of placing local religious on the margins of the community. Gossip is a subtle method of articulating power and boundaries that separate groups of people. The message is: one trusts the people with whom one gossips; those who are excluded are not to be trusted.[28]

Case study: Inculturation expectations collapse

One Mexican-American sister recorded her frustration and that of many others: 'I became a member of a North American congregation before Vatican II. We Mexican-Americans were (and still are) in the minority; the majority are white third- or fourth-generation Americans. During my training we had to divorce ourselves from our families, and I cannot even begin to express what this meant to me and other Mexican-American sisters. With the coming of Vatican II, I thought at last I can be a religious and a Mexican-American at the same time. Our chapters spoke of the need for inculturation and multiculturalism as priorities in our formation communities, professed communities and apostolates. When I and others attempted to take this priority seriously, all kinds of problems emerged. For example, members of my family began to visit frequently, openly using our language for conversation and prayer and other community members began to object, sometimes hinting or saying directly to me: "You are disturbing our peace with so many relatives, even distant ones, coming to see you. And why don't they speak in English? They should, because this is America!"'

Hispanic cultures traditionally emphasize the family as the basic unit of identity, in vivid contrast to the mainstream American culture in which individuals claim identity for themselves independently of family ties. When members of the congregational chapter in this case study enthusiastically support inculturation and multiculturalism, they are unaware of the implications for individuals and communities. Individualism has become such an unquestioned way of life for the dominant culture in the congregation that most members cannot conceive of any alternative lifestyle. Hence, the culture clash. The references to inculturation and multiculturalism in congregational chapters remain pure rhetoric.

Case study: Popular religiosity unappreciated

An international congregation founded in the nineteenth century in Europe with many communities in North America sought candidates for the first time among Hispanic Americans. For a short time it received candidates, but the formation leader reported that 'they did not survive for long either in the training programmes or later in our receiving communities'. Several who had left commented, and this is a representative view: 'My formation house was cheerless, without life, and the communities I lived in after profession were no better. Liturgies were dull, filled with words, but no colour or movement. I felt myself dying spiritually. I complained to the provincial, and she commented: "I cannot understand you. We provide you with highly trained formators, but you still complain." The director of formation tried to listen to me and said she understood, so the following month she bought Mexican rugs and ornaments and put them around the house, saying: "This will make you immigrant people feel at home with us!" It did not. She paternalistically decided, without consulting us, what she expected to make us "feel at home". We still feel like aliens, unable to pray in devotional ways that make sense to us. The sad thing is that no one understands. No wonder Hispanics leave religious life.'

In this case study there is a serious clash between popular religiosity, characteristic of many Hispanic peoples, and the standard ways of praying in contemporary North American Catholicism. Inability to appreciate popular religiosity and the tendency to condemn it as 'primitive super-stitious nonsense' continue to alienate countless Hispanics from the Church today.[29] At its core, popular religiosity is a storehouse of values offering answers of Christian wisdom to the great questions of life. It creatively combines the divine and the human, Christ and Mary, spirit and body, intelligence, imagination and emotion, in ways that are colourful and imaginative. Devotions to saints and pious practices – once part of mainstream American Catholic life – are integral features of popular religiosity.[30]

Case study: Congregational colonialism returns

A congregation had formally established a province in Africa. After some years it was decided unilaterally by the general government to suppress the province for reasons of administrative and financial efficiency, and to reunite the community of African sisters with the founding province in Ireland. The full provincial administration – all Irish – visited the assembly of African sisters to explain the situation, but to their surprise they were met with considerable anger. An African sister spoke feelingly for her group: 'Finance is not our primary need. We are prepared to be poor, provided we can govern ourselves. Now by the administrative change we again feel overwhelmed by the presence of Ireland, and we are made to feel small and unimportant. You have economic and political power. Now we have none and must submit all levels of our province, including our formation communities, to a culture of dependency and inferiority!' The provincial administration could not understand this, were 'deeply offended at the ingratitude of the African sisters' and reported to the general that the African communities 'had come under the influence of Marxism and liberation theologians'.

In their reactions to the administrative change, the African sisters are fearful of a return to a degrading congregational colonialism. The Irish administration is unaware that their African sisters have been made to feel inferior under earlier provincial administrations. This is an example of a residual myth (see Chapter 2), that is, a collective negative memory of oppressive past congregational colonialism. The residual myth becomes an operative myth for the Africans, revitalized by the failure of the provincial and general administrations to consult with them about the decision to suppress the province. Sadly, the provincial administration, by blaming the African sisters for negativity, sees no need to examine its own cultural assumptions nor to enter more deeply into the reactions of the African sisters. It remains trapped within its own monocultural view of the world.

Case study: A general chapter in confusion

An international congregation of priests met in general chapter in Britain for two months. A participant from a First World country reported his experience and that of many others: 'During the first two weeks, there was a great spirit of internationality and friendship. Each group explained through song, dances, food, and visual displays aspects of their cultural origins. We especially enjoyed the presentations from the joy-filled Third World countries; they made our Western productions look rather dull in contrast. Then something happened, and it still puzzles and angers me. Quite suddenly delegates from our Third World provinces began to complain bitterly in the general sessions that the translation facilities for them were not as good as for the Western delegates, that they were made to feel inferior in committee meetings by never being asked for their opinions. . . . I and others still cannot understand this anger, especially because we did everything possible to give them first place for their cultural presentations. These are the same people we have helped for so long with gifts to their formation houses and missions. They are ungrateful. Perhaps we have failed to teach them the right way to act in international gatherings. The chapter ended without these people realizing that they had undermined the good spirit of the gathering.'

In this case study the delegate, having unknowingly adopted a narrow classic view of culture, moves from enthusiasm for cultural diversity to disillusionment. Internationality for him and other Western delegates is restricted to such relatively inconsequential things as eating foreign food and admiring other people's exotic dances. Influenced by this approach to culture, he is prevented from understanding the requirements of authentic multiculturalism/internationality in the chapter and the congregation. He and others failed to move beyond the disillusionment stage of contact and left the chapter without having an authentic international learning experience or recognizing the need to develop the three competencies of cultural cognition, affectivity and operation. Third World delegates are reacting against a well-entrenched tradition of paternalism and cultural superiority on the part of the dominant culture. They rightly want to be accepted for what they are: members of the same congregation, with human experiences and insights of value to all.

176

Case study: A reflective and learning community

A multicultural formation programme was established in an atmosphere of considerable congregational enthusiasm, and the superiors provided a professional orientation programme for its members within a week of its establishment. Internal enthusiasm remained high for two months, then individuals found themselves becoming unusually irritable with other members of the group; some others no longer regularly attended community gatherings, claiming that their studies kept them away. Some complained of tiredness and headaches. At community meetings some participants would become emotionally upset, complaining that people were not listening to them. An outsider who visited the community came away feeling it was quite depressed and had nothing like the open atmosphere he had noticed when it was first formed.

The formator, with the help of a cultural counsellor, suggested a two-day evaluation. She invited the group first to ponder in a faith atmosphere the feelings of Mary and Joseph when they had to flee from their homeland with the child Jesus (Matt 2:13–15). They were asked questions such as: 'How do you think Mary and Joseph felt in a strange land and culture?' 'How would you feel in their place trying to communicate across the cultural boundaries with little or no knowledge of the local language?' In this faith sharing participants came to recognize their common culture shock reactions. In the earlier orientation they had been told to expect these feelings to emerge, but were unable to identify them in themselves until the faith sharing experience. The cultural counsellor was able to help participants to name the signs of culture shock; with a sense of liberation, members of the community were able to move forward to a new level of *communitas*.

The case study describes stages of culture contact, the second stage being the most difficult and problematic. Participants had achieved cognitive competency from their orientation programme, that is, they knew in theory about the symptoms of culture shock, but they had yet to identify them in their personal and group lives. In a faith context, and with the help of a skilled cultural counsellor, they were able to develop affective and operational competency. It became a powerful learning moment for them, and freed the group to move to a greater depth in faith and action.

Merging formation programmes: practical hints

Theoretically when organizations decide to merge they form a *substantially* new identity. In a federation by contrast the original organizations retain their separate identities and a high level of independence from one another, but create at the same time an overarching organization in which they agree to share various functions advantageous to themselves.

There is a trend in the Church today for both institutions and apostolates to merge: congregations, provinces of congregations, schools, hospitals, formation programmes. Various pragmatic and inspirational reasons are given, such as the need to use personnel and finances more effectively for mission. However, when it is a question of formation programmes, the word *merger* tends not to be used. Instead there are vague expressions like the following: 'uniting with another province for formation', 'combining our formation programmes', 'we have decided to send our candidates to be formed in another province', 'we are uniting with another province in a joint formation programme'. When pressed to explain the meaning of these expressions, however, administrators often describe what they propose as a *merger*, but they rarely define clearly what it means or demands of them. There is little awareness that nebulous statements, if left unclarified, can result in disaster or at least unnecessary pain and loss of apostolic energy in formation staffs and candidates.

Yet whatever expression is used – 'merging', 'uniting', 'combining' – the fact is that efforts to join together existing institutions, including formation programmes, commonly fail to meet expectations, because people do not appreciate that institutional interaction, as symbolized by these expressions, necessitates far more than a rearrangement of administrations. It necessitates the creation of a whole new culture. The contemporary struggle to unite East and West Germany aptly illustrates the point. When institutions seek to combine, they interact as cultures, and the resulting change is not a bloodless abstraction, but an intense human drama.

Since merging or even limited inter-institutional co-operation is a cultural minefield, this section concentrates on the dynamics of merging formation programmes within national cultures or across international boundaries. With the help of case studies, we will see that the purpose and the processes necessary for the merging of formation programmes must be clarified in the very early stages of discussions by the parties involved.

Lessons from experience

The literature on business amalgamations is filled with dreary warnings about the negative effects of mergers. Management consultant Tom Peters concludes that 'most studies suggest that, in general, (business) mergers do not pan out'.[31] Mergers have come to be associated not with increased profitability but with lowered morale, job dissatisfaction, unproductive behaviour, sabotage, petty theft, absenteeism and increased labour turnover, strikes and accident rates.[32] Management consultant Stuart Slatter advises that a merger of firms 'rarely brings increased efficiencies, unless accompanied by sound post-merger management. In fact, inefficiencies may actually increase as . . . divisive splits develop within the new top-management team as each manager retains loyalties to his former business.'[33] James O'Toole speaks of the contemporary stress on business amalgamations as 'merger-mania'. He says that 'the desire of large industrial bodies to merge is insatiable' and that the purpose and strategies for such actions are rarely thought through.[34] Charles Handy warns that organizations contemplating a merger are 'to some extent stuck with their past . . . their traditions. These things take years if not decades to change.'[35] Some authors wonder if the drive for mergers comes from authoritarian, patriarchal values dominant in Western society. These values, they claim, blind organizations to feminine qualities of creativity, of openness to other ways of co-operation than formal mergers.[36]

Overall, most commentators conclude that mergers fail because leaders neglect to clarify their purpose and insufficiently consider the human or cultural dimensions of change. In addition to sensitive leadership there must be, authors claim, a cultural compatibility (or what they term 'culture fit') between organizations that seek to merge. If there is insufficient culture fit, then cultural collisions will destroy efforts to merge organizations.[37] Anthropologists agree with these conclusions, but they complain that when management writers use the term *culture*, they do not grasp the complexity of its meaning. They uncritically accept a definition resembling the classic description of culture, that is *what people do around here*, not *what they feel about what they do*.[38]

Case studies: mergers in religious congregations

By way of summary, there are five significant insights from applied anthropology that need to be taken into account by formators and others wishing to merge formation programmes. I suggest that readers ponder them before studying the case studies, which illustrate the importance of these guidelines.

First, all organizations are cultures (or subcultures); hence, congregational provinces have their own cultures even if the provinces exist side by side in the same country; so also formation communities. Any interaction between them can become an experience of building a multicultural community.

Second, leaders ignore culture at their peril; people may change their behaviour with relative ease, especially under external pressure, but not so their feelings.[39]

Third, people are likely to resist change for two reasons: the fear of losing the known and tried, and unresolved grief following personal and group loss. Cultural interaction inevitably calls people to new ways of acting; the familiar must be left behind and few find this easy. Hence, any effort to merge cultures (for example formation programmes) may lead to varying degrees of overt or underground resistance. Furthermore, people experience grief when change occurs. Reactions of sadness and anger, unless they can be openly and freely expressed, can build up and then explode in ways that appear totally out of proportion to the provocation of the moment. The resistance has merely been deferred and stockpiled; they finally reach a breaking point and express it dramatically. People need the chance to grieve over loss.

Fourth, merging cultures is a highly complex and risky process requiring people of *refounding* calibre. Without such help, people resist change and mergers falter or fail.

Fifth, clarity and frankness of language are necessary. For example, mergers are not synonymous with takeovers, that is, the total assimilation of other cultures by a dominant one. True mergers recognize the need for honesty and dialogue between *equals*, so that the best of all cultures is preserved in the new emerging organizational culture.[40]

Case study: Confused thinking blocks merger

A provincial informed her province by newsletter about plans for the future formation of candidates: 'It has been decided, because of the small numbers of recruits and the lack of people to train as formators, to merge our formation programme with that of our neighbouring province where they have more candidates and better qualified staff. Our present staff will merge with theirs. The combined formation programme will be the best way to train our candidates for the mission of our congregation.' When the formation staff moved to join the host community they were well received, but soon discovered that they were treated as guests in the community, along with the candidates of their province. No dialogue was initiated through which both formation teams could share experiences and clarify goals for the new combined formation programme. Eventually, finding it impossible for anyone to understand their concern, the 'guest' formation staff resigned. Members of their province also reacted strongly by voicing support for their formators, complaining that they had not been consulted about the decision to close the local formation community. Vocations, they said, were bound to come and in good numbers and anyone could be a formator! Their provincial was astonished by their reactions. She responded to the criticism by saying that her decision just made good sense for a small province.

The provincial had not thought through what mergers involve. She was motivated primarily by the need to find a suitable place and staff for her province's candidates. The formation staff from her province understood that the word *merger* meant a dialogue among equals, from which a new culture for the formation community would emerge. The frustration of the staff could have been avoided, if for a lengthy period prior to the project being established, both formation staffs, with the full and official backing of their respective provincial administrations, had planned together the implications of the term *merger*. Formation communities symbolize ongoing life and a future. When they are closed down, or merge with other groups even of the same congregation, this action can cause a province to go into grief, as this case study illustrates. The provincial was unprepared for, and unable to handle, the grief responses, believing that the decision to merge was the only rational option and that others should see it as such.

Case study: Fears of 'provincial colonialism' revived

A congregational leader encouraged two provincial administrations to investigate the advisability of merging first their formation programmes and then their provinces. Investigation showed that for missionary and financial efficiency both levels of merging made perfect sense. However, reactions to the proposal to move ahead with the merging process were so negative in one province, which had been founded several decades earlier by the other, that the plan was dropped. The leader tried several times to encourage the merger, but the more he tried the more the resistance developed against the plan. Eventually he realized the need to seek the help of cultural interpreters and counsellors to understand and lessen the resistance.

The 'offspring' of the founding province suffers anticipated grief. Its members feel they will again suffer oppression from the dominant founding province if a merger takes place. The latter is remembered as an arrogant, 'congregational colonial power'. That memory is a *residual* myth; the thought of any merger makes the residual myth an operational force for identity and prevents any serious discussion about merging formation communities and provinces. The leader eventually recognizes that he needs professional assistance to deal with the anticipatory grief and the negative collective memories.

Case study: Failure to clarify and respect roles

Three provincials, with some consultation with their provinces, decided to merge their formation communities and agreed to use the formation residence of one of the provinces. A superior and staff were appointed for this interprovincial project. After a short period, however, considerable tension emerged at the staff and community levels. A candidate had been advised by the staff to leave, but members of his province objected directly to the formation superior, and the candidate's provincial wrote rejecting the decision of the staff. The staff complained that the provincial had no right to do this, but they were ignored. Before long, as other candidates were advised to leave the other provincials also directly interfered. With this, the staff's morale fell further. They felt unsupported by their respective provincials. Eventually the project broke apart in the midst of considerable anger and distrust at all levels.

The three provincials vaguely established on paper a new formation culture, the consequence of merging three cultures, but they did nothing to create it as a living entity. Each interfered without due reference to the other provincials or the staff. From the beginning they should have clearly defined the mission of the new culture and the levels of authority and responsibility of provincials, and a member of staff should have been appointed to liaise with the formation staff; any complaints should have been directed to him. The staff also failed in that it assented to the vagueness of the original agreement to merge. They should have requested clarification before accepting their appointments.

Case study: A successful merger

> Three provincial administrations agreed, with an outside consultant's assistance, that from a mission perspective it was essential for their provinces to merge. They consulted all members of their provinces, and most favoured the merger. Once the merger decision was finally taken, the provincial administrations sought professional advice on how to proceed. The merger was done over a seven-year period, in accordance with frequently evaluated strategies. As part of the merging process, all apostolates were assessed for their pastoral effectiveness in light of clearly stated criteria. It was decided that one formation community was sufficient, and that this should be the first stage of the overall merging process. Appropriate structures and lines of accountability were established for this formation community and people knew exactly where responsibility for decision-making rested. People with refounding competence were empowered to establish the new formation community so that a model of formation emerged radically different from anything seen before in the merging provinces. All members were invited to be part of the merging and evaluating processes, negative reactions were minimal and the ownership of the changes was at a high level.

In this case study the following factors guaranteed success: the purpose of the merger was clear; culturally sensitive leadership was aware that in-depth culture change is a slow process; professional assistance helped to clarify the vision of the merger and develop appropriate strategies; members of the provinces were involved in all stages of the merging; qualified people were used to implement decisions in formation.

Advice to leaders

The following advice to congregational leaders and formation staffs is a logical consequence of the theory of this chapter and the analysis of the case studies.

1. Clarify the vision and the strategies

The primary aim of any merger of formation programmes (as for provinces or any apostolate) must be to make the religious congregation better able to serve the needs of the kingdom of God. Thus, those responsible must ask questions such as the following: Is the merger apostolically justified, or is it just a way to maintain existing apostolates, including formation programmes, without evaluating them for their apostolic relevance or effectiveness? Are there better ways than merging to achieve the desired effects?

2. Involve members throughout the process

The amalgamation of existing formation programmes is an interaction of two or more cultures with the aim of creating a substantially new culture. In-depth culture change is slow and risky, demanding a radical, ongoing letting go of familiar attachments by all concerned. Hence, to ensure the achievement of this detachment, there must be involvement of members before, during and after the formal merger. People must feel they are realistically contributing to its development, with as much information available to them as is possible. Authority position persons must therefore ask themselves questions such as: What structures will best encourage the maximum involvement of members? Are the members being given adequate information? Are the most skilled cultural change agents being used to facilitate the process?

3. Foster group and personal grieving

When formation communities (and/or provinces) decide to merge, religious enter the liminoid stage of a spiritual journey. The old myth-ologies of the different formation cultures must be let go of to allow the creation myth of a new formation community to emerge and be confidently owned. Authority position persons, like Moses, must do two things: *first* encourage their members to share the stories of their formation communities with one another, together with their feelings of grief over the loss of the old; *second*, call them to share the vision or founding myth of the new formation programme or community. As Walter Brueggemann writes: 'Mourning is a precondition . . . . Only that kind of anguished disengagement permits fruitful yearning and only the public embrace of deathliness permits newness to come.'[41] This is a call to an ongoing process of personal and corporate conversion, which cannot be hurried; without it the merging of communities will fail.

4. Utilize cultural change agents and consultants

Change agents can be asked to assume responsibility for managing the process of moving from several cultures to one. They are transformational leaders who understand objectively the tensions involved in the process, can visualize the radically new, have acquired personal skills to cope constructively with personal and cultural change in their own lives, and are able to foster with empathy a positive approach in others to changes. In the merging of formation communities, such people are needed at all levels: as congregational leaders, ritual-grief directors and creators of new and relevant formation structures.

Because culture change is so complex, it is advisable for congregational leaders to seek advice at pivotal points in the merging process. A consultant's task is to collaborate with those entrusted with the merger in order to develop 'an understanding of the way things are done, thinking about the way they might be, and then working with (them) to consider what, how, and whether to change'.[42] The consultant cannot be effective unless he/she has well-developed cross-cultural skills.[43]

Summary

In recent years multiculturalism/internationality has been either championed as a symbol of the emerging paramodern culture (as described in Chapter 2) or condemned. The praise is often uncritical, the condemnation distorted. When people praise efforts to develop multiculturalism/internationality, they commonly downplay the complexity and problems associated with culture change. They expect too much too soon of people, and blind themselves to the mistakes that occur. When people condemn multiculturalism/internationality, it is because they often fear what it will demand of them – the giving up of power.

As followers of Christ we are committed to foster multiculturalism/internationality and as religious we must struggle to be exemplars in this field. Informed concern for multiculturalism/internationality must permeate all aspects of the formation process of religious, and at some stage in their training candidates for religious life need to live for a significant period of time in a multicultural/international community. When provinces within the same nation decide to merge their formation programmes they are also involved in a multicultural experiment because, though they belong to the same congregation, they have their own cultures. As few effective multicultural/international communities exist in the Church or society, efforts to establish them by formators will serve as examples of refounding. They will testify that such gatherings are possible. Nothing is more urgent in today's divided world than this.

Notes

1. Paul VI, Apostolic Letter, *On Evangelization* (Vatican: Vatican Press, 1975), para. 15.
2. A. Bellagamba, *Mission and Ministry in the Global Church* (Maryknoll, NY: Orbis Books, 1992), p. 123.

3. See W. Wink, *Engaging the Powers: Discernment and Resistance in a World of Domination* (Minneapolis: Fortress Press, 1992), pp. 195–272.

4. See D. Nygren and M. Ukeritis, 'The future of religious orders in the United States', *Origins*, vol. 22, no. 15 (1992), p. 272 and *Review for Religious*, vol. 52, no. 1 (1993), p. 48.

5. R. Hughes, *Culture of Complaint: The Fraying of America* (New York: Oxford University Press, 1993), p. 111.

6. See H. A. Giroux, 'Insurgent multiculturalism and the promise of pedagogy' in D. T. Goldberg (ed.), *Multiculturalism: A Critical Reader* (Oxford: Basil Blackwell, 1994), p. 336.

7. See G. A. Arbuckle, *Earthing the Gospel: An Inculturation Handbook for Pastoral Workers* (London: Geoffrey Chapman, 1990), pp. 15–20, 182–6;
   M. Amaladoss, 'Inculturation and internationality', *East Asian Pastoral Review*, vol. 29, no. 3 (1992), pp. 238–51.

8. B. Parekh, cited by Giroux, op. cit., p. 336.

9. See Arbuckle, op. cit., pp. 179–81.

10. See Chapter 3 above and G. A. Arbuckle, *Refounding the Church: Dissent for Leadership* (London: Geoffrey Chapman, 1993), pp. 15–66.

11. See F. Elashmawi and P. R. Harris, *Multicultural Management: New Skills for Global Success* (Houston: Gulf Publishing, 1993), p. 20.

12. The Report of the Committee of Inquiry into the Education of Children from Ethnic Minority Groups (Swann Report), *Education for All* (London: HMSO, 1985), pp. 767, 769.

13. See Arbuckle, *Earthing the Gospel*, op. cit., pp. 147–66.

14. See Y. Yun Kim, 'Adapting to a new culture' in L. A. Samovar and R. E. Porter (eds), *Intercultural Comunication: A Reader* (Belmont, CA: Wadsworth Inc., 1994), pp. 394–6.

15. Yun Kim, ibid., p. 395.

16. K. Oberg, 'Cultural shock: adjustment to new cultural environments', *Practical Anthropology*, no. 7 (1960) p. 177.

17. See R. Taft, 'Coping with unfamiliar cultures' in N. Warren (ed.), *Studies in Cross-Cultural Psychology*: Volume 1 (London: Academic Press, 1977), pp. 121–53; also Y. Yun Kim, *Communication and Cross-Cultural Adaptation* (Clevedon: Multilingual Matters Ltd, 1988).

18. S. Ting-Toomey, 'Managing intercultural conflicts effectively' in Samovar and Porter, op. cit., p. 360.

19. See Ting-Toomey, ibid., pp. 360–72.

20. See A. Adler and R. Taft, 'Some psychological aspects of immigrant assimilation' in A. Stoller (ed.), *New Faces: Immigration and Family Life in Australia* (Melbourne: Cheshire, 1966), p. 75.

21. R. Hostie, *The Life and Death of Religious Orders: A Psycho-Sociological Approach* (Washington, DC: CARA, 1983), p. 259.

22. See G. A. Arbuckle, *Out of Chaos: Refounding Religious Congregations* (New York: Paulist Press, 1988), pp. 128–30.

23. Document *Instrumentum Laboris* for the Synod of Bishops, *The Consecrated Life and Its Role in the Church and in the World* (Vatican: Libreria Editrice Vaticana, 1994), para. 91.

24. Ibid.

25. F. A. Hanson, 'Relativism' in A. and J. Kuper (eds), *The Social Science Encyclopedia* (London: Routledge and Kegan Paul, 1985), p. 696.

26. See E. Gellner, *Postmodernism, Reason and Religion* (London: Routledge, 1992), pp. 22–72.

27. See Arbuckle, *Earthing the Gospel*, op cit., pp. 162–3.

28. See G. A. Arbuckle, 'Gossip and scapegoating cripple pastoral innovation', *Human Development*, vol. 15, no. 1 (1994), pp. 11–16.

29. See A. F. Deck, *The Second Wave: Hispanic Ministry and the Evangelization of Cultures* (New York: Paulist Press, 1989), pp. 54–119.

30. See Arbuckle, *Earthing the Gospel*, op. cit., pp. 108–12.

31. T. Peters, *Thriving on Chaos* (New York: Alfred A. Knopf, 1987), p. 7. For a critique of corporate mergers in the United States see *The Economist* (10 September 1994), pp. 13–14, 93–4.

32. See G. Meeks, *Disappointing Marriage: A Study of the Gains from Mergers* (Cambridge: Cambridge University Press, 1977); S. Cartwright and C. L. Cooper, 'The psychological impact of merger and acquisition on the individual', *Human Relations*, vol. 46, no. 3 (1993), pp. 327–9.

33. S. Slatter, *Corporate Recovery* (London: Penguin, 1984) p. 245.

34. J. O'Toole, *Vanguard Management* (New York: Berkley, 1987), pp. 258, 250.

35. C. Handy, *Understanding Voluntary Organizations* (London: Penguin, 1988), p. 95.

36. See G. Morgan, *Images of Organization* (London: Sage, 1986), pp. 210–12.

37. See S. Cartwright and C. L. Cooper, 'The role of culture compatibility in successful organizational marriage', *Academy of Management Executive*, vol. 7, no. 2 (1993), pp. 57–70; B. J. Miller (ed.), *Mergers and Acquisitions: Back-to-Basics Techniques for the '90s* (New York: John Wiley and Sons, 1994), pp. 229–46.

38. For examples of the use of the classic definition by writers on management, see T. Deal and A. Kennedy, *Corporate Cultures: The Rites and Rituals of Corporate Life* (Reading, MA: Addison-Wesley, 1982), p. 4.

39. See S. A. Sackman, *Cultural Knowledge in Organizations: Exploring the Collective Mind* (London: Sage, 1991), pp. 16–23; J. Hunt, 'How people get overlooked in takeovers', *Personnel Management* (July 1987), pp. 24–6 and 'Managing the successful acquisition: a people question', *London Business School Journal* (Summer 1988), p. 215.

40. See A. F. Buono and J. Bowditch, *The Human Side of Mergers and Acquisitions* (San Francisco: Jossey-Bass, 1989), pp. 134–63.

41. W. Brueggemann, *The Prophetic Imagination* (Philadelphia: Fortress Press, 1978), p. 113.

42. E. Miller, quoted by R. McLennan, *Journal of Enterprise Management*, no. 3 (1981), p. 251.

43. See Arbuckle, *Refounding the Church*, op. cit., pp. 213–14, 217.

8 Formators: ritual elders of a rite of passage

A disciple is not superior to the teacher; but the fully trained disciple will be like the teacher.

(Luke 6:40)

The work of formation as a whole is the fruit of the collaboration between those responsible for formation and their disciples.

(Congregation for Consecrated Life)[1]

This chapter explains:

- the role of formators as ritual specialists whose task is to lead candidates through ritual initiation into religious and congregational life;

- the ways Moses helped to form the Israelite people in the Exodus and Jesus Christ trained the apostles;

- the competencies required of formators;

- the role of congregational authority position persons in formation.

In Chapter 3, formation was defined as a process whereby a person in and through community assumes responsibility for his/her growth in Christ in order to be of prophetic service to the Church and society. This means that the person is involved in a journey of liberation by which *under skilled guidance* he/she frees himself/herself from personal and cultural constraints. The task of a formator is to lead candidates on this sacred journey. What does Christ say to us about this formation process? What skills are necessary for the task of formation in light of the experience of Jesus as himself a formator? To respond to these questions this chapter draws insights first from social anthropology and then from sacred scriptures.

Cultures, rituals and ritual specialists

In Chapter 3 cultural models based on the variables of *group* and *grid* were applied to different cultures or groups within the Church. Ritual played an important role in each of them, but the nature of that role and the role of the ritual leader differed from model to model. In Chapter 2 ritual was defined simply as the visible elements of culture. Myth and ritual, writes anthropologist Edmund Leach, are but two sides of the same phenomenon, two ways of making symbolic statements about the social order: 'myth regarded as a statement in words "says" the same thing as ritual regarded as a statement in action'.[2]

Ritual must now be defined with more precision, because this will lead to a deeper understanding of the role of formators. Ritual is the more or less stylized or repetitive symbolic use of bodily movement and gesture in a social context, to express and articulate meanings, especially meanings about what people consider to be fundamental to the *purpose* of life.[3] A key quality of any ritual is that it is a form of repetitive behaviour that is not directed to any overt technical result. According to Victor Turner, rituals are periodic restatements that express and define social relations. Rituals create, or recreate, the categories through which people see reality – the axioms underlying the structures of society and the laws of the natural and moral orders. This function is clear in the rituals that surround Independence Day, Memorial Day, Thanksgiving Day in the United States or, in Britain, in the solemnities relating to the monarch's coronation or the annual opening of Parliament. Rituals restate certain values and principles of a culture, such as the ways in which new members are to be inducted into it and the manner in which members are to relate to one another, outsiders, gods and the natural world. Each culture has ritual elders or specialists who are formally or informally designated, because of particular talents they possess or status given them, to lead the society in its ritual life.[4]

In cultures in which there is a strong sense of rules (grid) and group identity, for example the pre-Vatican II Church, rituals[5] are many, highly elaborate and markedly stylized, and they reinforce the social and hierarchical *status quo*. They are under the direction of a specialized ritual elite with the task of maintaining the group's conformity to the established order. The personal attitudes of the ritual leaders, who have powers given them by the gods and officially sanctioned by the culture, are unimportant to the effective execution of their role. Their duty as ritual leaders is to recite the right words or perform the right actions as defined by tradition. Ritual leaders must not in any way prophetically challenge the accepted order of things. On the contrary, their task is to uphold tradition.

However, in cultures which strongly emphasize rules for social inter-action, but downplay the sense of group identity and obligations (for example the 'accommodationist Church', explained in Chapter 3), rituals exist primarily to serve the personal or self-achievement needs of individuals, not the group. Ritual leaders in these cultures are trained for this purpose and, as in the first model, their task is to support the cultural or religious *status quo*. For example, the rich and powerful in this culture depend on society and religion to support their individualism and lack of concern for the common good; political and religious elders are employed to make sure this self-centred way of life is maintained.

There are few traditional rituals, however, in cultures that have a very weak grid and a fragile sense of group bonding (for example 'protest churches' or countercultural groups). These are liminoid or pilgrimage cultures in relation to the surrounding world of cultural predictability. People of the latter see liminoid people as non-persons,[6] that is, they are 'out of order' or culturally 'unstable', 'polluting', 'dirty'. People of protest cultures hold a vision of society that threatens the identity of other cultural groups and for this reason they become ready targets for scape-goating. People want someone or some group to blame for their problems or fear of change, so they make the liminoid people the scapegoats. Ritual leaders in protest groups embody in their person the new vision of society, and their leadership ability comes not from tradition, but from their own inner conversion to the vision. They are founders or refounders of cultures, for example Mahatma Gandhi in India and Nelson Mandela in South Africa.

Case study: Formators become scapegoats

Over the last two decades a religious congregation of priests in the Third World has continued to receive a regular number of candidates. Successive provincial administrations have periodically selected pastorally experienced men to be trained as formators. Yet, despite their expertise in formation, they have been poorly received by the province as a whole. At provincial chapters, formators and the provincial administration have been subjected to considerable angry and ill-informed criticism. A proposal to consider the possibility of extending the novitiate from one year to two was bitterly and irrationally rejected by two chapters with comments like the following: 'There is no need for a two-year novitiate. We did not need this in our day so today's novices do not'; 'This is just another attempt by formation personnel to keep a hold on the resources of the province'.

A researcher employed by the provincial administration proposed this hypothesis to explain the vehemence directed at formators: 'Candidates are being formed today in intentional communities where they are developing apostolic qualities of collaboration, interdependence and mutuality. The majority of the members of your province, however, are patriarchal individualists uninterested in fostering these ministerial virtues. They see the intentional communities as a potential force to undermine their pre-Vatican II pastoral methods and power. This frightens them. Some want to change but are fearful because they do not know how to change or what it will cost them personally. They look for scapegoats for their

anxiety and find them in the formation staff and the provincial
administration supporting them.'

Historically, witch-hunting or scapegoating crazes flourish in times of
social, political, economic and religious upheavals or chaos. People
become confused and anxious and look intolerantly and simplistically for
some person(s) to blame for the chaos. Usually the scapegoats are people
on the margin, that is, individuals or groups who by their lifestyle and/or
ideas challenge the *status quo*.[7] Formators are such people because they
seek to form candidates who will prophetically challenge a congregation
that has lost its founding fervour. The researcher's hypothesis therefore
provides a logical explanation of the marginalization of the formators in
the province.

Rites of passage in a pilgrimage culture: functions of ritual specialists

Ritual leaders of rites of passage in weak grid/weak group cultures are
prophetic people, questioners of rigid social status systems in the
surrounding cultures and dreamers of a better world to come. In a true sense
they are not *doers* of ritual but are *themselves* the ritual. They concretize, by
their inner conversion and conviction, the idea that a new world *is* possible.
Myth specialist Joseph Campbell describes the ritual leader of this culture
of pilgrimage in this way: he/she is a 'hero', who 'ventures forth from the
world of common day into a region of supernatural wonder: fabulous
forces are encountered and a decisive victory is won. The hero comes back
from this mysterious adventure with the power to bestow boons on his
fellow man [*sic*].'[8] The ritual leader is a hero who has visited, and been
converted to, the vision of a new world and his/her behaviour mirrors this
interior transformation. The primary task of the pilgrim leader is not to
be a manager arranging accommodation and social events on the way,
but to inspire pilgrims with the hope that the destination can be reached.
Pilgrims, recognizing that their leader carries within himself/herself
the vision of their journey's end, are drawn to experience the same action-
oriented conversion.

The journey of formation in religious life is an extended ritual of
transition. It consists of two parts or sub-rites of passage, namely novitiate
with temporary profession as its finale, and the postnovitiate stage which
concludes with final profession. Formators are the ritual leaders. Although
they are appointed to this office, the primary source of their authority
to lead others is that they have become in themselves 'like the teacher'
(Luke 6:40) Jesus Christ. They certainly need the appropriate 'human
qualities and responsiveness' and 'necessary cultural competence',[9] but

their pre-eminent skill must be that they have undergone themselves the pilgrimage with Jesus the teacher and become one with him in their own lives, that they are swept up in the vision of 'the new heavens and new earth, where uprightness will be at home' (2 Pet 3:13) and yearn to draw others to share in hope this same dream. Having been a pilgrim on the journey of conversion they know its dangers and the qualities that travellers need to survive and grow.

We turn now to Moses and Jesus Christ who, as ritual elders, formed faith communities in their times. Both aimed through leading rituals of transition to create a new people of God; they were able to lead, however, only because they themselves submitted wholeheartedly to God.

Formators as ritual leaders: lessons from scripture

Moses: lessons for formators

Moses was involved in two interconnected journeys simultaneously: the journey of the Israelite people as a group, and his own inner personal one. He was commissioned by Yahweh to lead the people through a most difficult ritual of transition; he guided them through the wilderness to the threshold of the promised land. Moses followed the three-stage pattern of grieving and initiation with appropriate rituals at each phase as we saw in Chapter 5. He acknowledged the importance of the separation period in which people felt the pain of leaving the old and familiar world behind; there was hurting, anger, the move to blame others for their misery: 'To Moses they said: "Was it for lack of graves in Egypt, that you had to lead us out to die in the desert? What was the point of bringing us out of Egypt?"' (Exod 14:11–12). But Moses kept them on the task of conversion: 'Moses said to the people, "Do not be afraid! Stand firm, and you will see what Yahweh will do to rescue you today . . . Yahweh will do the fighting for you; all you need to do is to keep calm"' (Exod 14:13). Here is Moses the grief counsellor![10]

There are a number of lessons for formators in the way Moses exercised his formator's role in the exodus:

1. Appreciate the teaching power of chaos
Moses shrewdly understood the importance of permitting the people to experience the chaos (see Chapter 5). The old cannot be let go of and the new cannot take its place without the pain of chaos (Deut 8:2, 3, 5).

2. Constantly articulate the vision
Moses constantly kept before the people, especially at times when the chaos profoundly affected them, the vision of the new world to come, 'a fine country, a land of streams and springs, of waters that well up from

the deep valleys and hills, a land of wheat and barley' (Exod 8:7–8). He also mediated Yahweh's saving interventions – for example, the gifts of manna and quails – which foreshadowed in concrete ways the fulfilment of the promise in Canaan (Exod 16).

3. Keep contact with the founding roots during the time of chaos

Moses appreciated the need in the liminal period of wandering in the desert to keep links with the collective roots of his people back in Egypt. Hence, the bones of Joseph were gathered and the people carried them into the wilderness (Exod 13:19).

4. Model collaborative action

Moses was sensitive to the fact that the experience of chaos in the Exodus, a pre-condition for forming a new people, if not guided prudently, could lead to total destruction. Therefore, he sought the advice of Jethro, his father-in-law, who instructed him to group the people into manageable administrative units, under the direction of 'capable and God-fearing men, men who are trustworthy and incorruptible' (Exod 18:21). Moses was bluntly reminded by Jethro that he needed time to think and pray in order to discover the vision and plans required by Yahweh for the people to enter into a new land (Exod 18:19–20). He heeded the advice. Thus Moses as a formator modelled the need to cultivate team work, dialogue and subsidiarity, and to have personal space in which to contemplate God's presence.

5. Call people to be accountable

As a mouthpiece of Yahweh Moses taught the Israelites the values enshrined in the decalogue, that were to bind them together as a people and with Yahweh (Exod 20). He never hesitated to call the people to be accountable to these values: 'Be careful not to forget Yahweh . . . by neglecting his commandments, customs and laws which I am laying down for you today' (Exod 8:11).

6. Recognize that God alone calls and strengthens

Moses often reminded the people that the call to journey into the land of promise comes from Yahweh. No matter what gifts they may have had as individuals or as group, it was still Yahweh alone who called them and strengthened them for the journey: 'Beware of thinking to yourself, "My own strength and the might of my own hand have given me the power to act like this." Remember Yahweh . . . he was the one who gave you the strength to act effectively like this' (Deut 8:18). To respond to this call demands ongoing conversion: 'What does Yahweh . . . ask of you? Only this: to fear Yahweh your God, to follow his ways, to love him, to serve Yahweh your God with all your heart and soul . . . . Circumcise your heart then and be obstinate no longer' (Deut 10:12, 16).

7. Model the refounding role of the formator

Moses co-operated with Yahweh in the forming of the Israelites as the people of God and exhibited boldness of imagination, initiative and courage in the midst of the wilderness and its many trials. In this he is a model for contemporary formators who must, in co-operation with Christ, creatively devise radically new ways to initiate religious to serve in prophetic ways the post-Vatican II Church and world.

8. Model the role of grief leader

Moses is frequently depicted co-operating with Yahweh in rites of grieving. He allowed people to express the pain of their loss and used the occasions to re-articulate the vision of the promised land.

9. Pray as a formator

As a good formator should, Moses prayed repeatedly for the safety and conversion of the people he was leading through the wilderness and for the wisdom to guide them: 'If indeed I enjoy your favour, please show me your ways, so that I understand you, and continue to enjoy your favour; consider too that this nation is your people' (Exod 33:13). There was the touching scene in which 'Moses' arms grew heavy (at prayer), so they took a stone and put it under him and on this he sat, with Aaron and Hur supporting his arms on each side' (Exod 17:11–12). Over and over again Moses discovered in prayer that all things are possible to God the liberator from, and forgiver of, sin, the one who summons the poor of this world 'out of darkness into his wonderful light . . . a non-people (to be) the People of God' (1 Pet 2:9–10). Moses the hero and formator showed that formators who are close to God in prayer can help initiates to be intimate as mature persons with each other and with God. The seemingly impossible *is* possible through prayer.

10. Recognize the value of liturgical prayer

By his actions as Yahweh's agent in formation Moses illustrated the power of community prayer, and the need for it to be well prepared and to speak not just to the minds of participants, but also to their feelings.

11. Avoid creating dependency

Moses as formator was the servant of God. He sought to draw people to God, not to himself.[11] His detachment was eminently evident in his relationship with his successor, and in the manner in which he accepted his own death outside the promised land. Having told the people that Joshua would lead them across into the promised land, he did not criticize Joshua for lack of experience, as one less detached would have done, but went out of his way to support Joshua publicly (Deut 31:6). Then Yahweh called Moses to die alone on a mountain, after he had merely glimpsed the promised land from a distance. Moses accepted death and the circumstances in which it was to take place with a remarkable spirit of patience and detachment (Deut 34:1–7). A powerful symbol of Moses' detachment was the fact that people could not cling to him in death: 'to this day no one has ever found his grave' (Deut 34:6).

Scripture is at pains to tell us, however, that Moses could never have kept to this role as ritual specialist or formator of his people, if he was not at the same time struggling with his own inner journey of faith and conversion. Poor Moses, hardworking and zealous in the service of Yahweh and the people, experienced intense loneliness and social marginalization. Even his closest friends bitterly attacked him (Num 12:1). Yet he struggled to remain faithful, and we are told how 'Moses was extremely humble, the humblest man on earth' (Num 12:3). Moses was humble because he prayed. A naturally impatient man with a powerful temper (Exod 2:12; 32:19), he could never have survived the trials of ritual specialist without constantly praying to Yahweh from the anguish of his own inner chaos. Moses was truly a hero who frequently ventured into a region of supernatural wonder through prayer and faith-filled reflection on his own unworthiness. Once re-energized through prayer, he would return to share his wisdom with Yahweh's obstinate people.

It was his humility which gave Moses an authentic sense of humour. Humour is that sense within us which sets up a kindly contemplation of the incongruities of life. Humour is truly genuine when people recognize that, despite their sinfulness, God still loves them humanly speaking. This is an incongruous situation. The prophets saw this paradox for they acknowledged their own lack of gifts and reluctance to serve Yahweh on the one hand, but on the other hand, that Yahweh still loved them and wanted them to be his messengers. A highly incongruous situation![12] Not surprisingly, Moses had this gift of humour based on self-knowledge. He showed understandable reluctance to accept his prophetic role for he recognized his own inadequacies: 'Please, my Lord, I have never been eloquent . . . for I am slow and hesitant of speech' (Exod 4:10). Moses discovered that, despite his own hesitancy and sinfulness, Yahweh would always be faithful to his promises. Having accepted this incongruous reality, Moses had the confidence to lead with courage and hope. Through the gift of humour the seemingly impossible became possible for him: '"Who gave a person a mouth?" Yahweh said to him. "Who makes a person dumb or deaf, gives sight or makes blind? Is it not I, Yahweh? Now go, I shall help you speak and instruct you what to say"' (Exod 4:11–12). Without a gift of supernatural humour, similar to that of Moses, no formator today will survive the pressures of the task.

Jesus Christ the formator: lessons

Jesus initiated the formation of the apostles by calling them, and every Israelite, to conversion and faith in the good news (Matt 4:17).[13] They accepted their call by giving up all things and following Jesus: 'They left everything and followed him' (Luke 5:11).

It is consoling for contemporary formators to realize that for a long time these men, who followed Jesus and had received particular preparation from him, were in fact 'split-level Christians'. There co-existed within them two thought and behaviour systems which were sometimes in contradiction. At one level, they professed allegiance to the ideas, aspirations and example of Jesus, but at another level they held convictions that were not in tune at all with what Jesus was preaching.[14] After one lesson in private as his special followers, in which Jesus foretold for the second time that he 'will be delivered into the hands of men; they will put him to death; and three days after he has been put to death he will rise again' (Mark 9:31), they showed just how little they had interiorized the prophecy by quarrelling over 'which of them was the greatest' (Mark 9:34). The process of inculturation for them, as for the modern-day candidate, was slow and hesitant. The apostles found acculturation of the gospel to their previous ways of thinking more to their liking. It was easier to think of lording it over people, as the Pharisees and the Roman oppressors did, than to become prophetic servant leaders after the style of Jesus Christ. But at the end of it all, Jesus had only one failure out of twelve!

Jesus was *the* ritual specialist in transition to new life: 'I am the Way; the Truth and Life. No one can come to the Father except through me' (John 14:6). He was both the specialist *and* at the same time the transition itself to the kingdom and the Father, and his whole life was a testimony to this. The evangelist Mark began his text by linking the coming of Jesus to Isaiah's prophecy of a second exodus: 'The beginning of the gospel about Jesus Christ. . . . It is written in the prophet Isaiah: "Look I am going to send my messenger in front of you to prepare your way before you"' (Mark 1:1–2). On Sinai Yahweh assured Moses: 'Look, I am sending an angel to precede you . . . to the place I have prepared' (Exod 23:20). Jesus was the new Moses. As such, his style of initiating his apostles into the life of the kingdom was patterned on that of Moses the ritual specialist of the first exodus experience.

By reflecting on Jesus as evangelizer, it is possible for us to identify also the principles he used to form his apostles. We can imagine Jesus enunciating the same action-oriented principles to today's formators:

1. Repeat the vision often
'Where there is no vision the people get out of hand' (Prov 24:18). Both by word and action Jesus repeatedly retold the vision of the kingdom: 'Then fixing his eyes on his disciples he said: "How blessed are you who are poor: the kingdom of God is yours . . . . Blessed are you when people hate you . . . . Rejoice when that day comes . . . your reward will be great in heaven"' (Luke 6:20, 22–23). His healing the sick was a foretaste of the fullness of peace and healing in the kingdom.

2. Initiates must learn through chaos
Jesus was to be the new Israel, to be formed through the wilderness

experiences of the new exodus; to be one with Jesus, his disciples, always so slow to understand, must repeatedly go through their own exodus experience. The desert or wilderness theme was frequently to the fore in Christ's life and in his teaching of his disciples.[15] It was in the liminality of the desert (the symbol of chaos) that Jesus himself was initiated into his public ministry through testing purification, and it was to the wilderness of the desert that Jesus returned after incidents of successful teaching or healing. His call to his apostles came in a wilderness place, and he drew them back there whenever he wished to teach them matters of critical importance (Mark 6:31–2). Thus, 'Peter and James and John . . . are led . . . up a high mountain on their own' to experience the divinity of Jesus: '"This is my Son, the Beloved. Listen to him"' (Mark 9:2, 7). He allowed the apostles to be terrified by a storm on a lake in order to teach them the meaning of faith: '"We are lost!" And he woke up and rebuked the wind and said to the sea: "Quiet now! Be calm! . . . Why are you frightened? Have you still no faith?"' (Mark 4:39–40). Gethsemane and Golgotha were the testimonies by Jesus to the educative role of chaos in the process of initiating his followers.

3. Initiates must learn to pray

Jesus modelled for his initiates a life of prayer and action. Often he is pictured as withdrawing into the desert or up a mountain to pray (Matt 14:23), exhorting people to pray (Luke 18:1) or teaching his disciples how to pray (Luke 11:1–13). Without prayer initiates cannot survive (Luke 22:40).

4. Truths need constant repetition

Jesus had to reiterate to his apostles time after time in direct language, parables and action, the values of the kingdom, because they were 'slow to believe all that the prophets have said' (Luke 24:25). Dramatic experiences of dislocation left even his special friends, Peter, James and John, untouched in the depths of their hearts. After the transfiguration and the agony in the garden, they remained oblivious to the educative role of these events for themselves and others. Following the transfiguration they disputed with each other about who was the greatest among them and who should be permitted to perform miracles (Luke 9:46–50). Conversion was slow – desperately so. Formators, take heart!

5. Initiates must learn detachment and asceticism

The followers of Jesus enter a life-long journey of detachment and asceticism: 'No one who does not carry his cross and come after me can be my disciple' (Luke 14:27). To his disciples preparing to begin their preaching Jesus said 'take nothing for the journey except a staff – no bread, no haversack, no coppers for their purses' (Mark 6:8). They were to relive the detachment of their ancestors who on the eve of the Exodus were commanded to eat the paschal lamb 'hurriedly . . . your sandals on your feet and your staff in your hand' (Exod 12:11). Jesus lived this detachment himself: 'the son of man has nowhere to lay his head' (Matt 8:20). Initiates into religious life generally come from, and are to re-enter, a culture of consumerism and materialism. The gospel imperative of inculturation demands that they learn not to be seduced by the values of this culture; this is impossible without a spirit of detachment and asceticism in imitation of Jesus Christ.

6. Initiates are to confront oppression[16]

Jesus was sensitive to people who were oppressed, and he expected his followers to be like him. His words and actions were protests against systems and structures that oppressed and marginalized people. For example, the Samaritans were considered racially inferior to Jewish people, so Jesus directly attacked this prejudice by openly associating with Samaritans (John 4:1–42) or by making positive references to them (Luke 10:29–37). He associated with the marginalized: women (John 20:11–18), tax collectors and sinners (Luke 15:1–3). Many times he challenged verbally and by his conduct the hypocrisy of the Sadducees and Pharisees (upholders of the religious strong group/strong grid culture of his time), because they had lost the detachment of the Exodus experience and oppressed people with meaningless rituals (Mark 7:1–23). Conversion of heart and commitment to justice, not the mere external observance of precepts, must characterize the followers of Jesus: 'He has sent me to proclaim the good news to the afflicted . . . liberty to captives . . . to let the oppressed go free' (Luke 4:18).

7. Initiates are to be apostolically creative

Jesus exercised his imagination creatively in teaching, for example his use of parables, and his vivid descriptions of nature and human experiences (Luke 6:39). He was adaptable in his teaching, so he was able to preach to ordinary people or sophisticated scholars in language that they could understand and appreciate (Mark 12:37; Luke 20:19–44). And he expected initiates to develop similar qualities for the sake of the kingdom.

8. Initiates must develop empathy

Often Jesus, out of respect for the freedom of the person, went out of his way to avoid imposing his power on people. For example, he knew the sick man at the Pool of Bethesda had been ill for decades, but he still asked him 'Do you want to be well again?' (John 5:6). Consider the warmth of feeling that Jesus conveyed to people in the midst of his own agonizing death: Jesus prayed for those who were murdering him (Luke 23:34), and for the welfare of Mary his mother, and John (John 19:26–27). He was sensitive to known sinners or outcasts of society, for example Zacchaeus (Luke 19:1–10); he accepted Peter, though the disciple had just denied him (Luke 22:61).

9. Initiates need a sense of humour

In the Christian tradition holiness has too often been synonymous with gloominess. Down through the centuries people like Sts John Chrysostom, Augustine, Bernard of Clairvaux and Hugo of St Victor preached that a sense of humour was not to be cultivated by any serious follower of Jesus Christ, especially, of course, a religious. St Jerome in the fourth century gave the reason for this: 'As long as we are in the vale of tears we may not laugh, but must weep . . . . We are in the vale of tears and this age is one of tears, not of joy.'[17] After all, they claimed, Jesus is never reported to have laughed!

This is a total theological misunderstanding of humour and its expression in laughter, a point that the humorist St Teresa of Avila would have fully endorsed. Jesus, like Moses his spiritual predecessor, had in fact a most highly developed sense of humour and he showed his profound appreciation of the incongruous repeatedly in word and deed. Often difficult things could be said and not rejected when they were recounted with humour, for example in exposing the hypocrisy of the Pharisees: 'You blind guides! Straining out gnats and swallowing camels!' (Matt 23:24), or the example of Jesus when he reached detachment from worldly goods: 'Yes, it is easier for a camel to pass through the eye of a needle than for someone rich to enter the kingdom of God' (Luke 18:25). Neither Jesus nor his listeners would have kept straight faces at this imagery and its incongruity!

The life of Jesus, in fact, was a paradox of divine proportions! He, the King of Kings, was born in a stable, and died on a cross. Nothing could be more incongruous, yet nothing was more powerful in conveying the truth of his words: 'I have come so that they may have life and have it to the full' (John 10:10). And the source of Christ's humour? His detachment from self, his humility, his total faith in the Father: 'His state was divine, yet he did not cling to his equality with God but emptied himself to assume the condition of a slave' (Phil 2:6–7).

Initiates seeking intimate union with Jesus are not seriously committed to the task if they are unprepared to struggle to see in themselves the incongruous reality that, though they are sinners, God still loves them. They have yet to be personally converted to the implications of the divine incongruity of the incarnation: in order 'to shame the wise . . . (God) chose those who by human standards are weak to shame the strong, those who by human standards are common and contemptible . . . to reduce to nothing all those that do count for something, so that no human being might feel boastful before God' (1 Cor 1:27–28). If initiates show little or no signs of developing a sense of humour, I doubt they have vocation as frontline proclaimers of the good news or as religious, because they have yet to believe the heart of the message of Jesus, the grand master of humour.

10. Initiates must learn to grieve

Jesus, like Moses and the prophets before him, had the gift of grieving.

He recognized there must be death to the old before there is new life. By word and example Jesus taught his initiates this wisdom.[18]

11. Initiates must expect to suffer

Like Moses, Jesus was to create a whole new people and way of life. He and his apostles were consequently bound to suffer misunderstandings and rejection, and to be scapegoated by upholders of the political and religious *status quo*. If initiates are not prepared to be one with Jesus in this, then they must withdraw: 'If you belonged to the world, the world would love you as its own; but because you do not belong to the world, because my choice of you has drawn you out of the world, that is why the world hates you' (John 15:19); 'A servant is not greater than his master. If they persecuted me, they will persecute you too' (John 15:20).

12. Initiates must train to be refounders

The ultimate aim of the initiation of the apostles was for them to take up the challenge to 'Go out to the whole world; proclaim the gospel to all creation' (Mark 16:15). That purpose remains *the* priority in the form-ation of candidates. The Church's ministries need constant refounding so that the gospel is interacting with cultures in this world of change. This is a never-ending task. Yesterday's pastoral responses are rarely suitable for today. People who are unwilling to struggle to emulate the pastoral imagination and creativity of Jesus have no place as initiates in religious congregations.

13. Initiates are to have pastoral exposure

As we have already seen, Jesus structured pastoral exposure as an integral part of the initiation of his disciples. These are the 'teachable moments', events which dispose initiates to learn much about themselves as well as to recognize the need for more profound knowledge and skills.[19] The lesson for formators: if initiates remain unwilling to utilize the learning potential of pastoral exposure programmes, they have no place in religious life with its primary purpose of prophetic action.

14. Initiates must be multicultural

Jesus, sensitively aware of prejudice and discrimination within the culture of his time, by word and action challenged his disciples to be multi-cultural. Jews looked at Samaritans in a racist manner; they pictured them as stupid, lazy and heretical. The Samaritans had similar views of their Jewish neighbours. When Jesus told the story of the Good Samaritan, his listeners would have been left in no doubt about its meaning for them (Luke 10:29–37). They are to imitate the Samaritan's love of a person of a different culture and express this love by an openness to listen and a willingness to help: 'Go, and do the same yourself' (v. 37). Jesus himself models this directive in his meeting with the Samaritan woman at the well (John 4:1–42).

15. Initiates must avoid dependency

The charismatic leader is one who restores emotion, awe and magic to the conduct of affairs, and would appear to himself/herself and to others either to be endowed with divine, magical or diabolic powers or to be at least an exceptional individual.[20] Founders, refounders and prophets are usually charismatic people because proactive change requires such leadership, but there are grave dangers for charismatic persons and their followers to avoid, in particular the risk of domination and dependency. In times of chaos, people whose certitudes and sense of order have disintegrated are susceptible to manipulation by charismatic people, who consciously or otherwise can use their followers for their own narcissistic advantage. As anthropologist Charles Lindholm writes: 'it is an inevitable law that the passive should not only obey the active, but also adore them, since through obedience the weak and empty gain an identity, and the neces- sary illusion of potency and will . . . . And even though they are lost in slavishness, they feel immersed in love.'[21] Aberrant charismatic leaders may even twist sacred texts of a culture, for example the scriptures or founding national myths, to support their hold over their followers.

Jesus, like Moses before him, was at pains to avoid creating such a dangerous and immature culture of dependency. His focus was to lead his followers through personal conversion to the kingdom, not to becom- ing emotionally and unthinkingly attached to himself. At Capernaum admiring crowds had followed Jesus after witnessing the multiplication of the bread and fish. A lesser leader than Jesus would have been tempted to foster their emotional dependency. Instead he took the occasion to proclaim the truth of the eucharist which many found too difficult to accept, so 'many of his disciples went away and accompanied him no more' (John 6:66). He was even prepared to lose his special disciples, because he refused to compromise his teaching to maintain his following: 'Then Jesus said to the twelve: "What about you, do you want to go away too?"' (John 6:67). Throughout his preaching Jesus concentrated on the mission of the Father (John 2:17) and the Spirit: 'it is for your own good that I am going, because unless I go, the Paraclete will not come to you' (John 16:7). After the crucifixion he resisted Mary Magdalen's yearning to hold on to him: 'Do not cling to me, because I have not yet ascended to the Father. But go and find my brothers, and tell them: I am ascending to my Father and your Father, to my God and your God' (John 20:17). At Emmaus, just when the two disciples were in danger of developing undue emotional dependency on their guest, Jesus, he disappeared (Luke 24:31). They had to stand on their own feet as autonomous persons, owning the authority of their baptism, and acting accordingly.

Candidates are vulnerable to emotional dependency in at least two significant stages – on entering, and during the transitional phases of ritual initiation into religious life. The present chaotic state of the world causes many candidates to be less certain of their personal and cultural identity than in former ages. The transitional phases of their congregational formation emotionally dispose them to the manipulative power of a poorly integrated formator, who may foster an enmeshed or therapeutic community. If formators encourage such communities they obstruct the growth of candidates. The message of Jesus is clear: the cultivation of an unhealthy dependency in which formators make themselves the centre of the formation process is contrary to gospel values. The anger of Jesus in the temple, which was directed at people twisting the sacred to their own advantage, could be just as well aimed at self-centred formators: 'Take all this out of here and stop using my Father's house as a market' (John 2:17). When formators encourage intentional formation communities, they must keep a growth-oriented distance from their candidates, that is, a distance that fosters the emergence of a culture that supports individual autonomy and community growth.

Jesus, by describing and living himself what initiates must experience in their transitional ritual, was at the same time defining the capacities required of contemporary formators. For example, they are to be:

— people of faith, prayer, imagination, creativity, detachment;

— persons of refounding openness and humour, sensitive to the marginalized and voiceless, zealous for social justice;

— ritual specialists who are able to lead initiates because they themselves have earlier ventured 'forth from the world of common day into a region of supernatural wonder', personally discovering and owning there the mystery of Christ the pilgrim;

— persons of deep knowledge and love of the founding experience of their congregation, as a graced moment in which Christ revealed himself in a special way to a particular group of pilgrims;

— persons of such spiritual and human maturity that they do not foster a culture of dependency around themselves, but keep the formation process focused on Christ, 'the Alpha and the Omega, the Beginning and the End' (Rev 21:6), and his mission;

— people prepared to direct with firmness and compassion individuals who lack the necessary gifts to other vocations;

— people prepared to educate candidates 'for responsible love and . . . affective maturity';[22]

— people who readily appreciate the informative value of the social sciences in their apostolate.

Authority position persons: role in formation

By 'authority position persons' I mean provincials or their equivalent. They have overall responsibility for formation and the ability to delegate it to others (that is, formators). Their obligations are as follows.

1. To oversee recruitment of candidates

Leaders are to establish a process guaranteeing that *only* suitable candidates are encouraged to apply to enter the congregational training programme. The skills of a full-time vocation recruiter must be similar to a formator's:

– a deep knowledge and love of the founding experience of the congregation;

– a commitment to the values of Vatican II;

– the ability to co-operate with formators without interfering in the execution of their roles.

In today's Church the task of a recruiter is most difficult. A congregation may expect far too much of them and blame them for 'not producing the numbers as we had in the past'. As they will work in the stressful chaos of the Church and society, it will be especially challenging for them to maintain a sense of personal balance. If no appropriate person is available, no appointment should be made.

Case study: An unsuitable recruiter

A provincial, acting on the strong recommendation of a provincial chapter, had appointed a sister as a full-time vocation recruiter in a First World country. Theologically, the recruiter had fundamentalist qualities characteristic of restorationism. Most chapter members had not been convinced that there should be a recruiter at all, but they felt (to quote one delegate) 'it would do no harm to appoint the sister as she is so keen for the position and will feel let down if she does not get it'.

The formation staff, theologically Vatican II in orientation, became increasingly frustrated because the candidates proposed by the recruiter and accepted by the provincial were all psychologically and theologically unsuitable. The formation staff complained to the provincial who replied: 'The task of the recruiter is to get people into the formation house. Your duty is to sort them out! If no one is finally suitable, then at least you have helped them to grow a little more in the Christian faith.'

The chapter and the provincial acted quite irresponsibly, the chapter in pressing for the appointment of an unsuitable sister, and the provincial in colluding with the chapter's immaturity. Furthermore, the provincial ignored the nature of religious life and its formation requirements, because she accepted into the formation programme unsuitable candidates. In her view, formators had to be primarily counsellors or therapists for dysfunctional people who had no future in religious life. She also failed to realize that unsuitable candidates obstructed the development of individuals with appropriate qualities for religious life.

It is my experience that formation staffs, when consistently placed in impossible situations like the one described above, either resign from this apostolate, psychologically suffer burn-out, or leave the congregation. Some survive, but later regret the times in which they consented without protest to this 'congregational madness'.

2. To appoint a qualified formation team

The provincial must in justice appoint qualified staff, that is, people with human and spiritual maturity demanded by the task of formation. If this is not possible, and other alternatives are unavailable, for example using the resources of other provinces, then no formation programme should be established and all recruitment cease. In the Third World, where applications to enter religious life may still be numerous, congregations can be so eager to obtain recruits that they downplay the need for adequate screening and qualified staff. In my opinion this policy can never be justified.

In the First World, where candidates are few and there is great pressure to continue to staff other apostolates, provincials may hesitate to train and appoint qualified persons to formation communities. Sometimes a formator is left alone to form one or two candidates and may even be burdened with other apostolates at the same time. The task of formation is too complex and demanding for a person who is unqualified, alone, and/or holding down other apostolates at the same time. If a province cannot provide suitable formation on its own or in co-operation with others, justice demands it must cease recruitment and close down its training programmes.

3. To respect subsidiarity and support formators

The duty to form candidates is inherent in the office of provincial, but the authority is delegated to people trained for this task. The authority to train candidates comes to formators, therefore, from two sources: delegated authority from a provincial, and the authority of expertise from their own talents and training. The provincial, having delegated authority to formators, must now act according to the principle of subsidiarity: that is, whatever individuals or groups are able to do for themselves ought not to be removed from their competence and taken over by superiors. As Pius XII wrote: 'all social activity is of its nature subsidiary; it ought to aim at helping the members of the social body, never at destroying or absorbing them'.[23] In the contemporary chaos in the Church and religious life there is an ever-present danger that this principle will be broken in the formation apostolate.

Case study: A provincial is out of role

The staff of a major seminary of a clerical religious congregation unanimously concluded, after prolonged reflection on extensive evidence, that a temporarily professed student should not be called to final vows. The student, after being told by the superior that the staff would not be recommending him for profession, decided to leave the congregation before the expiry of his temporary vows. Later, under the influence of the vocation director, the student changed his mind and approached the provincial to be readmitted to the seminary. The provincial, without consultation with the seminary staff, told the seminary's superior that the student would be returning and that this information had been conveyed to the province. The staff became alarmed on hearing that the provincial had sided with the vocation recruiter and the student without any reference to them or the reasons they had given for their decision not to recommend him. The provincial retracted his support for the student only after the staff threatened to resign.

The example illustrates the danger of not respecting the principle of subsidiarity. Theoretically the provincial had the authority to over-rule the seminary staff, but subsidiarity demanded that this should not be done until he himself had thoroughly examined the evidence sent him about the student. The vocation recruiter, who had a very limited understanding of the theology of Vatican II, was well known in the province for his anti-seminary views. The staff rightly felt that the provincial, by supporting the vocation recruiter and by communicating his decision to the province *before* discussing the situation with them, had undermined their credibility in the province.

Case study: A superior-general ignores subsidiarity

A novice directress, acting for good reasons, advised the provincial that a novice should not be called to vows. The provincial duly acted on this advice, but when her decision was communicated to the general administration, the superior-general herself directly intervened. Without any consultation with either the novice directress or the provincial, the superior-general cabled the novice directress to inform her that she herself had called the novice to vows. The remaining weeks of the novitiate for the candidate would be spent under the novice directress. The novitiate staff had for many years been criticized for its firm adherence to strict standards of assessment. When the high-handed intervention of the superior-general became known, the critics in the province publicly rejoiced at the humiliation of the staff and the provincial (who was well known for her support of the entire formation staff).

204

The case is similar to the previous incident, but even more inexplicable because the superior-general has intervened. The latter was culpably unaware of the serious reasons given to the provincial for not calling the candidate to vows. The person did not in fact return to the novitiate because she herself had decided in the meantime that religious life was not her vocation. Moreover, it was later found that the superior-general did not have the authority in the constitutions to call anyone to the novitiate. Only the provincial could do so. Neither the novitiate staff nor the provincial, however, could defend themselves to the province at large because of the confidentiality of information about the ex-novice.

Both case studies are warnings to major superiors. Follow subsidiarity. If qualified formation staff are appointed, then support them, for their apostolate is an extremely difficult one, open to often ill-informed criticism from outsiders. Only in very exceptional cases, when supplied with sound information, should major superiors override their formation staffs. Intervention, however, must be done in a way that does not jeopardize the trust and ease of communication that must exist between the major superior and the formation staff.

Sometimes provincial chapters establish 'formation committees' to which they or provincials appoint members who are not involved directly in the formation apostolate. Often the task of these committees is vaguely defined, for example 'to advise the provincial on matters relating to formation'. When the objective of these committees is so ill-defined and people are appointed with little or no expertise, the situation is ripe for unnecessary tension and conflict. Formators have neither the time nor the energy to give to conflicts resulting from ill-informed members or committees of the province. The following guideline needs to be followed: let structures of accountability for formators be established that best serve the purpose of formation. These structures will protect formators from undue interference from members of other apostolates.

Provincials should expect formation staff to have regular supervision, like all serious-minded professional groups. A *professional supervisor*, as a skilled outsider, provides a supportive and confidential relationship, and helps to surface issues unrecognized by formators, placing them in touch with the dynamics active at different levels within the community's culture. For a specific issue, formators may wish to engage the services of a *consultant* who has skill in a particular area. The supervisor and consultant will act in such a way that the formators themselves retain both the diagnostic and remedial initiative; the problem will never be solved if the formators become unduly dependent on either the supervisor or the consultant.[24]

Summary

The functions of leadership are fourfold: to conserve, to nurture or empower, to manage and to be proactive. Of these functions the most difficult is to be proactive, because this means the leader must venture into the unknown, thereby disturbing the *status quo* and arousing the fears people have about change. Contemporary formation staff need to have the ability to exercise all these functions, especially that of being proactive. They are to create a formation process based on the values of Vatican II, and there are few signposts to guide them. For this reason they are truly called to be refounders of this apostolate. Their primary model throughout is the life of Jesus Christ and the manner in which he formed the apostles.

Mary the mother of Jesus has a unique relationship with each formator and initiate, since she was simultaneously a formator and an initiate. She helped to form Jesus the Saviour and became at the same time the first disciple of her Son. In her own pilgrimage of faith Mary became a disciple through an initiation into the mystery of salvific suffering, an initiation ritual that continued throughout her life. The thanksgiving hymn of Mary was a song of the oppositional themes of death/newness that all initiates into the life of Christ are invited to experience; the one who dies to his/her own selfish needs and lives for the Saviour can do great things for God (Luke 1:46–55). Mary was called to live this message in her journey with her son at critical, dislocating points of his life: a sense of lostness in a foreign land to escape the murderous hand of Herod (Matt 2:13–23), the warning by Simeon that she herself was to suffer with her son (Luke 2:33–35), anguish at the disappearance of her son in the temple (Luke 2:48), the sight of her dying son on Calvary (John 19:25–27).[25] Jesus himself revealed the secret of Mary's faithfulness as formator and initiate – she listened attentively in prayer to the word of God and she kept it (Luke 11:27–28). For this reason Mary remains a loving friend of formators and initiates.

Notes

1. Congregation for Institutes of Consecrated Life and Societies of Apostolic Life, *Directives on Formation in Religious Institutes* (Boston: St Paul Books, 1990), para. 32.
2. E. Leach, *Political Systems of Highland Burma* (Boston: Beacon, 1954), pp. 13–14.
3. See R. Bocock, *Ritual in Industrial Society: A Sociological Analysis of Ritualism in Modern England* (London: George Allen and Unwin, 1974), pp. 35–59.
4. See V. Turner, *The Drums of Affliction: Aspects of Ndembu Ritual* (Oxford: Clarendon Press, 1968), pp. 1–8. Also C. G. Helman, *Culture, Health and*

Illness (Oxford: Butterworth-Heinemann, 1990), pp. 192–3; C. Bell, *Ritual Theory, Ritual Practice* (New York: Oxford University Press, 1992), pp. 130–40.

5. See E. M. Zuesse, 'Ritual' in M. Eliade (ed.), *The Encyclopedia of Religion* (New York: Macmillan, 1987), pp. 419–20.

6. See M. Douglas, *Purity and Danger: An Analysis of Concepts of Pollution and Taboo* (Harmondsworth: Penguin, 1966), p. 117.

7. See G. A. Arbuckle, *Refounding the Church: Dissent for Leadership* (London: Geoffrey Chapman, 1993), pp. 68–72.

8. J. Campbell, *The Hero with a Thousand Faces* (Princeton: Princeton University Press, 1949), p. 30.

9. Congregation for Institutes, op. cit., para. 31.

10. See G. A. Arbuckle, *Grieving for Change: A Spirituality for Refounding Gospel Communities* (London: Geoffrey Chapman, 1991), pp. 151–6.

11. See G. W. Coats, *Moses: Heroic Man, Man of God* (Sheffield: JSOT, 1988), p. 41.

12. See G. A. Arbuckle, *Earthing the Gospel: An Inculturation Handbook for Pastoral Workers* (London: Geoffrey Chapman, 1990), pp. 214–15 and *Strategies for Growth in Religious Life* (New York: Alba House, 1987), pp. 67–87.

13. See Arbuckle, *Strategies for Growth in Religious Life*, op. cit., pp. 222–31.

14. See J. Bulatao, *Split-Level Christianity* (Manila: UST Press, 1966), p. 2.

15. See A. Stock, *The Way in the Wilderness: Exodus, Wilderness and Moses Theme in Old Testament and New* (Collegeville, MN: Liturgical Press, 1969), pp. 68–9 and passim.

16. See Arbuckle, *Earthing the Gospel*, op. cit., pp. 158–9.

17. St Jerome, cited by K.-J. Kuschel, *Laughter: A Theological Reflection* (London: SCM Press, 1994), p. 45.

18. See Arbuckle, *Grieving for Change*, op. cit., passim.

19. See R. Coll, *Supervision of Ministry Students* (Collegeville, MN: Liturgical Press, 1992), pp. 51–2.

20. See M. Weber, *From Max Weber*, trans. and ed. H. H. Gerth and C. W. Mills (London: Kegan Paul, Trench, Trubner, 1947), pp. 245–52.

21. See C. Lindholm, *Charisma* (Oxford: Blackwell, 1993), p. 47 and passim.

22. John Paul II, *Apostolic Exhortation: I Will Give You Shepherds* (Boston: St Paul Books, 1992), para. 44.

23. Pius XII (20 February 1949), cited by J.-Y. Calvez and J. Perrin, *The Church and Social Justice* (London: Burns and Oates, 1961), p. 122.

24. See E. H. Schein, *Process Consultation*, vol. 1 (Reading, MA: Addison-Wesley, 1988), p. 11; and D. Campbell *et al.*, *A Systemic Approach to Consultation* (London: Karnac Books, 1991), passim.

25. See Arbuckle, *Grieving for Change*, op. cit., pp. 102–5.

Index